DEADLINE SUNDAY

DEADLINE SUNDAY

A LIFE IN THE WEEK OF
THE SUNDAY TIMES

Brian MacArthur

Hodder & Stoughton
LONDON SYDNEY AUCKLAND TORONTO

British Library Cataloguing in Publication Data

MacArthur, Brian
  Deadline Sunday.
  I. Title
  070.4

  ISBN 0-340-50990-2

Book designed by Trevor Spooner

Published by Hodder and Stoughton,
a division of Hodder and Stoughton Ltd,
Mill Road, Dunton Green, Sevenoaks, Kent TN13 2YA.
Editorial Office: 47 Bedford Square, London WC1B 3DP.

Photoset by Rowland Phototypesetting Ltd,
Bury St Edmunds, Suffolk

Printed in Great Britain by Butler and Tanner,
London & Frome

Contents

Introduction

What readers see on the front page will help to form their thinking and their conversation over Sunday lunch.

The British read more newspapers – national and regional, daily and weekly, paid-for and free – than almost any other nation on earth. Nine out of ten see a newspaper at least once a week and 15 million buy a national paper every day. On their day of rest, so avid is their appetite for something to read, 17 million buy one of the 10 national Sunday papers. According to all the official statistics, that means they are read by up to 40 million Britons.

Journalism, even though it rarely lives up to its image, is one of the glamour professions. Journalists feed the dreams of the masses or meet the demand of the minority for sober analysis and comment. The best journalism catches history on the hoof. Yet even the best journalists soon learn that their reputation is only as good as their last story or column. That was last week or yesterday. Now there is the next story to write – and soon that, too, will be wrapping the fish and chips or, now that newsprint is bad for your health, recycled into wood pulp so that all those hard-won words can make still more newspapers for the scrapheap.

There have been many good novels and books about Fleet Street and many good autobiographies by journalists. As far as I know, however, there has never been a book which describes how a newspaper is made. *Deadline Sunday* is an attempt to describe a life in the week of one newspaper, *The Sunday Times*, one of the biggest and certainly the heaviest. It is a paper that has its detractors as well as its admirers. The book aims to be a report, enabling readers to form their own judgement on how the paper is made and edited.

We take our newspapers for granted. Yet I hope that this book will show the amount of effort that goes into the making of a newspaper – not only by journalists but by foresters, lorry drivers, advertising salesmen, circulation reps, printers and newsagents, among many others. I hope that it will also capture something of the excitement of journalism, whether of the foreign correspondent reporting on the headline stories, the critic attending a first night, or the assistant editor who helps to decide which stories make the front page. I hope it will show the influence of the editor as well as all the internal arguments and clashes that make a vibrant newspaper. It will certainly demonstrate that producing this one newspaper involved work not only on every continent but also in every corner of the United Kingdom.

My thanks are due to David St John Thomas, who helped to inspire the idea, Kevin Lyden, managing director, and Francis Davis of Shotton Paper, to Hilary Rubinstein of A. P. Watt, Ion Trewin, Simone Mauger and Bill Massey of Hodder and Stoughton who got it published, Trevor Spooner who designed it, Lynn Moorlen, my secretary, who lived with it on and off for months, and to my long-suffering family.

Deadline Sunday could not have been written without the unstinting help of many colleagues on *The Sunday Times*, whose names appear throughout the text. I thank them all and dedicate the book to them.

I had to choose one week (although there is a small element of cheating and a few of those who form part of that week's story have now moved to other papers) and it was one of the weeks when there was no big and dominant story that was certain to make the front page. That, perhaps, made it all the more interesting as the editor and his executives teased out and debated which was the most important report for the front page.

The power of newspapers can be overrated but they certainly have influence. What the readers see on the front page will help to form their thinking and their conversation over Sunday lunch. *Deadline Sunday* will have served my aim if it shows that the decisions made that week on *The Sunday Times* were seriously taken by serious men and women who also had quite a lot of fun on the way – and if it makes a few newspaper readers take their newspapers just a little less for granted.

Brian MacArthur
June 1991

Sunday

The paper on sale today contains more than 500 items and reports from every nation in the United Kingdom and every continent on earth. Six days ago nobody knew what the news would be.

As dawn breaks over Highgate in north London and the first rays of the sun light up the tower blocks far down below, the streets are silent and deserted. The steady rumbling of the traffic on its way to the nearby M1 has given way to the soul-stirring melody of the birds. A stirring of the soul is needed at this time on a Sunday morning when sensible men and women are still asleep.

At 5 am at a small newsagent's shop in the village High Street, however, six men and two women are already at work. It is their busiest morning and they need to start early. They are assembling the Sunday papers and the shop is piled with 6,500 separate bits of 2,000 newspapers.

The biggest – or the worst – is *The Sunday Times*, with eight sections, two magazines and a comic. Soon the papers will be delivered to the doorsteps of Highgate and the richest areas of Hampstead, where the sheikhs and the sultans and the millionaires live in their £10 million mansions on the borders of the heath. The same work is going on at 40,000 newsagents all over Britain.

From this shop Sunday papers are delivered to 1,500 homes before 8 am. Since this is Highgate and Hampstead, there is a big demand for the "heavy" Sundays. So they are assembling 200 *Sunday Telegraphs*, 463 *Observers* and 765 copies of *The Sunday Times*, apart from all the other big Sunday papers. *The Sunday Times* is the most time-consuming of the papers. The magazine has to be stuffed between the back three sections. That pile is then stuffed into the next four sections – and the main news section is then wrapped round the lot. It takes about 20 to 30 seconds to assemble each paper, and doing that 765 times is heavy work.

After an hour about 6,500 newspaper sections and magazines have been assembled into the 2,000 multi-sectioned newspapers. Five hundred will be on sale in the shop, the rest have to be delivered. The manager consults a computer print-out which sets out the individual orders, street by street, avenue by avenue, flat by flat. After another hour the papers are sorted into piles for each delivery route. A *Times* and an *Express* for Number 50, a *Telegraph* and *News of the World* for 27, *Observer* and *Mail* for Number 13. At 6.45 three Suzuki vans arrive and the papers are loaded. Each van covers one of three zones. The men set off and the vans stop every 250 yards, while two men deliver the papers to the doorsteps or through the letter-boxes.

As a deliverer of newspapers, and I joined the team this Sunday morning, you quickly became obsessed with letter-boxes. We have just spent more than two hours assembling all these huge papers. Now, faced by the average British letter-box, an eight-inch wide slit, we have to take them to bits again with frozen hands. At many letter-boxes it takes up to six separate "postings" to get the paper into the home. What a waste of effort it all seems. First you spend hours assembling them all. Then you unravel them so they can get through the boxes.

That is why *The Sunday Times*, the biggest offender in the eyes of newsagents, has sponsored research into "doorway furniture", which is how the marketing men describe the urns or boxes or clips in which the paper could be left outside the door so that the reader gets an unmangled copy and the job of the delivery boys and girls is made easier. It's going to take a long time, though, before they catch on.

When *The Sunday Times* expanded its number of sections, many newsagents grumbled about all the work involved in delivering them. Some even refused to deliver the paper and insisted that readers collected *The Sunday Times* themselves. Yet selling Sunday papers is good business if it is done efficiently, using modern methods such as the computer print-out to list every customer and delivery vans instead of boys and girls understandably groaning under all that weight.

Indeed the main difficulty nowadays is finding boys and girls to deliver the papers. They have to get up early, it is lonely out there at 7 am delivering papers, some parents are worried about their children's safety, and they don't get much more than £10 to £15 a week. They can earn as much in a Saturday morning on a Tesco or Sainsbury's check-out till. That is why more newsagents are using vans, particularly for the heavier Saturday and Sunday papers, and why *The Sunday Times* sponsored a £5,000 competition in 1988 to design a trolley for papers to go on the back of bikes, a delivery system which is slowly catching on.

Although *The Sunday Times* is heavy, it is puny by comparison with the Sunday edition of the *New York Times*. An average edition weighs six pounds and runs to more than 750 pages, including several magazines and supplements. It costs $1.25 on the street. Its publishers allegedly make a million dollars per pound of weight and in a good week it weighs up to seven pounds. Within the delivery areas of New Jersey, Connecticut and New York State, it is delivered to households in vans or cars by contract carriers. Further away, it costs more – as much as $2.25 in southern

Home delivery

The winner of the competition was Tom Winters, a professional designer from Bristol, who created a collapsible trolley that could be pulled by hand or attached to a bicycle. Remploy, which he approached for costings, suggested that it could be sold for about £40. It was subsequently put into production.

Apart from variants on the trolley, the other most popular suggestions from readers were for receptacles and plastic bags (an unpopular idea with newsagents: guess who has to put the papers inside the bags?).

A nationwide research programme was conducted to test readers' responses to receptacles for newspapers and some of the results were put on show to the trade. They included special urns, newspaper holders that could be attached to doors or walls, as well as various clips, all selling for between £10.69 for a brass newspaper holder and £39.49 for a giant milk bottle into which newspapers could be stuffed. Some were put on sale at B & Q but there was no great demand. The most popular option was box containers.

A survey by National Opinion Polls, commissioned by newsagents in the north-west, showed that:

THE average number of rounds was six, covering delivery to an average of about 288 homes.

MOST employed eight deliverers, who stayed for an average of 17 months.
95 PER CENT of deliverers were school-children.
THE average delivery charge was 20p per week.
NINE out of ten customers paid for their papers at the shop.

New Jersey, depending on how much the local distributor charges. Since the paper is too big to be delivered by children – not quite the situation yet in Britain – fathers and children often make money by delivering the paper around the neighbourhood in a station wagon, with father driving and the children running from house to house.

The newsagent I visited in London uses only adults to deliver the papers and charges each customer 70p a week to help cover its costs. On top of that the newsagent gets 20p back for every copy of *The Sunday Times* he sells. When you're selling 765, and charging 10p a day for delivery, that's good business. So the revenue earned by this newsagent for *The Sunday Times* alone out of which, of course, he has to pay wages and overheads – is more than £150 a week. And he is selling another ten newspapers. This newsagent is not complaining about *The Sunday Times*.

On sale this morning, midway through 1990, is a typical *Sunday Times* with eight sections, two magazines and the *Funday Times* comic, selling at 60p. It has not been a dramatic week for news but it is still a paper that is full of interest. The front page reports that Mrs Thatcher, still Prime Minister then, is planning a "golden scenario" for an election victory and that President de Klerk has said he wants to abolish apartheid. There is also a new drug which may cure breast cancer. The Sport section reports that Tracy Edwards and her all-woman crew on the *Maiden* are nearing England at the end of the Whitbread Round-the-World Yacht Race. At the Saatchi advertising agency, eight staff have defected to set up a rival, a story that leads the front page of the Business section. The comedian Rowan Atkinson has won three awards at the Montreux Television Festival. That is the cover story for the Arts, while the Style section features the last days of the late Greta Garbo. Glasnost Galore, describing the joys and the dreams of eastern Europe after the fall of the Iron Curtain, is the cover story of the magazine. There is still more variety on the front pages of other sections, whether it is the Lords of Tartary in Books or a bachanal in Reykjavik in Travel.

As the circulation department starts work to ensure that *The Sunday Times* is distributed throughout the United Kingdom and to 61 countries around the world, another gruelling week is over for the journalists. Although the presses ran until 4 am, their work finished at 2.30 am when Tony Allaway, the night editor, updated the last few pages with the very latest news.

As they awake, later this morning, there will be many different reactions. Reporters, columnists and critics will instantly turn to their section to make sure that their articles have been used and that they haven't been mangled by the sub-editors who cut the copy and write the headlines. Only then will they turn to the front page. After that they will once again savour

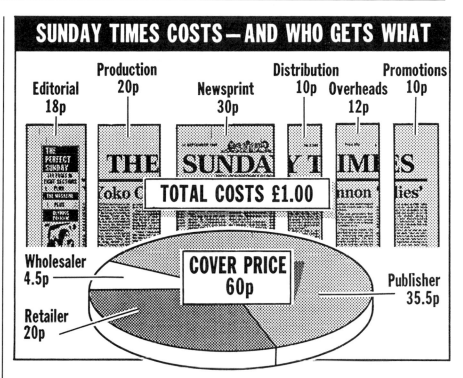

The economics of newspapers. The cover price is now 80p.

their own words and enjoy the transient glory of their by-line and their beautiful but often heavily-edited prose. Many will realise, too late, that – dammit – this sentence and that sentence could have been so much better written. There is never quite enough time. Never mind, say the cynics, it will be wrapping fish and chips tomorrow. Assistant editors will check the other Sunday papers to see if they have been scooped or their rivals had better ideas. Quite soon this Sunday morning they will start worrying about how to fill the paper next week. That is the nagging worry that never quite goes away, even on a Sunday.

The paper they produced in the past six days will sell more than 1.1 million copies this morning and will be read over the next few days by more than 3.5 million, since most papers are read by two or three people. It contains more than 500 items. There are 41 British and 16

Saturday night/Sunday morning: the roar
of the presses at Wapping.

foreign news stories, two long Focus specials on major news subjects of the week, and 37 pictures in the news section. Sport includes results for athletics, American baseball, cycling in Italy, football in West Germany, golf in Italy and Britain, hockey, motor-cycling in Italy, motor-rallying in the Isle of Man, shooting at Bisley, snooker at Grantham, speedway, table tennis in Japan and tennis in Italy and Germany. There are 33 articles or columns and 20 letters to the editor in the News Review section which leads on the Tiananmen Square uprising, 76 articles or reports in Business, nine in Style and 17 in Travel. There are 68 reviews in the Books section and ten features in the magazine. The paper has reported from every nation in the United Kingdom and from every continent on earth.

Although it will soon be consigned to the dustbin, *The Sunday Times* will meanwhile amuse, irritate, anger, upset, inform, educate and entertain millions, and help to make the livelihoods of hundreds. Yet six days ago nobody, not even the editor, knew what the news was going to be. This is the story of how those 250 pages were filled – of many lives in a typical week of *The Sunday Times*. The story would be very similar on any other newspaper.

Something for everybody: the range and variety of Britain's best-selling paper.

Deep in the Forest

For every tree that is felled, another is planted. That is the law, a statutory obligation on owners of forests.

Off to the west are the mountain crags of Snowdonia. The salmon-stocked river Dee winds slowly through a valley far down below. We are in the Cefn Clwyd woodlands, a tranquil 1,300-acre Welsh forest of Sitke spruce, where the only sound is the cry of birds. It is one of many forests around the world where the story of *The Sunday Times* begins.

Cefn Clwyd is one of three North Wales forests owned by Shotton Paper, one of the world's newest newsprint manufacturers. It now produces 450,000 tonnes a year, of which a quarter is recycled from old newspapers and magazines collected from Britain's dustbins and newspaper banks.

Newspapers are often accused of raping forests, particularly when editors get pious about such issues as the felling of the Brazilian rain forests. Angry readers, who hap-pily eat from teak tables, enjoy mahogany furniture, throw away crisp packets and drink milk from Tetrapack cartons, all of which are much more damaging to the environment, write to accuse editors of hypocrisy.

So I had imagined a scene of devastation with hundreds of men scything through the forest felling thousands of trees in a cacophony of sawdust, noise and dirt. I was wrong. The forests where the trees that make newspapers grow are silent and lonely. Twigs crackle underfoot and the air is sweet with the smell of wood and leaves. Nobody is at work. At Cefn Clwyd a forester inspects the forest once a week and decides which areas are to be thinned and which to be felled, perhaps one or two hundred at a time. A few days later the trees are felled. Shortly afterwards they are collected and sent to the paper mills at nearby Shotton on the

Dee estuary near Chester.

The Sitke spruces, which make newsprint, are farmed as a crop. They are grown and harvested in a continuous 40-year cycle. As you walk through the forest some parts are still densely packed with row upon row of trees, planted 15 to 20 years ago. Then one row in three will be thinned so that the others flourish. Then one row in two will be thinned. On one sunlit upland are row upon row of baby spruces, a foot high, a few yards apart as far as the eye can see. They will not mature until 2025, although they will start to be thinned and felled soon after the year 2000.

For every tree that is felled, another is planted. That is the law, a statutory obligation on owners of forests. They indeed would like to plant still more trees. When accused of raping forests to make newspapers, they point out that nine million seedling trees were burnt in 1988 simply because there was nowhere to plant them.

One end of Cefn Clwyd is the forest of all our imaginations – overarching trees stretching towards the sky, mature trees that are up to 100 feet tall, the sunlight shafting down through their branches. This was the part of the forest that was planted in the 1950s and which will be felled within five years, only to be replanted with new seedlings; and even as this part of the forest is cleared, so another will be ready to replace it year after year after year.

The manufacturers who use the Sitke spruce describe it as "green gold". That is because it grows four times faster in the moist humid climate of western Britain than similar varieties in eastern Canada or Scandinavia. It can be used to make newsprint after 18 years and is fully matured within 40 years. Sitke spruce also provides the best sort of fibre for making newsprint.

At Shotton the spruce is quickly transformed into newsprint. Once the trees have been stripped of the bark (used later to create steam for the mills) they are chipped into fragments before going into the pulp mill, where the wood is softened with steam and separated into long fibres which are eventually transformed into a pulp like lumps of wet blotting-paper. Recycled pulp is blended with the new pulp, water is added and the resulting mixture is propelled on to the papermaking machine. It emerges in giant rolls, ready for delivery by road to *The Sunday Times* and most of Britain's other big papers.

The most amazing sight at Shotton is the 4.5-acre warehouse attached to its new recycled fibre mill. Inside it at any one time are millions of old newspapers and magazines, stored in piles at least 100 feet high, now about to be recycled yet again into newsprint. Shotton uses 160,000 tonnes of old newspapers a year, which makes 120,000 tonnes of newsprint – and saves some 600,000 trees.

The technology of recycling is now advancing rapidly. Within the past five years the Bridgwater Paper Mill has produced more than 1 million tonnes of recycled newsprint, saving 13 million trees. Out of nearly 1 million tonnes produced in Britain in 1990, more than half is made from recycled fibre.

As Britain's biggest newspaper, aware that it is open to the accusation of destroying the environment, *The Sunday Times* uses as much recycled fibre as it can get. It has also sponsored a nationwide campaign for the recycling of newsprint. The destruction of trees is a live political issue, at least for the environmentalists, as a letter to the

Ten things you didn't know about trees

ABOUT 15,000 to 20,000 trees are felled to make 1.3 million copies of a 124-page issue of *The Sunday Times*.

78 PAPERS are produced from one Swedish tree; up to 100 from a British tree.

ABOUT 250,000 trees are cut down each week to make into newsprint for the 15 million national newspapers read in Britain every day.

SOME 5,000 acres of forest are cleared every year for national newspapers.

TREES are replanted at a much faster rate than they are felled. SCA, one of the biggest Swedish newsprint manufacturers, plants 60 million seedling trees every year.

NEW trees are planted on 100,000 acres in Britain every year.

NONE of the hardwoods, oak, ash or beech, is used to make newsprint.

RECYCLING old newspapers creates toxic effluent. Since chemicals have to be used to bleach and de-ink them, the effluent is specially treated with hydrogen peroxide and sodium hydrosulphide to remove any residual chemical effluents before it is discharged into rivers.

1 MILLION tonnes of recycled newsprint saves the felling of 13 million trees.

THE only part of *The Sunday Times* where chemical pulp is used is the magazine, which is made of glossier, higher-quality newsprint. Magazine newsprint is made from 65 per cent Norway spruce, 24 per cent filler (usually Cornish china clay) and 11 per cent chemical pulp. The pulp is treated so that there is no toxicity in the effluent and the paper is bleached by using oxygen instead of chlorine.

editor demonstrates this very week. It is from the acting environmental health officer of Leeds City Council, who is encouraged by *The Sunday Times'* recycling campaign. A Save Waste and Prosper campaign in Leeds, he says, has recycled more than 35,000 tonnes of materials from 120 newspaper and magazine banks, but the price per tonne has been forced down from £5 to £2:

> The need to develop demand for recycled newsprint is paramount and a fixed minimum recycled fibre content for all newsprint that can be increased year by year is a required step. In the short term the used newspaper merchants and recycling mills need to be forced into accepting that a price has to be paid for the secure and steady supply of this material, a service that bodies such as ourselves have and will provide. Why the price has plummeted so much, with supplies at mills still around the six-week mark, is most confusing. Is it perhaps that unscrupulous merchants and mills, with large control of the market, are using the situation to make a quick short-term profit at the expense of public concern and long-term environmental issues?

Some newspapers are likely to grow still bigger over the next decade – and the issue of newspapers and the environment won't go away. The use of recycled newsprint will grow. Newspaper readers, anxious to escape guilt for destroying the environment, whatever the strict controls on newsprint manufacturers, will see to that.

Monday

"My job is to be a conductor of words and pictures but it's not coloured wallpaper. We make the magazine refreshing, enticing and alluring so readers keep flicking through the paper."

After working throughout Saturday, Monday for most Sunday paper journalists is a day of rest. A few, however, are working early. Iain Johnstone, film critic and radio panellist, is on Radio 4's *Start the Week* with Melvyn Bragg, Sir John Harvey-Jones, former chairman of ICI, Sir Peter Hall, theatre director, and Edwina Currie, the controversial Tory MP. Television critic Patrick Stoddart has just got to bed after a heavy night at the Montreux Television Festival. In Hong Kong Jon Swain, the Far East correspondent, is deciding how to spend his week – should he concentrate on the debate over the future of United States' military bases in the Philippines or the saga of the *Goddess of Democracy* dissident radio ship? Its mission to broadcast programmes on the benefits of democracy to China is in tatters since it became stranded in Taiwan without a transmitter.

For Johnstone it is an important day: later he is off to Cannes for the annual film festival, one of the big events of a film critic's year; meanwhile he is promoting his new book, *Cannes: The Novel*. The *Start the Week* panel is a competitive, upstaging crowd. Harvey-Jones tells Hall he prefers Chekhov in the original Russian. Currie steals Johnstone's notes and uses a quote. "I let her off," says Johnstone, "because she's rather sexy." Then they all agree to go to Cannes with Johnstone – Currie (who's off to Romania to supervise the elections) to supervise the Cannes jury, Hall to show them how to direct, and Harvey-Jones to be troubleshooter for the Hollywood accounting system that can turn a $30 million film that earns $300 million into a trading loss. In the event, only Johnstone catches the plane for Nice.

It is the season for European festivals – not only film at Cannes but also the annual television beano at Montreux on the shores of Lac Leman, the most important competition in the television year.

"It is also a vital week in a television writer's year," says bearded Stoddart, one of the wittier critics. "You get your hands on people who are inaccessible for much of the time. For the other 51 weeks commissioning editors, channel controllers and programme-makers are busy ploughing their furrows while you plough yours. In Montreux we are all Brits abroad, in town for the same purpose and appalled by the same things – Norwegian comedy, the cost of beer, how much of it we manage to drink. There are rules of engagement. It is a week in which anything goes and most things can be said without fear of comeback. The reporters tell the practitioners where they have been going wrong and the practitioners get their own back for all the unpleasant things we have written about them in the past year. Vernon Lawrence, who is head of comedy at Yorkshire Television, snipes amiably at me on an hourly basis for not having written about *A Bit of a Do*. I do not have the heart to tell him I just didn't like it very much."

Today the week is almost over for Stoddart. He arrived last Wednesday and the awards are announced tomorrow. It has been a good week for Britain. The ITV entry, Rowan Atkinson's mime show *Mr Bean*, was shown on Friday; on Saturday there was the BBC's *Alexei Sayle*; on Sunday Channel 4's *Norbert Smith: A Life*, with Harry Enfield. They are competing with more than 30 other shows from nearly 30 countries.

"They all count as light entertainment, which just goes to show what some people do for entertainment," says Stoddart. "There are plodding comedy sketch shows from Austria and East Germany, ethnic music shows from Spain and Hungary. Comedy travels unhappily even when it is done for the best of reasons. When it is done for the worst of reasons it usually ends up dead in the water. Atkinson's show is different, however. It is a mime show in a classic tradition and it is obvious from the moment it starts that the crowd understands it perfectly. They also love it, which is a bonus. British shows traditionally get a respectful viewing here because Britain has been at it longer than most and our shows are expected to be well made, technically superb and clever. They don't always make people laugh, though, and Atkinson did that in a big way. Already by Friday lunchtime the British contingent knew they had an award winner – which is nice for Thames TV, who made it, but irritating for the BBC, for whom Atkinson has done most of his most famous work, such as *Not the Nine O'Clock News* and *Blackadder*."

As Stoddart wrestles with his hangover and Johnstone jets to Cannes, the offices of *The Sunday Times*, once Napoleonic rum warehouses, are almost deserted. The three one-storey buildings were converted into newspaper offices when Rupert Murdoch staged the overnight flit of his four main papers from Fleet Street to his new non-unionised site at Wapping, near the Tower of London, in 1986. They are airy and pleasant to work in. But for a year after the move, Wapping was unpleasant for the staff who worked within the compound which was protected by barbed razor wire. Every day they had to walk through jeering pickets. On Saturday nights there were bloody

Patrick Stoddart

Television critic. Aged 46. Started writing about television on the *Evening News* in London in the mid-seventies before freelancing as producer, writer and presenter of TV programmes. He then spent eight years in radio, including a stint on the BBC *Breakaway* programme. Moved to *The Sunday Times* in 1986. Watches up to 40 hours of television a week, usually at home, occasionally at London previews, often on special videos sent by the television companies.

clashes between police and angry pickets outside the plant. Yet the shedding of 5,500 print workers did not cause all that many tears among the staff of *The Sunday Times*, whose Saturday night production had been jeopardised for decades by union disruption. With their new Atex word-processors at Wapping, journalists were back in control of the production of their paper – and the increased profits of News International were the main reason that *The Sunday Times* was able to expand to eight sections.

Some sections of the paper – Business, Books, Style, Travel and Arts, which go to press on Thursday and Friday – are working; but the throb of activity which hums through the offices from Tuesday to Friday, when all the staff are at work, is missing today. There is work to do but there is a Monday-morning feeling about the place, especially for Jeff Randall, the City editor, who is just back from a golfing holiday and feeling far from dynamic. Awaiting him, moreover, is a long letter from Storehouse, the High Street retailing group, making nine criticisms about an article in yesterday's paper. Still, that's not unusual. There are always complaints about all sections of the paper. No paper is doing its proper job unless it is upsetting somebody.

Away from Wapping, however, one section of the paper is very busy. *The Sunday Times Magazine*, working from the paper's former offices at Gray's Inn Road near Bloomsbury and King's Cross, has the most difficult production schedule of any section of the paper. Much of the magazine goes to press up to six weeks before publication and in any one week Philip Clarke, its editor, is dealing with the ongoing production of six different magazines, all in different stages of production.

A tall man in his sixties who walks his dog in the Essex countryside every morning at six, Clarke has worked for four editors and seen it all. He is one of the characters of *The Sunday Times*, where he has spent most of his career. Although occasionally world-weary with the foolishness of editors or managers and always avid for the latest gossip from Wapping, he has an infectious enthusiasm for his work, a flair for big reader-grabbing ideas, and a penchant for memorable *bons mots*.

After being deputy editor of the magazine to several editors, always the best man never the groom, he entered his destiny late in his career. He is the all-round, experienced and professional journalist, one of the founders of the Business section, who has worked in all sections of the paper. Under his editorship the magazine has expanded, added new special extra magazines, and the quality of its journalism has been rewarded with several national awards for excellence. Magazine editors voted Clarke Editor of the Year in 1990.

Clarke is an enthusiast with a clearly thought-out philosophy of the role of the magazine within so big a newspaper. "It has to be a sharp counterpoint to the paper," he says. "The worst trap that its editor can fall into would be to run the sort of features the newspaper runs with colour pictures. That isn't what the magazine is about. It has the potential to range far and wide over every subject. It has the skills and the ability to present a range of different subjects, each with a tone and flavour that is different. With that goes a realisation that if it is ranging in that kind of way, one of the classic weapons in its armoury is surprise, its ability to change pace

Philip Clarke

Editor, *The Sunday Times Magazine*. Aged 61, he is now the longest-serving member of staff and has been on the paper since 1965. Joined after working for *Sheffield Telegraph* and *Sunday Graphic*. Has been property correspondent, transport correspondent, founder of Prufrock, the Business News gossip column, assistant editor of Business News and editor of the Scene pages. Joined magazine in 1978, became editor in 1986 and has overseen its continual expansion.

by switching from one kind of feature to another. My job is to be a conductor of words and pictures, but it's not pictures in colour or coloured wallpaper. We have to imagine the reader on a Sunday. It's not our business to produce 500 stories but four or five main features with a few bits and bobs. We mix them so that the magazine is so refreshing, enticing and alluring that the readers keep flicking through the pages."

One of the great tests is PS, a characteristic Clarke *bon mot*. Have we got page-stoppers, articles so enticing that readers stop and say to themselves "What's happening here?" On other occasions he describes that as the "dippability factor", the editorial tactic of forcing the reader to stop and dip.

Clarke admits that the general expectations of newspaper magazines are not high, at least compared with such magazines as *Country Life*, and an unexpected feature reaps high reader-satisfaction. "Ours is a popular, general interest, quality magazine and by and large people don't have a finely honed perception of what it is they are going to get and enjoy. That means that when you succeed in producing a good magazine, their satisfaction level zooms out of the charts."

He starts flicking through the magazine that is now in production. It's a good, eclectic issue, he says. It starts with a mystery story. When builders found a skeleton in a Cardiff garden, police turned to Richard Neave, who specialises in reconstructing faces from skulls. His work showed that it was the skull of a teenage girl, whom police were able to identify. "Everybody loves a mystery. We have cracked the mystery."

Then there is a change of pace, a

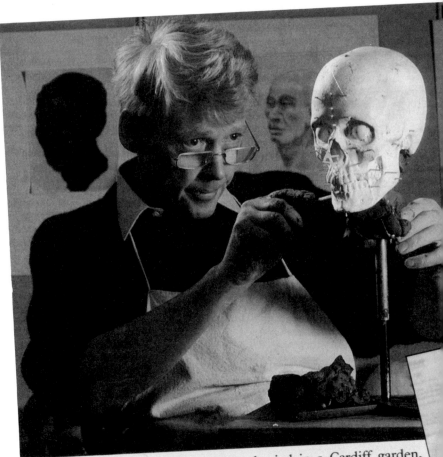

When builders found a skeleton buried in a Cardiff garden, police, in their quest for an identity, turned to Richard Neave, who specialises in reconstructing faces from skulls. With little more scientific than modelling clay, tools and a few cocktail sticks, Neave went to work. Report: Amit Roy. Photographs: Jerry Young

MAKING THE FACE FIT

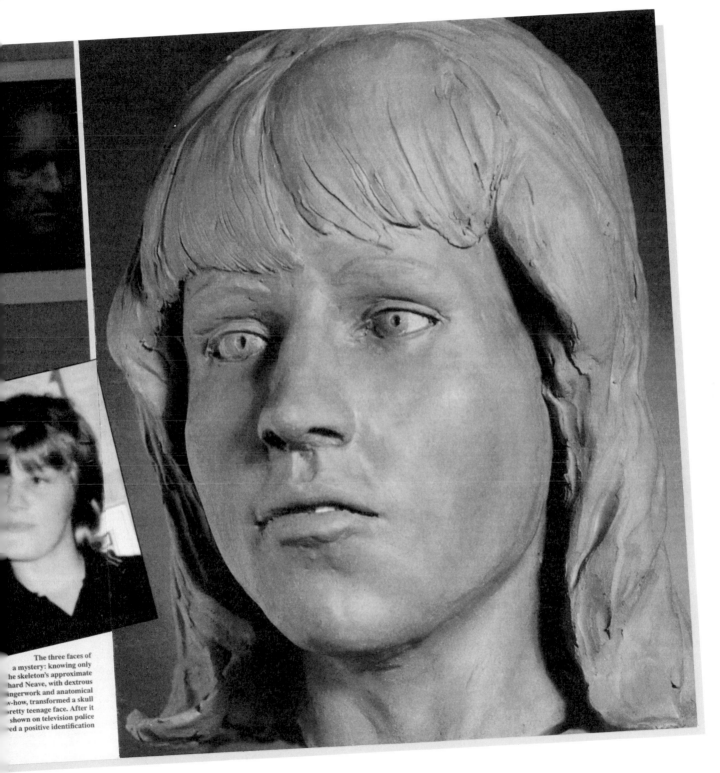

The three faces of a mystery: knowing only the skeleton's approximate [age], [Ric]hard Neave, with dextrous [fi]ngerwork and anatomical [kno]w-how, transformed a skull [into a p]retty teenage face. After it [was] shown on television police [receiv]ed a positive identification

"Everybody loves a mystery," says Clarke.

feature wittily headlined "Hide and Sequin": after the grisliness of murder, an explosion of colour devoted to fashion, sequins that add sparkle to slinky leggings, spangly jackets and stunning shifts. It's a brilliant bit of positioning, says Clarke. "You need a bit of relief."

Then there is another contrast – a report by Jon Swain, the award-winning foreign correspondent, on Aung San Suu Kyi, a national hero in her native Burma after her detention by the government. That is followed by an article on the Isle of Man TT races, due again the following week, which publishes the name of every rider who has been killed in the race since 1911. Statistically, at least, one or two riders will die this year, it says. Admittedly the magazine is going to be oversubscribed on death this week, says Clarke, but this article tells the reader the truth about every death. "It's a straight piece of reporting. It doesn't moralise but what it does *par excellence* is to put a major research effort into a story and produce a definitive piece of journalism."

Now there is another change of pace, an article about the pop star Chrissie Hynde, with yet another punning headline: "Benefit of Hynde Sight". Pop stars are two a penny, Clarke admits, but Hynde is a star with a difference. She has gone green and become a propagandist for saving the planet.

OK, he adds, his excitement mounting, so we've had a murder mystery, fashion, motor-cycle racing and a personality interview with a point. Now we are in the back of the book with the semi-regulars – design, health, wine and architecture. So this week there are articles on the art of the silversmith, flamboyant men's waistcoats, and tranquilliser addicts. "That's how you put it together. Then you have to ensure that every issue is different so that readers aren't reading about the same sort of subjects every week. Simple, isn't it?"

Clarke presides over a staff of 50 and a budget of £3.2 million, with an extra £750,000 for the London magazine, which appears in London and the South-East. Although they work several miles away from the main offices, Clarke is frequently at Wapping, either to see the editor or to attend news conferences. Soon the magazine will move in with the paper and its splendid isolation will be over. (It finally moved in March 1991 to Admiral House, a building across the road from the main plant at Wapping, where Clarke's office commands panoramic views over St Katharine's Dock.)

The magazine works at a totally different pace from the weekly deadline of the rest of the paper. The copy is set in nearby Leather Lane, the pictures are processed in Finsbury Circus and the magazine is printed in Scarborough (a headache for the circulation department, which has to get the paper and magazine delivered to newsagents from printing plants at London, Manchester, Glasgow and Scarborough).

The Sunday Times Magazine was the pacesetter in Sunday journalism, the first in the field – and Rupert Murdoch has been determined to keep it on top. With one bold stroke in 1988 he decided that the magazine should differentiate itself from the opposition, and that its pages should be bigger. It has also spawned a mini-empire of ancillary magazines devoted to such subjects as House Style, Fashion, Business and Motoring so that there are some Sundays when it comes as three magazines plus the

Funday Times comic. Three magazines and an eight-section paper make a good bargain for 60p.

Every so often Clarke devotes the magazine to one major piece of journalism. When I met him he was looking at the proofs of a sumptuous issue in which more than 40 pages were devoted to "A Vanished Realm: The Lost Treasures of Britain", written by Sir Roy Strong. "This will smash 'em in the aisles," he enthused. "The competition can't get near this. Most of them haven't got the resources, the talent or the flair to clear the decks and go for a bold stroke of journalism." Among the treasures it covers are Inigo Jones's masterpiece, the old St Paul's, centuries of monastic treasure, Holbein's portrait group of the Tudor dynasty and the royal palace of Westminster.

He studies one of the spreads. "Just look at this," he says, admiring a treasure that was pulled down: Nonsuch, Henry VIII's finest palace. "This takes time and patience. Look at the detail in that artwork, the crowd of people, the gardens, the parterres." It was obviously a biased assessment – but true for all that.

Although every other Sunday paper eventually followed *The Sunday Times* by publishing a magazine, its birth in 1962 was difficult. A British Sunday newspaper magazine had been a pet project of Roy Thomson, the avuncular Canadian who then owned the paper. On the afternoon the first issue was due off the presses, Thomson attended a tea-party at Watford and after the cucumber sandwiches made a brief speech. "What we are doing here today is something that many newspapers have wanted to do for a long time – but everyone said it was impossible," he declared proudly. "Now we have proved that it is

"This will smash 'em in the aisles," says Philip Clarke.

possible and we are doing it. I and all of us here know that it will be a great success."

Then he moved to the press hall, pushed a button and started the run. He peered hard at the first copy. Then he peered even harder through his large pebble glasses.

"My God," he said, turning to Denis Hamilton, then editor of *The Sunday Times*, "this is going to be a disaster."

Hamilton, once the youngest brigadier in the British army, who served under Montgomery and survived, was an editor with a reputation for remaining cool under fire. He raised one eyebrow, marginally, and allowed a protracted silence to follow – a classic Hamilton tactic for making somebody else break cover. Eventually a printer who could bear the tension no longer pointed to Thomson and said in an edgy voice, "He thought it was going to be full of funnies!"

Eight Things You Didn't Know About the Magazine

LORD Snowdon was the first magazine photographer – and maybe the only one – ever to be tipped on a job. He was photographing some Blackpool landladies. They didn't realise who he was, and he hated people knowing. After seeing him working for several hours one of them pressed a £1 note into his hand as he was leaving. "You've worked bloody hard, lad," she said. "I know they don't pay you boys much. Go out and treat yourself to a real good dinner."

THE one picture which received a record number of reader requests for copies was a magazine cover. It was for an issue about public attitudes to animals. The lead feature was a powerful report from inside a slaughter-house. The art department went to some trouble to produce the worst cover ever: grossly sentimental, schmaltzy, perfect chocolate-box stuff. In short it was a send-up. It was meant to demonstrate the public's double standards about animals. So the worst cover ever was an enormous success for the wrong reasons.

THE design director, Mike Rand, has designed over 1,250 issues and worn a beard for every one of them. His considerable and talented presence has given the magazine a great sense of continuity – something not possessed by any of the others.

THE biggest internal hiatus concerned an issue on the female form. The cover was a nude, front view of a girl – up

That first magazine was greeted with universal derision. The rest of Fleet Street gloated. Advertising agencies hated it. Soon the magazine was losing £20,000 a week. Yet what the detractors failed to notice was that the magazine had increased sales of *The Sunday Times* by more than 150,000 a week.

"At that moment," Clarke says now, "I doubt whether anyone involved realised the overall importance of what had happened. For this was a watershed in British publishing, the beginning of a new epoch. Three months later circulation was holding at 1.1 million, an increase since the launch of the magazine of 127,000 copies. Nothing which had been added to the paper could have caused *The Sunday Times* to pull so strongly away from its traditional rival, the *Observer*. A year later the magazine, described by its first editor, Marc Boxer, as the culture shock of the sixties, had spawned a new journalism and encouraged a new creativity from the advertising industry."

Since then it has many achievements to its credit – the war photography of Don McCullin, the first partwork on the "1,000 Makers of the Twentieth Century" and in 1988 its biggest-ever package, a 124-page main magazine, a 16-page partwork on "The Taste of Italy", the inserted London magazine with 44 pages, and a banded-on 84-page magazine on house style, a total of 268 pages.

Yet thirty years later the culture shock for Iain Johnstone is not the size of the magazine but the sudden transition from London to Cannes. Johnstone is wetting his novel's head at a party on Long Beach and basking in the acclaim of fellow film critics from Toronto, Sydney and the *New York Times* who read the

book on their flights to the South of France.

"They are amazingly keen on it," says Johnstone as he drinks champagne on the sand and watches the Mediterranean sun set over the Old Port. "Perhaps it needs to be consumed with jet-lag and a few vodkas. Nevertheless life is tolerable."

Something of an understatement that, especially for all the reporters and executives at Wapping who envy the seeming lotus life as he wanders off to dinner at L'Esquif with his publisher Catherine Eccles.

The lotus life? Stoddart would disagree. He has been to so many dinners – up a mountain for Thames, in town for Central Television, up the mountain again for Channel 4 – that his personal hallucination is beans on toast and a cup of tea, which is always his first meal when he gets back to England. "You mustn't imagine that the week in Montreux is all spent eating and drinking," he says. "Some of it is spent watching Moldavian soot jugglers, Portuguese ferret dancers or whatever else the programmes offer up. You sometimes need a drink rather badly after an afternoon's viewing. As for eating, the joys of fancy food run thin after a couple of days and you hear yourself ordering omelette and green salad with monotonous regularity."

He admits nevertheless that you do drink more than is good for you, mainly because nobody goes to bed in Montreux and everybody wants to talk. "This is the week in which the world is set to rights, the television industry is re-invented and the universe put to better use. Discussions that start at midnight end at dawn, without anybody noticing the night steal away. My earliest bedtime has been 4 am. The latest, twice, was 8 am."

It is a much lonelier life for Jon Swain, the paper's farthest flung foreign correspondent in Hong Kong. He has decided to talk to John Witherow, the foreign editor, in the morning and recommend a trip to the Philippines, a country, he says, that is neglected by British newspapers. "Two young American airmen were shot dead last week near Clark airbase by the secret killers of the Communist New People's Army. The approaching talks about the base have given rise to enormous demonstrations, with people waving banners with Yankee Go Home on them. That provoked silence from the US embassy in Manila and a confrontational crackdown on demonstrators by the police."

As Johnstone and Stoddart carouse the night away, Swain starts packing his bags for an early start tomorrow.

THE EVOLUTION OF THE FEMALE FORM

THE SUNDAY TIMES magazine
How we use animals

Stop the presses. *Top*, the cover that went too far and how it was changed. *Above*, the schmaltzy cover that received the record number of requests from readers for copies — a send-up by the art department of the lead feature from inside a slaughter-house (right).

to the shoulders and just above the er, er . . . mysterious, semi-lune of the pelvis. It was set against an outline of the Venus de Milo with her measurements. C. D. Hamilton saw it when it was already on machine, shouted stop the presses and ordered that her form be clothed with a body stocking. Some people think it looked more suggestive then than the first version.

IT takes 7 to 10 days to print the magazine at 40,000 copies an hour. Ideally it is completed the Tuesday before publication.

IT takes 6 days to distribute. The first copies go out Monday pre-publication, the last on Saturday pre-publication.

THE most letters ever received on any one subject resulted from A Life in The Day of Mary Philpott, a total unknown. She was a woman of 57 who had spent her life looking after elderly parents. She was living on her own in very deprived circumstances, with just her cat Tosca for company. There was an amazing response from readers — an American sailor even arrived in the office to take her out for a good dinner. (See page 156.)

IT'S not generally known that another magazine is produced three times a year — spring, summer and autumn — which has a circulation of 30,000. It's called *Watchword*, and goes to members of WATCH, the young people's environmental club jointly sponsored by *The Sunday Times* and the Royal Society for Nature Conservation.

Tuesday

The editor is dissatisfied: "These are all issues. What people can be written about? We've got to get some humanity into these pages. Otherwise we shall be calling ourself the *Sunday Suicide.*"

Rosemary Collins

Home news editor. Aged 31. New Zealander who started career on *Auckland* and *Christchurch Star*, where she was political correspondent. After a stint on the *Daily Mirror*, she joined *The Sunday Times* in 1988 as a reporter and was subsequently deputy foreign editor.

Some journalists seem to get all the luck, especially seen through the jaundiced eyes of *Sunday Times* assistant editors, stuck for up to 12 stress-filled hours a day at Wapping and unable even to see the sun. Not for them the high life of Cannes or Montreux – even though deputy editor Ivan Fallon awoke with Iain Johnstone to a beautiful sunrise over St Tropez. Fallon is now driving to Marseilles and hoping to be in London for the editorial conference. Not for them, either, the excitement of being a foreign correspondent. As Rosemary Collins, the flame-haired news editor drives to Wapping, Jon Swain is jetting from Hong Kong to Manila, James Blitz, the Moscow correspondent, is following the dramatic events in the Soviet Union, and Tony Allen-Mills is reporting the excitement surrounding the first Romanian election since the downfall of the Ceauşescu government.

They have the glamour and the excitement. Collins, a young New Zealander who moved to *The Sunday Times* from the *Daily Mirror* and quickly became a star reporter and the first woman news editor, has power. That power takes its toll. She works 12-hour days and the nervous tension that goes with the job shows in her nails: they are bitten to the quick. Stress levels at Wapping are measured on the Richter scale and hers is six to seven.

Awakened by her alarm at 6.45 am, Collins immediately switched on the BBC news. Her working week started last night, however, when she watched *Newsnight* on BBC2UF195. *Newsnight* on Monday is a must for this news editor. It gives her a feel for the news that is dominating the start of the week. If she is out on the town, she tapes the programme and watches it when she gets home. Even in the shower this morning, she was listening to the radio. Then she collected all the papers and set off for Wapping, meanwhile switching the car radio to LBC to listen to Andrew Neil, editor of *The Sunday Times*, who is chairing the morning news programme this week. Now she knows what is on the editor's mind this morning.

By 8.30 Collins is at her desk reading the papers for leads on news stories and making phone calls to reporters. The first editorial conference of the week with Neil, attended by every section editor, starts at 11.30. Now she is making sure she is thoroughly prepared.

Managing editor Tony Bambridge is also reading the papers. It is the way most newspaper executives start their day, whatever paper they work for. What they are looking for is ideas – stories that can be developed from yesterday's news. It takes Bambridge about an hour to work through the *Daily Mail*, the *Daily Telegraph* and the *Independent*.

"I start at 7.30 with the *Mail*," he says. "Of all the nationals it has the sharpest feature ideas and is essential reading. Next the *Telegraph*. All the news that's fit to print – and more if I'm lucky. It is the best paper for news. Having read it carefully, I feel ready for the day. Then the *Independent*. A quick look through for something that catches my eye that will spark an idea. All ideas are carefully noted down in a large ledger that goes with me everywhere. The start of each day means a fresh page and a date at the top: ideas on the right-hand page, jobs to be completed that day on the left. All notes are saved. You never know. My wife points out, once again, that I have the mind of a clerk – a highly qualified clerk but none the less a clerk. I ignore her."

Bambridge is in his car by 9.10 and at the office by 10, where he settles down to read all the rest of the papers before going off to see all the managing editors. "Ideas in a vacuum are not good. It is chat, chat and still more chat that refines them into workable journalism."

Tuesday is the symbolic start of a Sunday paper's week. Although there are still five days to go before the paper is printed and it ought to be a relaxed day, Tuesday morning is one of the most frantic of the week. The editorial conference is at 11.30 and by 10 am the editors of the eight sections are putting together the lists that will be scrutinised by Andrew Neil. All too often, since he is a demanding editor, they are found wanting. Nobody wants the humiliation, so enjoyed by all their colleagues, of a public dressing-down at the conference.

A lot of news can break between now and Saturday, but it is important to get the staff working and to lay strong foundations now. Many of the decisions made this morning will be reflected in the paper that appears on Sunday. Some will be started but killed because they have been thoroughly covered by the national daily papers and become stale news by Sunday. Some, the ultimate frustration for Sunday reporters with only one day a week to aim at, will be written after days of work but squeezed out by better or newer stories.

With so big a paper, Neil also has to ensure that a balance is struck between politics and show business and stories that are important and those that are entertaining. The paper would not sell nearly 1,200,000 copies a week if it reported only domestic politics and international affairs. There are eight sections and

Anthony Bambridge

Executive editor. Aged 54. A London School of Economics graduate, he started on *The Economist* before joining *The Observer*, where he was business editor and news editor. Joined *The Sunday Times* in 1977 and has been business editor, news editor and managing editor of both News and Features. As executive editor, he has a keen eye for design flaws and says he is a problem-solver, sweeper-up, adviser, and wise counsellor. "No paper can afford to be without one."

Robert Tyrer

Managing editor, Features. Aged 44. Started on *Chatham, Rochester and Gillingham News* and was then a uranium miner in Canada before joining Fleet Street News Agency. Moved to Australia as a sub with a news agency. He then worked for eight years as Latin America correspondent for the BBC World Service, before joining *The Sunday Times* in 1986 and becoming foreign editor in 1988. Responsible for Review section and Focus articles in News section.

eight front pages. Each of the front pages should make a different appeal to the reader and offer changes of pace. Otherwise *The Sunday Times*, since it is so big, becomes too unrelenting. If that happens it loses sales.

The Arts newslist is being drawn up by Tony Rennell, managing editor of the four back sections, and David Mills, deputy reviews editor. There are three big stories this week: the future of Glyndebourne (they hope to get the first drawings of its new building), a Rolling Stones concert in Holland on Friday night, and an interview by Bryan Appleyard with Sir Peter Hall, the theatre director, and Peter Palumbo, chairman of the Arts Council. That, they think, is probably too academic, too much about policy rather than people, for the front Arts page.

It is a good week for the arts. There is the Cannes film festival (an offering for the front of the Style section, so out of the running for the Arts front); the Montreux Festival, where Patrick Stoddart is tipping Rowan Atkinson's *Mr Bean* to win three of the awards for comedy series (in which case Atkinson could be a subject for the paper's main profile); a new Peter Hall production of Ibsen's *The Wild Duck*; and a scoop on the new Madonna album which the other critics won't hear until next week.

Rennell and Evans opt for Glyndebourne: "The unsubsidised opera house seems set to lead the way for opera in the 1990s"; and the Rolling Stones: "The most lucrative rock band tour ever reaches Europe. The Rolling Stones Urban Jungle show opens in Holland, awash with sponsorship and spin-off merchandising after their successful Budweiser endorsements and tough negotiating over televi-

sion rights in the USA." Their list is ready.

The taciturn Bob Tyrer, managing editor of the Review section and the two long News Focus articles, has the most difficult of the lists to prepare. Not only does he always open the batting at conference but his is the list that most engages the editor and causes most debate. That is because the News Review is the intellectual heart of the paper.

So far he has jotted down four main thoughts, the IRA, child molesters, mad cow disease and the desecration of Jewish graves in France and Britain. The Romanian elections are due at the weekend, which could be a Focus subject, and he has also noticed in the *Independent* a report that a vase bought for £20 in the 1960s has been sold for £25,000. That could make a good light story. By 10.30 he has already had six people in his office, made six phone calls and still hasn't read all the papers. A man of few words and an abrupt manner, he is in a hurry. An hour later he has decided to put forward four options for Focuses: Romania, mad cow disease, paedophile hysteria (a story about attempted kidnaps of children by bogus social workers) and a report from inside Russia's prisons, which he has commissioned himself.

John Witherow, the foreign editor and a rising star, is discussing world news with his deputy, Richard Ellis. Their main problem is to guess what will be news by next Sunday. It is futile to despatch their foreign correspondents on stories that will get so much coverage in the dailies over the next five days that readers will be bored by them on Sunday. There are some stories they know will still be live news by Sunday – the Romanian elections, the South African president's meeting with Mrs Thatcher on Saturday, the meetings between James Baker, the American Secretary of State, and Soviet leaders in Moscow that are due to end on Saturday, and the likely election of Boris Yeltsin as president of Russia.

They are also looking for subjects that are in the news and which will make good reads. Ellis has heard that Soviet women are making videotapes to attract foreign husbands. That seems a good subject. What about the impact on France of the attacks on Jewish graves? But will that story still be of interest by the end of the week? Perhaps it would be worth investigating the fate of General Noriega, the deposed Panamanian president, now that he is in gaol awaiting trial on drug-trafficking charges. Perhaps, too, Rajiv Gandhi, the deposed Indian Prime Minister, would be worth a report: apparently he is still insisting on being called Prime Minister. Jon Swain is in Manila.

Roger Eglin, editor of the Business section, is also preparing his list and reflecting that he is short of journalists this week – his City, production and design editors are on holiday and the editor of the Innovation page, devoted to new developments in science, has chickenpox. At the moment the future of Philips, the electronics giant, seems a promising subject for his main Focus article, which runs at 2,000 words. Philips sees itself playing an important role challenging the Japanese push into Europe but it has internal management problems and needs a shake-up. Eglin has also noted the half-yearly results of Marks and Spencer: they are excellent and against the dismal trend in High Street trading. By comparing and contrasting Marks and Spencer with Storehouse/BHS he would get another good Focus for the City pages.

He taps the two top items for the Business list on to his screen:

A tale of two groups: Marks and Spencer confounds the sceptics with bumper results. But Storehouse is sacking 1,500 and making provisions for losses. What makes the difference?

Philips in crisis – the Dutch giant has always seen itself as Europe's electronics champion. But can it survive, never mind beat off the Japanese? Even its own chairman says it's in trouble.

A keen yachtsman himself who sails every weekend off the Isle of Wight, Eglin is also working up a long feature on the America's Cup. He wants to look at the reasons so many business tycoons pour millions into the race. San Diego has said it will get £1 billion from staging the cup. He sets up a worldwide team of reporters to write it – John Huxley in Sydney, Philip Robinson in Los Angeles, Peter Hadfield in Tokyo and Keith Wheatley in England.

For human interest amidst some of the other pages, which will be devoted to the American economy and privatisation in eastern Europe, he adds to his list a story about Gwendoline Lamb. "She lost nearly £100,000 after being ripped off by the Manx Savings and Investment Bank and a bent commodity dealer eight years ago," he says. "For eight years she has driven the media – especially us – mad, ringing up and campaigning to get something done about it. She may have got results and deserves a reward for her persistence. A good personality piece."

Meanwhile Bambridge is talking to Insight, the investigative team of *The Sunday Times*, renowned over three decades for several sensa-

John Witherow

Foreign editor. Aged 39, Witherow worked for Reuters in Madrid and London before joining *The Times*, where he worked for the home and foreign desks and reported the Falklands conflict. Joined *The Sunday Times* in 1984 and was defence and diplomatic correspondent before becoming foreign editor. The pleasure of his job on a Sunday paper is finding the unusual stories and angles that the daily papers missed.

Roger Eglin

Business editor. Aged 50, son of journalist who worked on *Liverpool Post* and *Picture Post*. Graduate of London School of Economics. A former business journalist on the *Observer*, he joined *The Sunday Times* as industrial editor in 1972 and reported all the great industrial battles of the sixties and seventies, including the Laker and Concorde battles. After a spell as deputy business editor, he was appointed editor of Business News in 1983. A keen yachtsman, his boat *Fruesli 2* won its class six times during one Cowes Week.

tional scoops that have often become stories reported throughout the world. They seem to have a good story about the European Community subsidising the sale of high tar tobacco by BAT, the giant British manufacturer, to Third World countries. That is one candidate for the newslist but on Tuesday it is much too early for Collins to make any commitments.

She has the same difficulty as Witherow on the foreign desk. She must initiate stories rather than simply react to the news of the week, for fear of setting her reporters on trails that will be stale by Sunday. Her main job is therefore to think of stories that will still be original on Sunday. On her mind today as ideas worth consideration after reading the papers are the growing number of beggars in London, workaholics (she has noticed a report that the Japanese are turning their backs on overwork and is debating whether to check on the attitudes of Britain's captains of industry), Britain's biggest-ever claim for compensation against Glaxo over its drug Myodil, and the Thatcher–de Klerk meeting. After a call from Neil in his car she is also planning a story on the Lockerbie Pan-Am bombing, the report of the Bush Commission is due shortly, he says.

At any one time in any newspaper office, there is always at least one member of staff who is deeply unhappy and grumbling about his treatment by the editor, the newsdesk, his section head, or, at *The Sunday Times* Peter Roberts, the managing editor who handles expenses and guards the editorial budget. This morning there are two.

One of the business journalists is having a row with his immediate boss about relationships between business journalists and City public relations men. For Eglin this is a familiar grouse. "Some feel that City journalists get a bit too close to the PRs in wheeling and dealing for stories – run this one, ease back a bit there on the criticism and next time we have an exclusive we'll see you right. It is a dangerous trend. Journalists fall for it because they fear PRs will go to the opposition with stories. The journalists should have more faith in the power of *The Sunday Times*. The aggrieved journalist has strong investigative instincts and has been accused by his superior of treading on a few PR toes." Eglin has been on *The Sunday Times* for nearly three decades and knows how to deal with such familiar complaints. He tells the reporter he hopes he had his boots on.

The other disgruntled journalist is Michael Jones, the political editor and one of the paper's elder statesmen. Jones, who blows a fuse easily but quickly recovers, is fuming with rage. He had wanted to go to a meeting of the Council of Europe in Strasbourg, but Roberts has insisted he flies economy class. Jones believes that the political editor should fly club class. "Mine is a very high pressure job," he rages. "The meeting of the council might have made a Focus or a report for the foreign pages which would have been an exclusive. *The Sunday Times* is the foremost Sunday political paper and the editor is passionately interested in politics and well-informed."

That is not Jones's only grouse about Roberts. A visit to Strasbourg was a guarantee of a story. Now he has lost it. "We have a lot of space to fill – it's bayonets fixed from Tuesday onwards, when we have to fire on all cylinders," he says. "I would have had to fly back on Thursday, go to a CBI dinner and still write my column, pick up news for Atticus and get political stories for the weekend. Still I've made my point. I'm not going on an economy ticket. The political editor deserves club class."

On that seething note of disgruntlement, he goes into conference.

11.30: Editorial conference
Neil is even better informed than usual this week since he has been dealing with the news since dawn on LBC radio, which is attempting to rival the BBC's *Today* programme. He is fully abreast of the news and anxious to show it. He turns first to Jones. What's on the political menu? There's the new Labour Party policy review – but that may not be news by the weekend, says Jones. There is a by-election in Ulster and another in Bootle. Then he flicks unhappily through the other newslist headlines. All the stories are about money, money, money, he says.

What about mad cow disease? Isn't it always a fair assumption that the government is being complacent?

A lively discussion follows. Are the farmers or the manufacturers of animal feed to blame? asks Bambridge. What's happening abroad? asks Michael Williams, managing editor of the News section. What readers really want, says Neil, is a child's guide, covering the farmers, the butchers, the scientists and the politicians. Why not use the fears of parents to raise the questions that readers are asking themselves? Then Philip Clarke intervenes. What about looking at what is happening behind the closed doors of the supermarket chains, he suggests. He hits the right button. The editor decides. "Let's get the story going as a Focus."

Next on the agenda is paedophilia. Neil, a Scot, suggests that the story has been ignored by the national papers because all the early incidents were in the north of England. Only when cases were reported near London did the national papers get interested. Tyrer is sceptical but the rest of the conference think it is a good story. Neil wants it followed up: "It may not make the paper – but let's see." He rejects the idea of Russia's prisons and the Romanian elections as Focuses. They should be reported on a foreign news page.

The big story, says Neil, is the Bush Commission report on the Lockerbie disaster. It's going to say security was a mess, Iran and Syria were the culprits, and recommend surgical strikes against them. "Insight have got to gut the report, marry what it says with what we know from our own inquiries, and take the story on."

Then Bambridge and Rennell, who tend to work like Siamese twins, each sparking ideas off the other, raise the subject of the M1 Kegworth air disaster inquiry, which is making riveting reading in the daily papers. Under cross-examination the pilots have revealed that the wrong engine was shut down. A reconstruction of what happened on the flight deck would make a good story, they suggest. Neil agrees. Asked what Insight has to offer, Nick Rufford, its editor, mentions their story about Third World tobacco which was originated by Neil, who learned about it when interviewing Teddy Taylor, the Tory MP, on his LBC programme. "That might get you on to page one again," says Neil.

He is, however, still dissatisfied. These are all issues, he says. What people can be written about? Rennell, a graduate of Oxford and

Michael Jones

Political editor. Aged 54. After a varied career on the *Manchester Evening News*, *Northern Echo*, *Financial Times*, *Daily Telegraph* and *The Times* Business News, he joined *The Sunday Times* in the seventies and was news editor and political correspondent. Appointed political editor six years ago, he leads two political correspondents and the economics editor. He is also chairman of the Parliamentary Press Gallery. Asked about the joy of his job, Jones said: "The freedom and the stress." Asked about the aggravation, he replied: "The freedom and the stress."

Andrew Neil

Editor. Aged 42. A Scot from Paisley and graduate of Glasgow University, Neil worked in the Conservative Party research department before joining *The Economist*, where he was lobby and labour correspondent, America correspondent from 1979–82 and then UK editor before being spotted by Rupert Murdoch, whom he had gone to lobby for a satellite television consultancy. He was appointed editor of *The Sunday Times* in 1983 and presided over the move from Gray's Inn Road to Wapping, as well as the expansion of *The Sunday Times* into a multi-section paper. *Who's Who* names his club as Tramp — a characteristic snook at the establishment — and his recreations as dining out in London, New York and Aspen.

Cambridge with one of the keenest journalistic minds in the office, suggests Rowan Atkinson if he wins at Montreux. Somebody else suggests Richard Lacey, the Leeds professor who has been making statements about mad cow disease (and who was at the centre of the salmonella and listeria scares). Another thought is Adnan Khashoggi, the millionaire arms dealer now on trial in New York. That could be fun, Neil concedes. But he is still unhappy. So far, the diet is air crashes, the Arts Council, poverty, Russia, paedophilia, and anti-semitism. "We've got to get some humanity into these pages. Otherwise we shall be calling ourselves the Sunday Suicide."

By now it is 12.15 and lunch is looming. The rest of the lists are considered at greater speed. Neil is happy about the de Klerk–Thatcher meeting. It isn't often that there is a good news story on a

Saturday. He asks if John Cassidy, the American correspondent, has got the latest CIA assessment on Gorbachev, and suggests a feature on the professors of Marxism in East Europe, say in Prague or Budapest. What are they going to do now that Communism is on the way out? He decrees that the Arts section should always carry a story about a personality or a performance on page 3; is delighted that Cannes is the subject of the Style section front; suggests diagrams to go with its feature on the newest dance craze, the Slide; and checks finally that the newsdesk is doing a story on begging in London. After 80 minutes, the conference is over.

Afterwards Neil says it was a meeting that started badly but developed as it went along. At first the suggestions – inside Russian gaols and the Romanian election – were dull, but he is happier now that several varied and promising sub-

Tony Rennell

Managing Editor, Arts, Books, Style and Travel. Aged 43. A Cambridge graduate, who trained as a teacher at Oxford, he decided to become a journalist instead and worked for the *North Herts Gazette* and *Oxford Mail* before joining *The Times Educational Supplement*. Joined *The Sunday Times* Business News section in 1978 and subsequently became News Editor and managing editor News. He resigned in 1990 but still extracts books for the Review Front serialisations.

What's in the news? The editorial conference for heads of departments.

Ivan Fallon

Deputy editor. Aged 47, son of Irish poet Padraic Fallon and graduate of Trinity College, Dublin. Started career on *Daily Mirror*, then joined *Sunday Telegraph* and became influential City editor before moving to *The Sunday Times* in 1984. Author of *De Lorean, The Rise and Fall of a Dream-maker*, and *The Brothers: the Rise and Rise of Saatchi and Saatchi*.

jects, such as mad cow disease, child abuse, Lockerbie, the Kegworth crash and the Insight scoop on tobacco, are being worked on.

The Tuesday conference, he says, gives a kick-start to the week. It gives the assistant editors a sense of direction and starts hares running. After lunch, the chasers of the hares will start to hit the telephones. The week has really begun.

As Neil sets off for lunch at the Savoy with Lord Stevens, chairman of United Newspapers, Ivan Fallon's plane from Marseilles has been delayed, his plan to attend the editorial conference was dashed and now he is also late for his lunch at Smith New Court, one of the largest securities houses in the City. He has phoned from his car and is greeted graciously when he finally arrives at 1.30. Fallon, one of the most experienced City journalists in Britain, writes a column in the business section and what he learns over lunch is an essential ingredient of what he writes. You learn far more over lunch than you ever get by sitting in the office and relying on the phone.

His host is Michael Marks, the chief executive, who has four senior colleagues with him. The feeling around the table is that the tide has turned for Thatcher with the result that optimism is flowing through the markets.

"These people have the keenest market antennae in the City," says Fallon, "and Marks is legendary for his instant decisions, his willingness to take large amounts of stock on his books, and his market feel. They are not much interested in politics as such but passionately interested in its market implications. Marks has just hired Peter Walker [who had recently resigned as a Cabinet minister], who had arrived for his first day yesterday. Why had

he wanted Peter Walker as a director? Because he will bring in lots of business, Marks explains – and indeed he already had. He has extraordinary contacts all over Europe, and superb Japanese contacts too. They don't want him for decoration, he will earn his money."

By Tuesday Christine Walker, editor of the Travel section, is well into her week, most of the section is already organised and she is already planning for next week. When the going gets rough many journalists indulge in fantasies about becoming a travel writer. It seems one of the soft and glamorous options in newspapers. Yet it is not as easy as it looks, according to Walker. Good travel writing, she insists, is rigorous journalism: "Our readers now go on at least two holidays a year. We have to keep them interested 52 weeks a year, writing about five destinations a week."

Her front page this week is an extract from a book, *Last Places* by Lawrence Millman, who has traced the route taken by the Vikings from Norway to Newfoundland. Walker has chosen an excerpt where he describes a weekend bacchanalia. It is a beautiful piece of writing and rare, according to Walker, because it is so natural. The travel writer has to do an immense amount of research and groundwork, she says. "After that you hope that the muse will help you to write a story that takes the reader with you on your journey. Millman writes effortlessly but packs a lot of information into every sentence and creates a great sense of place and character."

The amount of research and groundwork that goes into a really useful travel feature is demonstrated on the next two pages in a spread devoted to Sicily and her islands, written by David Wickers

"*Ja, ja*. Tycho Brahe died. His bladder exploded while he was waiting to meet the king of Denmark."

"Things like that will happen. If you have a bladder."

"Kindly do not explode your bladder around me, Johann."

"I'm Haukur. He's Johann, son of Bjartur, grandson of Egill, great-grandson of Thorgeir. The only alcoholic stalinist in the country."

"My mother was a stalinist. If I didn't support Stalin, I'd be insulting her memory."

"How's your bladder?"

"Full. *Skal!* "

"*Skal!* "

"Better the little fire that warms" — raising the *brennivin*

international conference on motorcycle gangs in Copenhagen and seemed eager to show off new methods of making their bikes backfire. More horns honked. More drunks drank. I kept running into old acquaintances who didn't recognise me and total strangers who did. A bearded man who looked like Walt Whitman on a binge asked me what I was doing on board his trawler (he *did* seem to be bobbing up and down on the high seas). When I said this was downtown Reykjavik and not, unfortunately, his trawler, he gazed around in amazement. "*Allt er a tja og tundri*," he told me. Everything's topsy-turvy.

Everything *was* topsy-turvy. I

> **❛** One woman lurched over to a man and butted her head against him. Others just careened around until they happened to crash into a member of the opposite sex **❜**

bottle — "than the Great Fire that burns. *Skal!* "

"Oh, five or six."

Near the telephone exchange, a dozen teenage boys were lifting a teenage girl on top of a stop sign. She was doing her best to help them. While they push... she was shinnying up the One of the boys, whose proclaimed him the most of all...

attributed this at least as much to the Midnight Sun as to inflation or alcohol. From th... nobody is truly... nod off... conv... do...

On the bottle: a weekend bacchanalia.

Christine Walker

Editor, Travel section. Aged 41. A *Sunday Times* veteran, who joined the paper in 1975 and has worked for it ever since, apart from a brief spell on Weekend World with Peter Jay, with stints on Tried and Tasted, the picture desk, and the television section where she oversaw the TV listings.

and Hester Delooze. Apart from giving details of 14 towns in Sicily, it tells readers how to get there, when to go and what guidebooks to read, as well as full details of the Aeolian and Egadi islands.

A reader who is thinking about a visit to Etna is told: "It is easily reached from Taormina, either by bus or by driving along the autostrada to Giarre, then following the Etna sign west to the base of the old cable car." Wickers packs in the essential information with superb

economy, "From here, four-wheel drive vehicles climb to 2,900 metres. Allow five to six hours for the whole trip." That is the sort of detail that really helps readers.

Yet why run a feature on Sicily on this particular Sunday? That is because Europe is a good place to go in May, according to Walker. "The sun is shining and you can still book on the spur of the moment." Judging by the number of delighted tour operators and travel agents she meets, it is also obvious that the

ALTERNATIVE AFRICA The former field director of Voluntary Service Overseas, Bob Ashworth, has set up Insight Travel (09952-6095) for a different way of visiting Ghana. Visitors will stay with local families and — unlike the majority of holidays to Third World countries, which offer little financial benefit to the host country — 90% of the price on an Insight holiday will be returned to the Ghanian economy. Above all, Ashworth maintains: "Insight holidays are for those who want to understand more about a country and its people and who want to get involved, rather than just be a spectator." Price: £780, inclusive of flights, airport transfer, one overnight hotel and 10 nights' half-board accommodation with the host family.

THUMBS UP Even ardent walkers need a lift sometimes. From July 13, CountryWays Travel (0903-32112) will operate minibus services from London and the south coast to the hills and mountains of England and Wales. Buses will drop and collect walkers from areas difficult to reach without a car.

FRANCE AT A GLANCE "A must for every home" is how France Travel Service describes its new, free, six-page leaflet which lists umpteen possibilities and permutations for anyone travelling from the UK to more or less anywhere in France. The leaflet, obtainable from Abta travel agents, covers Motorail services, charter and scheduled flights, train and fly-drive options, together with prices, and offers a direct booking service (081-750 4262 with a credit card).

guides are well used by readers.

She has two other pages to fill this week. She has decided to fill one with two articles on ideas for those who want holidays with an "ecological punch". One article describes a tour of duty with the British Trust for Conservation Volunteers clearing rhododendrons from the banks of the Aberglaslyn Pass in Wales, the other an obviously memorable holiday as a volunteer warden on a Royal Society for the Protection of Birds nature reserve at Leighton Moss on Morecambe Bay, where Jenny McClean took her 11-year-old son Thomas. He did not want to leave: "I look at him, covered in grubbiness and new-found confidence. Nature has cast her spell. He says he has never felt so free. He knows, as all children do, that this is how the whole planet ought to be. And as we drive over the Pennines towards hot baths and clean linen, the thought persists that down in the reedbeds the otters are playing, the bitterns are booming and the harrier has landed."

Walker fills her last page with the weekly Weekend Break feature, written this week by Richard Binns and describing a visit to the heart of Warwickshire. Again it is packed with useful details and also recommends five good restaurants and two hotels as well as which maps and guides to use – another article to cut out and keep, which is not often the fate of a news journalist's work.

The last job of the Travel section week is to decide which news item to select for the Compass Points column about new travel bargains and which of the readers' Travellers' Tales to select for publication. Neither is easy, especially the selection of news, since travel editors are bombarded with public relations handouts and invitations to

test holidays. (*The Sunday Times* has a strict rule that it pays its own way. On the few occasions when it accepts free travel, it credits the source of hospitality.)

There were 20 invitations in the post this morning alone (and an average week brings at least 50), among them invitations to Disneyland, Deauville, Cyprus, San Antonio and San Francisco. Walker eventually decides to lead with the news that there are real bargains for winter holidays if travellers head for distant lands.

Travellers' Tales is a small but invaluable feature in which readers pass on tips they have picked up on their own holidays. Today Walker chooses three – about pickpockets on the Metro in Lisbon, the attraction of going to Vindolanda before a visit to Hadrian's Wall, and a warning about Naples from Pat Brown Clopper of north London: "Be prepared for a sharp intake of breath if you take a cab from the airport. The fare will be double that indicated on the meter. Staff at my hotel confirmed the practice goes on and no amount of protesting helped, even though my Italian is good," she advises.

All Walker has to do now is to persuade the design department to lay out the pages and the picture desk to find illustrations for the articles so that she can start concentrating on the next week. She plans a major feature on "Cool summers" featuring canoeing in Finland and riding in Iceland, with the front, as a contrast, featuring Bombay.

A few offices away from Walker, Kate Carr, editor of the Style section, is savouring the prospect of a front on the Cannes Film Festival by Iain Johnstone. As a subject, it is a natural. Glitz, parties and famous people – all the ingredients that make good material for Style are

● IT'S that time of the year again — when considerate locals try to ease the tourist's load by unburdening them of their wallets, photographic equipment and, if at all possible, their passports too. A timely reminder to keep a watch-out for these types comes from Linda Elley, of Vicars Cross, Chester.

"As we boarded the Metro in Lisbon recently, my husband's way was blocked by a seemingly bemused man. Three others then closed in and began to jostle my husband." As the Elleys had lost camera equipment in a similar incident in Las Palmas six years earlier, they realised it was an attempted robbery and escaped by shouting "pickpockets", clutching their wallets and ~ving their way clear

TRAVELLERS' TALES

had delivered a swift thump to the ribs of one of the offenders).

● *TALKING of daylight robbery, Pat Brown Clopper, of Cannon Hill, London NW6, has a warning for those heading to Naples. Be prepared for a sharp intake of breath if you take a cab from the airport.*

"The fare will be double that indicated on the meter. Staff at my hotel confirmed the practice goes on, and no amount of protesting helped, even though my Italian is

● CONSIDER a detour, suggests Margaret Brown, of Bletchley, Milton Keynes, after reading William Green's article on Hadrian's Wall (Fortified for going to the emperor's wall, April 22). She recommends a trip to nearby Vindolanda beforehand.

"Vindolanda is the site of successive Roman forts, some of which predate the Wall. When we walked the three miles of the Wall from Steel Rigg to Housesteads, the experience was enhanced by the knowledge gained at Vindolanda as we had some understanding of what life was like for a Roman soldier."

Have you
travell
Sus
T

Travel tips from readers.

represented in Cannes. It also has the added advantage for Carr of not being London or New York, so often where all the glitzy parties are held.

Style is different in tone from every other section of the paper — more concerned with social froth and light articles based on person-alities and social events, such as the highlights of the London season, but written sceptically and with edge. It is the *Tatler* section of *The Sunday Times*, a contrast with the Review section, which is more like *The Economist* or *The Spectator* in tone, Unflurried, competent and cool, Carr, who moved to *The Sun-day Times* from women's maga-zines, is another woman who has risen quickly within the hierarchy.

She also oversees the paper's coverage of fashion, which is always decided a week in advance so that the photographs can be organised. The subject this week is how British

women are always outshone by the international jet set when it comes to dressing for the big social occa-sions. Carr has been hoping that the pictures would be shot at Glyn-debourne — but Glyndebourne has refused to co-operate, so they are being shot even now in Richmond Park.

The weekly Tried and Tested fea-ture, in which a panel of experts test food products, was also set up a week ago. Carr decided to look at sparkling mineral waters, such as Perrier and Badoit, and the test was done at Leith's, the famous London caterers, last Friday.

Now, with two days left before the section has to go to bed, she has a range of choices. She wants to do an article on Country Cousins, the romantics who left London for the

Kate Carr

Editor, Style section (now managing editor, Arts and Leisure). Aged 33. Started career as sub-editor on *Good Housekeeping* before moving to *Company* magazine, where she was arts editor. Joined *The Sunday Times* Look pages in 1987 and was founding editor of Style. "The aim was to leaven the rest of the paper so that readers weren't overwhelmed by news and politics. We were spicy and more light-hearted and are probably read by more younger readers and women than are other sections of the paper."

Jokes and banter. Walsh with Harrie Ritchie (left), Cheryl Younson (centre) and Jo Duckworth, their secretary (seated).

John Walsh

Literary editor. Aged 37. Born in London of Irish parents, Walsh is a graduate of University College, Dublin, and Exeter College, Oxford. Varied career includes spells as assistant editor of *The Director*, selling advertisements at *The Tablet*, courting publicity for the publishers Gollancz, and as assistant literary editor of the *Evening Standard*. Author of *Growing Up Catholic*, an autobiographical reflection on being a Catholic.

country but who now, disillusioned, are returning. The problem is to find the right people to interview. Two writers are desperately trying to find them. Valerie Grove, one of the paper's main columnists, is offering a piece on a new book about Laura Ashley; and Carr is also hoping that the story she sold to the editor at the editorial conference, about the Slide taking over from the Lambada as the hip dance, will work out.

The Books editor, John Walsh, an Irishman who lives in a state of constant tension spiced with jokes and banter with his deputy Harrie Ritchie, a benign Scotsman who makes a perfect foil for the Walsh rages, probably has to make more hard choices than the editor of any other section. He gets hundreds of books every day – the bookshelves on the walls are packed tight with them and there are piles all over the floor that you have to step over to move round the office. Only a tiny proportion, however, can be reviewed, even though *The Sunday Times* is the only paper with 16 tabloid pages to devote to books. Unlike the *New York Times* Book Review section, which according to

an envious Walsh has eight sub-editors who read every book they are sent, Walsh and Ritchie have to make snap judgements.

"User-hostile" books, as Walsh dismissively describes them, typically by authors with PhDs, are instantly rejected. There is a special "schlock" shelf for blockbusters, romance, horror and sci-fi, stored against the days when the editor insists that Walsh reviews at least some of the books that the readers are buying instead of the literary books that appeal to literary critics. All children's books go to the author Susan Hill and all paperbacks go to Austin MacCurtain who edits the weekly Paperbacks section. Then there are piles for fiction (where the novels that get reviewed are selected by Penny Perrick, the fiction editor), biography, politics, history, poetry and so on.

On any one day Walsh is not only planning for next Sunday but also commissioning reviews that will appear one, two or three weeks later. A reviewer will normally get at least ten days to read a book and write his review. Among the decisions Walsh has to make this afternoon are who should review a new

Charles Darwin biography, a new Patricia Highsmith, the T. S. Eliot lectures of John Carey (the chief book reviewer, so an awkward choice), a new Mordecai Richler novel (subsequently nominated for the Booker Prize) and a new Arthur Hailey blockbuster. There is also a new book by the poet Craig Raine. Walsh has tried his old tutor Hermione Lee, who cannot do it, so he is now trying Christopher Ricks.

Often, too, themes occur. The 50th anniversary of the Battle of Britain is due shortly and he now has eight books about it, all of which will make the subject of one review. There are also several books on Englishness – a new Marc Girouard on the English town, the biography of Laura Ashley, a book on historical gardens, another on English interiors, and yet another on 90 years of *Country Life*. All of them go in one bundle to the social historian Christopher Hibbert for an essay-review.

Meanwhile the advertising department have rung to say that they cannot sell an advertisement scheduled for page 11. Walsh tries to get a rhythm in his pages so the decision about what review to use has to be judged against the reviews published on the opposite page. They are a combination of pop sociology – a review of two Debrett books on etiquette, manners and correct form and another book about the nature of masculinity. Walsh decides to complement that with a review by Julia Neuberger of a book about American school-children and a poem by Carol Ann Duffy about schooldays, entitled "The Captain of the 1964 Top of the Form League".

Around the office meanwhile, the staff of each section, oblivious of the work of the others, are going about their jobs. The pace of Tuesday is more leisurely than the end of the week but there is work to do and an opportunity to catch up on jobs left over from the previous week.

Michael Williams joined *The Sunday Times* only five years ago as deputy News editor. Now he is managing editor of the News section, one of the most senior assistant editors, who selects and allocates its contents from what is offered by Collins and Witherow. Managing editors are the editor's cabinet. An occasional air of abstractedness conceals William's sharp and creative brain for news and, with Witherow and Tyrer, he is another rising star. Each is conscious of the others. Saturday is the highlight of his week as he makes up the news pages. "Even though the pages are made up with scalpel and paste and the first proof comes, not hot off the presses but cold out of a photocopier, I still find it impossibly glamorous," he says. "Glamorous in just the way I imagined it as a young graduate trainee journalist in Liverpool 20 years ago."

Tuesday, however, is not so glamorous. Today Williams is being coroner, conciliator and psychotherapist. "This week the inquest is into how two identical stories ended up on different pages of the Manchester edition on Sunday. Bad mistake though it was, I am secretly pleased to discover it was the printer's fault. Now he won't dare complain next time I shoehorn a late story in at deadline time."

Now he has to conciliate between the investigative reporters of Insight and the newsdesk, who are peeved that Insight want to send their own "undercover" reporter with the fans to the World Cup.

Penny Perrick

Fiction editor and fiction reviewer. Daughter of Eve Perrick, the former *Daily Express* columnist, and Ben Perrick, publicity director of Foyles. Author of *Late Start: Careers for Wives*, and *The Working Wife's Cookbook*, she started on *Vogue* and was a *Sun* and *Times* columnist, before founding *The Sunday Times* Books section. Favourite authors: Saul Bellow, Richard Ford, John Updike, William Trevor, Martin Amis and Edna O'Brien.

Margarette Driscoll

Reporter and feature writer. Aged 31. A former feature writer with the *Daily Mirror* and *Today*, she enjoys the variety of reporting. "You never know where you will end up during the week." Sent at an hour's notice in 1991 to cover the plight of the Kurdish refugees after the end of the Gulf war, she spent a month on the Turkish border. With Jon Swain, the unluckiest reporter in the week reported in this book.

"Will it compromise the regular man who is on his way to Italy already, put him in danger?" Williams muses. "The answer is simple. It's too expensive. The budget rules, as well as news values."

Next into his office is a specialist reporter who is worried that he is not getting enough stories into the paper. Is he writing the wrong stories – or not writing well enough? he wants to know. Williams knows the reasons. His specialism, until recently the obsession of every newsdesk, is now mildly out of fashion. "I don't tell him this," says Williams, "but remind him of all the good articles he has written over the past six months. A cop-out? Not really. The job of a news manager is to maintain the confidence of the team."

Williams also agrees that Margarette Driscoll, one of the best reporters, should fly to Monte Carlo tomorrow. For more than six months Driscoll has been chasing a bizarre story about the mysterious disappearance of Friderike Dunhill-Woolrich, the wife of one of the founders of the Dunhill tobacco dynasty. She discovered that Italian police believed she had been kidnapped by her maid, Gabriela Mayer, whom she had adopted as her daughter and had subsequently signed her Italian home to her. When the adoption was annulled after an action by Mrs Dunhill's sister, the two women fled to Austria. Mayer was adopted again and Mrs Dunhill died, leaving Mayer as her heir and occupant of the Monte Carlo house.

A week ago an Italian court, due to try Mayer on criminal charges of kidnapping and extortion, had ruled that the second adoption was legal and the case was adjourned. But a *Sunday Times* photographer, Alistair Miller, calling at the house in Monte Carlo had been invited in by Mayer. What set Driscoll's newshound's blood racing was her agreement to pose for a picture if Driscoll came from London to interview her and put her side of the story.

"This was a remarkable breakthrough," Driscoll said excitedly. "I had tracked her down to Monte Carlo while writing my initial stories but our conversations had been over the telephone and hysterical and brief." She had spoken to Miller over the weekend, who reported that Mayer kept changing her mind. Now she is flying off to see if she can solve the riddle.

For Valerie Grove, a *Sunday Times* star whose long weekly interview with a celebrity is one of the main features of the News Review Section, it has been a better Tuesday than usual. Grove is one of the joys of *The Sunday Times*, well-read, beautifully dressed, a fierce guardian of standards of writing, an often wicked sense of fun – and a husband who edits one of the paper's main rivals, the *Sunday Telegraph*. According to the success of her interviews, her moods swing between elation and despair; and she is a working mother who tries to leave the office in time to meet her children from school.

Often the decision on whom she should interview is not made until Wednesday or Thursday. Often the idea is hers; sometimes she yields to Tyrer or the editor, who have to strike the right balance of interest, either for the section or the paper as a whole. Today, however, the sole suggestion at conference was that she should see Jim Swire, spokesman for the British relatives of the Lockerbie dead. Then there was one small setback. There was only one brief cutting on Swire in the Wapping library. She wasn't downcast for long: "As soon as I reached him on his portable phone, I knew he was the man: despite being a busy full-time GP and much in demand – a 6 am date with TVam tomorrow morning – he was willing to talk," she says, a very happy woman. "He had an air of quiet obsessiveness and he gave such amusing directions about how to drive to his house in Bromsgrove – three motorways, uphill, down dale, along winding lanes and uncharted dirt-tracks – that I have decided to take the 5.10 train tomorrow, and to meet him after he has finished his surgery."

After the go-ahead from the editorial conference, Margaret Park, a City reporter in the Business section, is trying to set up an interview with the bosses of Marks and Spencer. Eglin, meanwhile, has established that Philips don't want to talk to him about their problems. "I'm not surprised," he says. "If they were bright enough to see the wisdom of briefing the quality press on their problems, they probably wouldn't have such serious problems in the first place. But we will do our best to do their job of enlightening their 18,000 UK employees and numerous shareholders. We have some useful contacts with deep knowledge of the company. I shall use a Dutch journalist who is very good."

Eglin has also spent an hour interviewing a candidate for a job. He is Andrew Davidson, editor of *Marketing* magazine, owned by Haymarket Press, who have just poached Philip Beresford from the Business section to edit *Management Today*. Eglin is keen to hire him and rings Bambridge, who is holding his weekly meeting with the editor of Insight, and asks him to see Davidson quickly. Bambridge fixes an interview with

Davidson for tomorrow.

City editor Jeff Randall, meanwhile, has forsaken his usual news meeting with the City staff and flown to Shannon in Ireland, where he has accepted an invitation, issued through a London intermediary, to interview Larry Goodman, one of the country's most powerful and secretive businessmen. "The City suspects Goodman is about to bid £1 billion for Berisford International (owner of British Sugar) so this is a coup," says Randall, who is spending the afternoon hopping around Ireland in a helicopter looking at Goodman's agribusiness operations before meeting him for dinner at the Savoy of Dublin, the Shelbourne Hotel.

It is, perhaps, harder work at the House of Commons, where David Hughes, the chief political correspondent, is trying to arrange interviews with ministers to get stories for Saturday. He is a happier man when he is successful with John Selwyn Gummer, the agriculture minister – a good interview to get in a week obsessed with mad cow disease. After attending a briefing on the new Labour Party policy review, Andrew Grice, political correspondent, is talking to Labour MPs to try to find out what happened at the private meeting of the national executive which approved it. For them, however, there are still four stressful days to go before the paper goes to press – and the political correspondents of the daily papers can destroy all their potential stories until Saturday morning.

Now suddenly it is all change for the Style section. Neil has spotted an article in a New York magazine on the last days of Greta Garbo. At 4.30 he rang Rennell to tell him it would make a strong front for Style. Within half an hour, Rennell has

Jeff Randall

City editor. Aged 36. A graduate of Nottingham University, he studied journalism at the University of Florida and worked as a freelance for the *Wolverhampton Express and Star* and the *Investor's Chronicle* before joining *Euromoney*, *Financial Weekly* and then the *Sunday Telegraph*. As city editor he directs a team of five reporters and has written several scoops including Robert Maxwell's bid for Spurs and George Walker's bid for William Hill.

David Hughes

Chief political correspondent. Aged 40. After working first for the *Merthyr Express,* he went to the Commons in 1979 for the *Western Mail,* the morning newspaper of Wales, and then worked for the *Daily Mail* before joining *The Sunday Times.* The best stories, he says, always come from Westminster. That is the joy of the job.

called New York, bought the rights to publish the article in Britain for 500 dollars, and organised the despatch of pictures from New York (due to arrive tomorrow). Several of the decisions made at the conference only four hours ago now have to be junked.

Since Garbo is on the front and Cannes will still be published – but on an inside page – Rennell and Carr decide to ditch an interview with the comedienne Pamela Stephenson: they do not want the section to be top-heavy with show business articles. They also decide to hold over two other features for another week. Out, therefore, go the articles on the Slide and the launch of a new perfume by Oleg Cassini, Jackie Kennedy's favourite designer.

"I would normally be reluctant to make such hard decisions so early in the week," says Rennell, who has a volatile temper and is no sycophant of Neil. "When the editor says he wants something, you have to guess whether he is making a suggestion, a request or an instruction. I sensed this time that it was an instruction – but I agreed with it anyway. Often we would discuss such requests with him."

Stoddart has also phoned in from Montreux to announce that Rowan Atkinson's *Mr Bean,* as expected, has won three awards – the first-place Golden Rose, the comedy prize and the press jury prize. Nobody has ever won three of the five major awards before. Not only that but Channel 4 came second with *Norbert Smith,* and independent British companies have won first and second prizes in the competition for independent productions. Even though the story will appear in all the daily papers tomorrow, Rennell decides that Atkinson should be profiled in the Arts sec-

tion: "He is interesting enough to make a good weekend read."

At 5 pm the 15 news reporters meet Rosemary Collins for a weekly session to bat around ideas for news stories. There are three good ideas. Richard Caseby suggests an investigation of the plight of the veterans who attended the first nuclear tests; Greg Hadfield, the Education correspondent, has got some new research on rowdy and disruptive school pupils; and Tim Rayment, the chief reporter, has discovered that some new cars are sold when they already have 1,000 miles on the clock. All three could make good stories.

Eglin, meanwhile, is smiling. An earlier hunch has been vindicated. "Bingo! It's just come up on my screen that the Manx government is refunding at least some of the investors' money. Well done, Gwendoline!"

By 7 pm, the office is almost deserted. Tuesday is an early night. Outside the office, however, life still goes on, particularly for Chris Nawrat, the Sports editor, and Iain Johnstone in Cannes. Nawrat is now going out to dinner to try to lure the brilliant sports writer Matthew Engel from *The Guardian* to *The Sunday Times* – but he has already done four days' work by now.

This is the story of his week so far, which started last Saturday, even as he was putting the previous week's Sport section to bed. With Nick Pitt, his deputy, he had decided then that the Whitbread Round the World Yacht Race, due to end on Saturday this week, would probably make a front page picture and that the main story would be the Middlesex versus New Zealand cricket match. With New Zealand due to play two one-day internationals against England, that would be a way of spotlighting the Kiwis. He also set up an off-beat feature about Monday night racing at Windsor by racing correspondent John Karter, and decided which cricket matches to cover this Saturday.

On Sunday – this is a man who seems to work a seven-day week – he rang round his correspondents organising coverage of the World Cup, the Whitbread, English cricket, and athletics. It is a strange athletics season, with no Olympics or world championship. "I still think we should keep athletics in the paper and ask the athletics correspondent to think of a person to profile. We talk about live coverage next Saturday and settle on the age-old attempt to break Roger Bannister's first sub-four minute mile at Oxford." Then yesterday he made still more calls, in particular to Peter Roebuck, the Somerset cricket captain who writes for *The Sunday Times* and wants to do a feature on Jimmy Cook, the Somerset batsman. Nawrat is initially dubious: it would be the fourth article in succession on a Somerset player. "I decide that only insiders would think that important. After all it was a brilliant innings and he was there to witness it. Journalists often believe their readers have the same sort of encyclopaedic knowledge of what has appeared in the paper as they do. This is patently nonsense."

Now, tonight, with his plans in place, he is off with Pitt to meet Engel. "We are attempting to poach him. He would be a wonderful catch, one of the handful of sports journalists whose writing I admire. My move was opportune. He is at a crossroads." During the meal he spoke to Roebuck on the phone and agreed the article on Cook. At midnight he is watching a video of the England–Denmark match, in which a typical Gary Lineker goal extends England's unbeaten run to 17 matches. As he goes to bed he is confident that Engel will join – but Pitt disagrees.

In Moscow James Blitz works three hours ahead of London. His was a typical day for a foreign journalist in the Soviet Union, often frustrating, sometimes successful. His day started at 9, when it was still 6 am in London. When he rang Witherow, the office was keen on a story about Boris Yeltsin, who is standing for the presidency of the Russian parliament this week. It will be a big blow for Gorbachev if he wins, but Blitz thinks he will lose even though he made a brilliant speech in Moscow last night.

James Baker, the American Secretary of State, is in Moscow for arms talks but they are likely to be over by Friday and will have been covered by the daily papers. One news lead may be the situation in the Baltics, he thinks, even though the newsdesk in London is weary of the story. Nevertheless he rings up the foreign ministry for permission to fly there, just in case, but meets a tough man to deal with. "Usually I can just say I want to go and they let me go after 24 hours have elapsed. Now he wants all my flight details before he registers me, which will delay my flight by a day while I try to get tickets."

Witherow has also asked him to follow up a story in the *Wall Street Journal* about dating agencies which arrange international marriages for Russian women who want to emigrate. "I think it will have to be the focus of a piece about the particular difficulties life in Russia presents for women – no Tampax, no contraceptives (115 abortions for every 100 live births). After all dating agencies here are probably

Andrew Grice

Political correspondent. Aged 35. Started on *Slough Observer* and *Liverpool Echo* before joining *Coventry Evening Telegraph*, where he first reported politics from the House of Commons in 1982. Subsequently political correspondent on *Daily Express* and *London Daily News*. The joy of the job, he says, is not only being at the centre of events but also the unexpected – the sudden eruption of the Westland crisis, for instance, or the outcry in 1991 about killer dogs.

Chris Nawrat

Sports editor. Aged 42. An Essex graduate, after being a sports journalist on the *Morning Star* and editor of *National Student*, he joined *The Sunday Times* in 1983 and was deputy Sports editor until promoted in 1988. "It's the best job on the best paper in Fleet Street," he says. "I have no further ambitions. I mean that."

no different from anywhere else in the world."

Blitz has been trying to get an international line installed in his flat. "Amazingly I'm asked to take my case to the deputy minister for telecommunications – a bit like getting a visa for the US stamped by James Baker. I sit in his office for 15 seconds. He says 'OK, regard it as done.' I left, got back to the office and suggested writing a story about it."

Meanwhile Irina, his assistant, has arranged an interview with a dating agency. "I went round to find a stream of women queuing up in a tiny flat. The agency is in fact a side venture to an exhibition of Jewish art that is being taken round America this year. It's a good story. When I got back to the office, there had been big demonstrations by ethnic Russians in Latvia and Estonia. I must get up there."

Now in Manila, Swain has reached his destination and is staying at one of the most sumptuous colonial-style hotels in Asia, the Manila Hotel. His first impressions depressed his spirits. "The crumbling chaos of the airport resembles more the dilapidated atmosphere of the sub-continent than the sanitised efficiency of Singapore, Bangkok or Kuala Lumpur. It is an instant reminder that I have arrived in a country that is not only beset by convoluted political problems but also by a sagging economy and a crumbling infra-structure. It is a constant sorrow each time I come to Manila that it has not moved forward since Aquino was assassinated. Everything that is working is just a faded image of what it was under Marcos."

Even the sumptuousness of the hotel fails to remove his disillusionment. "Even here, where the opinion of the visiting international community is gently massaged into believing that all is well in a country that sees an attempted coup every six months, are confronted by rocketing corruption, a Communist insurgency and an atrocious human rights record, appearances are deceptive. Behind the languid, smiling faces lurks an incredible inefficiency. The city is crumbling. There are frequent power cuts. Appearances cannot be kept up any longer." Swain is now ready for bed and a round of appointments tomorrow.

Elsewhere abroad, *Sunday Times* men are enjoying more cheerful evenings. After dinner with Goodman in Dublin, Jeff Randall is confident that he has got a good story. He believes Goodman will be a serious bidder for Berisford. Now he is enjoying a quick drink with Alan Parker, Goodman's British public relations consultant. "One drink turns into four and I stagger off to bed at 2 am."

Meanwhile, with his wife Mo, Iain Johnstone is working Cannes for his Style article. Since he had seen the films for the first three days at London previews, he stayed in London for *Start the Week*, missed the early parties, and took his children to Windsor Safari Park on Sunday while Mo went on ahead to Cannes. "Windsor is very similar to the festival," he points out, "lizards, alligators, killer whales, tigers, snakes – all the types already assembled on the French Riviera."

So tonight is for serious party-going with the snakes and the lizards – and unlike the Schwarzenegger–Stallone party at the Hotel du Cap last night there are no men with guns to stop journalists gatecrashing. The first stop was the party given by Jake Eberts, whose book on Goldcrest, *My Inde-*

cision is Final, is also being published this week. They move on to the British Film Institute party, where the drink has already run out. Two down, still two to go – and there are no problems about the drink at the next stop.

"At the Front Line–Medusa thrash at the old château at La Napoule, the champagne is coming out of the taps," says Johnstone. "David Soul is there without his wife – they came down by bus and babysit on alternate evenings. There is a different banquet from different countries in each room of the château. I remember Soul filming Wolfgang Puck as a humble chef working here ten years ago. Now he owns Spago in LA." The last stop is Jane's disco, where Roger Daltrey is giving a party.

At last the long Cannes night is over – and at last, back in London from Montreux, Patrick Stoddart is tucking in to his beans on toast.

A party with Anna and Rupert Murdoch

It was a week when Rupert Murdoch was in London with senior executives of the worldwide News Corporation, mainly for sessions on 1990–91 budgets and strategic meetings on his newspaper and television interests. He hosted with his wife Anna a party for his senior executives at his penthouse apartment in St James's Place, off Piccadilly, with stunning panoramic views across Green Park. One of the guests was Ivan Fallon, deputy editor.

"The invitation says 7 to 9 and I arrive at 7.10 to find the room already full. The Murdochs on these occasions are impeccable hosts, greeting their guests and spouses with great warmth. Rupert kisses my wife Sue, I kiss Anna and pass on for the champagne.

"A small orchestra is playing, the patio doors are open, the place is filled with flowers and it looks lovely. I enjoy this type of party immensely and increasingly it feels very much a family occasion. There are people here I spent days with at Aspen (where the senior executives gather occasionally for a worldwide think tank on the future of News Corporation) but haven't seen since and we spend the next hour moving round greeting people.

"All the other London editors are there, as well as Andrew Knight (executive chairman of News International), Sir Edward Pickering, and the senior London directors as well as the rest of the gang from New York, Los Angeles and Sydney.

"We leave at 9.30 after a superb sit-down buffet. The Murdochs never seem to sit but move through the crowd, continually topping up glasses, offering more food, making sure they miss no one. They are still smiling at the end. Often there are many outsiders at these occasions. Tonight it is News Corp only, a family reunion."

Since inheriting one Australian daily paper in the 1950s, Rupert Murdoch, chairman and chief executive of The News Corporation, has built one of the world's top five media empires. News International, its British arm, owns *The*

Sunday Times, *The Times*, the *Sun*, the *News of the World* (the two biggest selling newspapers in the English speaking world) and *Today*. It also has a 48 per cent stake in British Sky Broadcasting. Among many other papers, News Corporation also publishes the *Australian*, founded by Murdoch as Australia's only national paper, and the *South China Morning Post* in Hong Kong.

News Corporation owns Twentieth Century Fox in Hollywood and Fox Television, America's fourth television network, as well as Harper-Collins, one of the world's three leading English language book publishers.

Murdoch transformed the fortunes of the British national newspaper industry in 1986 when he transferred production of his British newspapers from unionised Fleet Street to union-free Wapping, shedding more than 5,000 print workers, and dramatically cut the costs of production.

Anna, his wife, is a director of News Corporation and writes novels.

Wednesday

At 3 pm Roberts is due to meet Rupert Murdoch for a grilling on the editorial budget. It is a difficult year. There have to be cuts. The debate is over who suffers most.

Peter Roberts

Managing editor from 1978 to 1991. (He is now managing editor of *The Times*.) Aged 56. After being chief sub-editor of the *Northern Echo*, he was chief foreign sub of the *Daily Mail*, chief assistant to Harold Evans when he was editor of *The Sunday Times*. He was then foreign manager and worked in the sports department before moving into his slot as guardian of the budget.

Some journalists do business over lunch. Quite a lot of my own is done over breakfast and by 8 am today I am at the Goring Hotel near Buckingham Palace, chosen because it is the closest restaurant to the new headquarters of Random Century, one of Britain's biggest publishing houses. As the buyer of serialisations for the paper, I am meeting Gail Rebuck, managing director of the Century, Hutchinson and Ebury imprints, and Richard Cohen, editorial director of Hutchinson, to decide whether any of their books for the next year would be worth considering for serialisation.

They have several strong candidates – not only the memoirs of Ronald Reagan but also the memoirs of Roy Jenkins, *The New Russians* by Hedrick Smith, a biography of Elton John, Vanessa Redgrave's autobiography, and the final instalment of Callanetics. That boosted sales of *The Sunday Times* by nearly 100,000 when it was first serialised. When the books are written we will read them, and then, if we decide a book is worth serialising, negotiate a contract and a price, which can vary between £10,000 and £100,000. After this meeting, however, I know some of the books that will be candidates for serialisation over the next 18 months.

Eggs and bacon are a long way from the mind of managing editor Peter Roberts as he slips on to the M1 on his journey to Wapping from his cottage in a sleepy Oxfordshire village. He is brooding on the most important day of his year. At 3 pm he is due to meet Rupert Murdoch, chief executive of News Group, which owns *The Sunday Times*, for a grilling on the proposed editorial budget for 1990–91. Unassuming, softly-spoken but with the skill of a ferret in unearthing editorial extravagance – some reporters accuse him of believing it's his own money – Roberts is an old stager who has worked for three editors and is recognised by the management as a strict guardian of the sanctity of the editorial budget. As editorial manager dealing with expenses, contracts, budgets and, quite often, sackings or redundancies, his is not a job that is coveted by his colleagues – but his sympathetic treatment of his colleagues is widely acknowledged. After 12 years in the job he is moving shortly to *The Times*, and James Adams, his successor, is understudying him in the week before taking over.

Now as he sits impatiently in the daily jam as the M4 reaches the outskirts of London, Roberts is thinking through every detail of the editorial budget. He knows that it will be ruthlessly examined and any weakness quickly exposed by the sharp, incisive mind of Murdoch. He also knows that he is in a strong position. In 1980 it took 155 *Sunday Times* staff journalists to produce papers that averaged 67 pages a week. In 1988, 152 staff journalists produced papers averaging 127 pages. Over those nine years the editorial budget rose from £8.2 million to £16.2 million. Given inflation of 85 per cent, that amounts to a doubling of productivity on only a slight increase in budget. Editor Andrew Neil believes it represents one of the best productivity records of the Thatcher years – and that the paper has practised what it preached.

Today is different for Roberts but usually there is a lull in the tempo of the week on Wednesday, when deadlines for the news-based sections are still days away. It is the day when news reporters start working on their stories, making their first inquiries, calling contacts or setting off abroad.

Margarette Driscoll is in Monte Carlo to meet Gabriela Mayer. She is already sensing that this is a story that is doomed. She has driven to the house with Alistair Miller, only to discover that Mayer is out. Yet when she calls Rosemary Collins in London, she discovers that Collins is talking to Mayer on the other line. Through Collins, Driscoll tells Mayer that she has checked into the Mirabeau Hotel and that Mayer should call her there. "By the time I got to the hotel reception, there was a message saying she had called," says Driscoll. "Then nothing." This is proving a frustrating story.

Also travelling is Michael Williams. He is on his way to Belfast to meet Ulster correspondent Liam Clarke, who has ideas on how to improve the edition for Northern Ireland. "Even seasoned newsmen can be surprised and, not having been to Ulster before, I am overwhelmed by the soft green countryside around Aldergrove Airport and the provincial normality of Belfast," says Williams. "It strikes me as about as dangerous as Leicester but without the traffic – a view confirmed by a tour of the city, including such notorious spots as the Shankill, the Divis flats, Gerry Adams' house and Bobby Sands' grave. Why doesn't some enterprising person do 'Troubles' coach tours? We end up talking about this, and the differing qualities of Belfast and Dublin Guinness, rather than more serious matters."

Valerie Grove has two interviews to do today. The first this morning, for Style, with Anne Sebba, "a terrific-looking blonde", who has written the new book on Laura Ashley. They meet at the Gilbert-Sullivan pub in Covent Garden so that Sebba can be photographed

James Adams

Managing editor and Defence correspondent. Aged 40 and a suave Harrovian, described by editor as "thorough, loyal and irreverent". Started on *Evening Chronicle*, Newcastle, and *Eight Days* magazine before joining *The Sunday Times* foreign desk. Writes for *Washington Post* and *Los Angeles Times* and is author of several books including *The Financing of Terror* and *Secret Armies*. First thriller, *The Final Terror*, published in autumn 1991.

outside the Laura Ashley shop, and then repair to a café for black coffee. It is an effortless interview for Grove. "She was very forthcoming about her dealings with Sir Bernard Ashley, all fascinating stuff. She also showed me a letter she had had from one of Laura's daughters which was very revealing about her father – not, alas, for publication but very useful for background."

The main political columnist of *The Sunday Times* is Brian Walden. Once one of the brightest Labour MPs, Walden left politics to become an incisive television interviewer and the Sunday lunchtime Walden interview regularly makes headlines in Monday's papers. Given his sympathy for Margaret Thatcher – at least until his notorious grilling after the resignation of Nigel Lawson – his column is widely read for clues to Thatcherite thinking. Wednesday is the day he finishes writing his column.

His subject this week, as so often, is the Labour Party. He has read the new policy review and found it wanting. "I was struck by the emphatic nature of the pledges – pledges that they cannot withdraw," he says. There was a dissonance between their social and financial aims that was so obvious. They were pledging to spend an enormous amount of money but without increasing taxes.

"I thought about it over the weekend, started writing yesterday, finished this morning and it will be telexed tomorrow. What takes time is the thinking, seeing all the logical consequences, not the writing. Is it true, for instance, that the review means the practical abandonment of socialism? Does socialism depend on the spending of money? I spent most of Sunday thinking about that. I think the line through to see if it is logical and

Kinnock t

Last Tuesday, Neil Kinnock made a significant commitment on behalf of a future Labour government: "We have no design, no intention for raising the taxation of the huge majority of ordinary people who are working for their living. We have to meet the bills of society out of improved performance. It cannot come out of an extra great slab of taxation. That would be folly."

Much that politicians say contains less than meets the eye, but this commitment is not only important in itself; it has far-reaching consequences. It could be dismissed as the sort of thing Kinnock would say in order to get elected, except that the language is unusually emphatic. If Labour wins the next election and dishonours this pledge, it has scant chance of re-election. Disclaiming the wish to raise "an extra great slab of taxation" to pay for social improvements may strike the casual observer as nothing to get excited about. Would not any modern politician with any sense say the same?

That may be the way the matter is seen in the saloon bar, but the majority of Labour party members have always seen it differently. They want society transformed and accept that this is a costly undertaking. Heavily taxing individuals to promote social good is a traditional Labour policy. The effect of Kinnock's pledge is that, whether or not the Labour party has abandoned socialism in theory, it has abandoned it in practice.

There is no way that any major aspect of a socialist society can be

makes sense. Some columnists think their job is to stir things up. If they turn out to be wrong, so what? I don't regard my job like that. I want the reader to say: 'I think that chap has got it right,' to feel that it makes sense and that he can rely on what I write. I don't care if it's exciting. I seek thoughtfulness and simplicity. It doesn't necessarily

’ows socialism from the sledge

The Labour leader has committed himself to policies that negate the party's ideology, says **BRIAN WALDEN**

st taxpayers are not quired to shoulder ens. I offer one ob- The Labour party, ht-wing leadership, mmitted itself to a distribution of Healey, who repre- most realistic face, od-chilling threats But standard-rate the overwhelming ax revenue and, if ng to be asked to ere can be no mas- n.

minority are not ock's pledge. But tle pledge all to our will not in- rate beyond 50%, al insurance sur- creases will raise are no more than ess socialists who e underclass is y financed by the t on a number of t considered a tever the rights ch a measure, I body that, as a enue raiser, a o a dud. Social atisfying to left- s not put much y. If one wants be paid for — to by "the huge ry people".

el at the dexter- of Kinnock. He t reassure mod- that this means ermanently off re people point

out that this is what he is doing, the better pleased he will be. Naturally, he will deny it when faced by any unreconstructed socialist body — if such a thing still exists — and he can obscure and confuse the issue for those who want to be deceived.

Kinnock's conversion to capitalism, tinged by the faintest pink of social democracy, goes far beyond anything I asked for when I was in the Labour party. I am forced to agree with Tony Benn, who commented, plaintively, that the new policy was a "breathtaking revelation of the extent to which revisionism has gone in the party."

The Labour party is going to swallow this unpalatable programme, because it is tired of losing general elections. If socialism has to be thrown off the sledge and left for the wolves in order that the race be won, then that is a price the party is prepared to pay. Benn will

pay it too, because, whatever the sincerity of his convictions, he is being dragged along by the impetus, together with the rest of the parliamentary left. They are powerless to alter the direction. If Labour is well on the way to following the trend of most socialist parties by discarding its distinctive ideology, it still has much to do to reconcile its various pledges.

I shall suspend final judgment until it produces its election manifesto, but meanwhile the words of that great American fixer, governor Al Smith of New York, are in my mind: "Somebody is going to be cheated. The only question is, who's it gonna be?"

Contemplate what it means when Kinnock describes the control of inflation as Labour's priority in government. How can that be squared with Labour's constant claim that much more money ought to be spent on public services and on public sector employees? Should this statement now be amended by the addition of the crucial phrase "when the economy expands at a rate which makes such spending possible"?

Surely all those disaffected public employees who demonstrate, brandishing placards and booing the prime minister, are not doing so to make the point that when the economy expands they expect better treatment? An innocent like me thought they wanted more money for themselves, and more resources for the service in which they work, immediately. If all they want are non-inflationary increases at some future date, why would they suppose that this is

something only a Labour government will concede?

As its statements stand, the Labour party can offer the public sector no more than any other party. It is not going to raise the taxes of the "huge majority" and it regards inflation as its priority. This precludes borrowing billions of pounds for release into the economy, because everybody knows the inflationary consequences of doing that. Labour has, at least, one promise too many and it looks as if some large group will be cheated.

Charitably, I shall not list a further string of Labour pledges, which look to me as if they would prove costly. If it does not face the inherent contradiction between its declared financial aims and its social promises, I can make the safe and banal prediction that the Labour party will be increasingly discomforted by the queries that will be hurled at it. It is the social promises that have gone beyond the bounds of what is possible.

Never forget that under Margaret Thatcher's regime, which we are told has but slight regard for social provision, the burden of taxation has increased. I get the impression that the prime minister is ashamed of this fact, because it is the opposite of what she intended. But it highlights in the clearest possible way our present situation. A sharp increase in public expenditure can be paid for only by an increase in taxation.

If Kinnock's "ordinary people" want the state to spend more money on them, they had better be ready to provide it. Which doesn't make much sense, does it?

---

have to be fine English but it must be comprehensible."

Walden is an unusual journalist – his column is ready two days before his deadline. At Wapping, as their early deadlines draw nearer, John Walsh, Christine Walker and Kate Carr start yelling at the picture desk for the photographs and illustrations they need to complete the de-

sign of the Books, Travel and Style sections so they are ready for the presses by Thursday night.

"It's like a snakepit in here," says John Walsh in the Books office. He is still waiting for his picture for the front page and cannot, therefore, do the layout. The advertisement dropped from page ten means the page has to be redesigned. The

Brian Walden

Columnist. Aged 59. A former president of the Oxford Union, Walden was Labour MP for two Birmingham seats from 1964 to 1977, when he became presenter of Weekend World and subsequently The Walden Interview. He has since left *The Sunday Times*.

bestseller lists have been sent but the machine at Wapping will not accept them – another source of frustration. Another review is late – and he ought by now to have completed five pages.

Christine Walker also wants pictures to illustrate the Travel front on the bacchanalia in Iceland. Those she has got are "terrible" – an audience at a Tom Jones concert at Reykjavik. She rejects them. She has been offered instead an engraving of Vikings on the rampage, which works, she thinks, but only just. Now she is reading all the proofs and checking every telephone number in every article. Nothing irritates or frustrates readers more than to try the wrong number when they want to book a holiday. Style is also yelling for pictures. Kate Carr cannot get decent pictures of Greta Garbo and the pictures from Cannes have still not arrived.

It isn't all bad news, however. After getting rejections from Christopher Ricks and Jonathan Raban, Walsh has persuaded A. A. Alvarez to review the book by Craig Raine. Gerald Kaufman, the Opposition spokesman on foreign affairs, has agreed to review the memoirs of Caspar Weinberger, the American Secretary of State during the Falklands War. He has persuaded Roy Porter, the British social historian, to review the new book by Simon Schama, his former tutor.

Walsh is also pleased by another coup. Mrs Catto, the wife of the American ambassador to Britain, has agreed to review the new Arthur Hailey airport blockbuster. It is about television news – and Catto was also once a news reporter in America. Like Christine Walker, he is solving his problem over a front page illustration by going for an engraving. It depicts the Great Game, the Victorian cold war played out between the Caspian Sea and the Karakorams, between Afghanistan and Tibet, and the subject this week of the lead review.

For Alex Butler, the chief sub-editor, a cool disciplinarian and mordant wit, the week starts on Wednesday. He works such long hours on Fridays and Saturdays overseeing the subbing and head-lining of the news and review sections, often doing 16-hour days, that he works a four-day week. The chief sub is one of the central personalities in any newspaper office. His team of "subs" correct reporters' copy, cut it down to size and write the headlines, always, if reporters are to be believed, cutting out the most vital bits of their copy and writing headlines which fail to tell the true story of their report. Subs learn to be hard and cynical.

THE GREAT GAME: On Secret Service in High Asia
by Peter Hopkirk *John Murray £19.95 pp562*
Nicholas Richardson

Butler is both and as he arrives this morning he needs to be. Awaiting him on his desk is a stinging memo from the editor, a Scot.

"Who was responsible for changing 'fish suppers' to 'fish meals' in the Scottish edition last Saturday night?"

A classic case, Butler reflects, of the north–south divide. The story had been subbed and revised by Englishmen when the only Scottish "revise" sub – the chief sub's longstop – was on holiday. Butler is forced to eat fish supper and humble pie but makes a mental note to ensure that the guilty sub suffers too.

Thousands of miles away in Moscow, James Blitz's assistant, Irina, is trying hard to get him tickets for Latvia – unless he gets there by tomorrow he will be too late to check the situation and file by Saturday. Blitz himself is trying to find more women to interview for his report on Soviet dating agencies. He has phoned a feminist friend in Leningrad who has given him good quotes on the misconceptions Soviet women have about life in the west. In return she wants a favour. Can Blitz phone the British Embassy to hurry along her application for a visa to England? Blitz phones a friend in the Embassy.

In Manila it has been a frustrating morning for Jon Swain. "My request to see the American ambassador falls on deaf ears. He does not want to speak to non-American journalists at a time that highlights the sensitive position of the US in its former colony. The only person who might be available is a political officer, an unreconstructed Vietnam war veteran whose main contribution to intelligent comment is: 'Goddam, I don't know how we lost that war.' He said that Clarke and

Subic naval base remain vital to US global strategy despite the diminishing Soviet threat." As usual, Swain says, the Australians are the most lucid and offer the most insights. "I see someone from their political section. Their presence in the region has been so long and lasting and usually on the sidelines that their powers of observation and political commentary are more astute than most."

After yesterday's enthusiastic report from Roger Eglin, executive editor Tony Bambridge is interviewing Andrew Davidson about a job with the Business section. "He's charming and bright. Just get down to things when Ivan Fallon (the deputy editor) rings. Can I spare a few moments? He has got Barbara Conway in his office and thinks I should speak to her. I explain I'm interviewing but he won't be put off. Excuse myself and go to Ivan's room. Yes, I do remember her. One hell of a reputation for financial investigations. But where would she fit in? Biznews? Insight? No, that's no good. Insight is a team effort and she is a loner. Anyway they already have a financial man in Chris Blackhurst. What is more she doesn't really want to go on doing financial investigations. A picture flashes through my mind: all those journalists who become brilliant in a special area and then immediately want to go and do something else. No, this is an interview that is going nowhere. I excuse myself and hurry back to my office."

The interview with Davidson resumes. He strikes Bambridge as full of ideas and he is impressed by his cuttings – the examples of his work from other papers and magazines. "He's very stylish," Bambridge reflects to himself. "I am reminded of myself at the same age. Fatal. I'm about to start recalling my own

Alex Butler

Chief sub-editor (now night editor of *The Times*). Aged 39. Started on *Newham Observer* and became news editor before moving to *Southend Evening Echo* at Basildon, where he was splash sub-editor. Joined *Pulse* in 1982, where he became chief sub-editor. Joined *The Times* in 1986 as a home news sub and moved to *The Sunday Times* as deputy chief sub in 1988, subsequently being promoted to chief sub-editor.

career but just manage to check myself in time. He's 30 and earning £32,000, going up to £35,000 in July plus a motor-car. Shit! This is going to be hard."

He takes Davidson to meet Fallon, who confirms Bambridge's view. When Andrew Neil wanders into his office for a talk he tells him Davidson should be hired, gets the go-ahead and tells Roger Eglin to start negotiating with Peter Roberts on pay. "It won't be easy," Bambridge thinks, "but I'll save myself for the second line of attack" – the moment when Roberts says the proposed salary is too high.

Just as hiring journalists is part of everyday life, so is dealing with writs. As Fallon and Bambridge were interviewing a new member of his staff, Eglin has been talking to Antony Whitaker, the legal manager of Times Newspapers. A story in the Business section has said that Asher Edelman, the American businessman, was friendly with shady characters in the American gambling industry. Edelman has sued and the battle between him and *The Sunday Times* is hotting up. The bill for legal costs could run into hundreds of thousands of pounds. Now Whitaker wants the journalists who wrote the report to go to America for a fortnight to research some loose ends.

With Fallon, Bambridge, City editor Jeff Randall and industrial editor Andrew Lorenz, Eglin is now off to the weekly highlight of the Business week – the Business lunch in the Mikado room at the Savoy. It is an off-the-record meeting, nothing that is said is ever used except as background, but it is an entertaining way for the senior editors of the Business section to get to know the captains of industry and to learn what in the business world is making them happy or unhappy.

An added advantage is that when the guests become involved in big stories the staff can call them on first-name terms. As usual they are met by the major-domo: "Everything all right, gentlemen?" A smile, a big bow. "We've been coming here for ages," Bambridge thinks, "and each lunch must set the paper back £500 a time but I bet the old boy has no idea who we are. 'Everything all right?' 'Yes thanks.'"

The guests today are Lord King, chairman of British Airways, Arthur Walsh, chairman of STC, Richard Duggan, managing director of the Trade Indemnity Group, and Simon Bentley, chief executive of Black's Leisure Group. Over drinks they gossip – they have all been reading *Liar's Poker* and *Barbarians at the Gate*, the two bestselling business books of the year so far, and they have all been following the Guinness trial. Over lunch King dominates the table. His plan to take a 20 per cent stake in Sabena, the Belgian airline, has been referred to the Monopolies Commission and the European Commission has also been involved.

He was horrified to discover that officials from Brussels had the right to inspect anything in his offices and to look at any document – but only to photostat and take away those that were relevant to their inquiry. They had gone through all his personal papers, including his income tax, though they finally decided to photostat only six documents. King's secretary, who speaks fluent French, heard one say to her two colleagues as they entered his office: "So this is how rich capitalists live." They were his own pictures, King says. There is also an important principle at stake, he insists, as they enjoy the smoked salmon. If the Sabena deal is stopped, BA's growth will be severely restricted. Eglin senses a good story on how the powers of the Brussels Eurocrats are making life tougher for top businessmen. Back at the office that afternoon he briefs the Brussels correspondent, Iain Jenkins, to start working on it.

Arthur Walsh is also on good form, insisting that the British economy is in much worse shape than anybody realises. That view is supported by Duggan, who insures trade credit, who says that in terms of bad debts and companies going bankrupt the situation is as bad as in 1979–80. (A recession was declared only a few months later.) As they leave, Bambridge confirms Eglin's view that there is a good article to be written on the power of Brussels, based on King's anecdote.

There have been other lunches too. Andrew Neil is meeting a fellow editor, Robin Morgan of the *Sunday Express*. Kate Carr lunched with Stuart Wavell, recently appointed as the paper's new Paris correspondent. She wants him to write from France for the Style section. All the newsroom people are at a Mexican restaurant in Soho, giving a lunch to one of the reporters, Ian Birrell, who is getting married on Saturday. David Hughes is lunching with a contact from the Treasury. He gets some useful background on how the Treasury sees inflation developing through the summer, as well as guidance on British policy on the European Exchange Rate Mechanism. That finds its way by Saturday into the lead story on the front page.

Chris Nawrat lunches with Peter Lawson of the Central Council for Physical Recreation. *The Sunday Times* promotes the annual Women's Sports Awards with the CCPR and Moët & Chandon. They talk about the plans for 1990, but also about the idea of an exhibition of British sport, which both are keen on. "We believe that the only thing Europeans have in common is sport, not language, culture, religion or food," says Nawrat. "As Britain gave sport to the world, why not, as our contribution to 1992, put on a six-week exhibition of sport – paintings, artefacts, trophies, seminars, films, books, displays and so on. The Queen and Prince Philip would allow their collections to be part of the exhibition and would probably open it. We are both excited by the idea."

There was no glamorous lunch for David Walsh, the group sales controller for the advertising department, even though at least half *The Sunday Times* consists of display and classified advertising, which pays the journalists' salaries and defrays the cost of their expense-account lunches. Few journalists ever meet any of the advertising sales staff. One reason is that they work in a different building. The real reason, however, is that journalists loathe advertisements – they get in the way of the words or are arranged in awkward shapes that the editorial designers have to beat if the writers' words and pictures are to overcome the messages from the ads.

Walsh is number two to Dorothy Cumpsty, advertising director. His job is as stressful as any journalist's but his infectious enthusiasm for the job and enjoyment of the tension is just as great. He has 60 staff to sell advertising to *The Times*, *The Sunday Times* and *The Sunday Times Magazine* and they bring in £1 million a day.

This is week 46 of the News International 1989–90 fiscal year and Walsh is wishing now that he hadn't set the budget so high in February

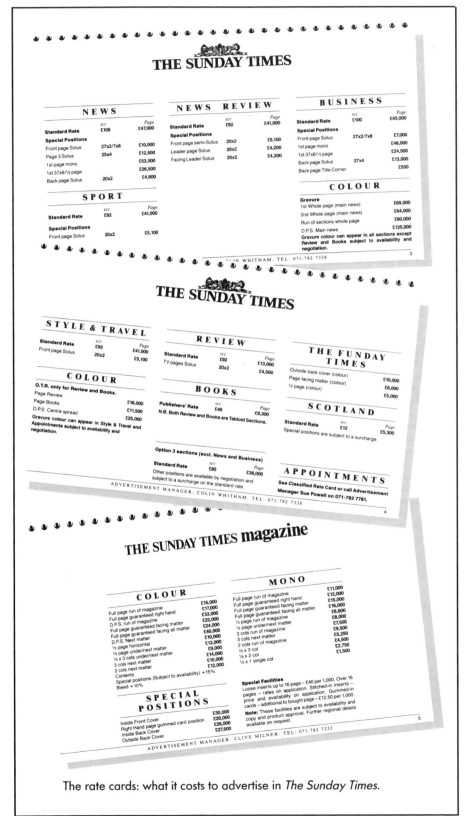

The rate cards: what it costs to advertise in *The Sunday Times*.

1989. Then advertising in newspapers was hitting the roof. There were big takeovers and mergers, big government campaigns for privatisation and it looked as if the advertising boom was never going to end. He set what he thought was a realistic target for this fiscal year, an increase in revenue of 15 per cent, based on an increase in volume and on selling an extra 5 per cent ads.

Fifteen months later the situation looks very different. There is not only a slump in advertising because of the economic recession, but two new papers, the *Sunday Correspondent* and the *Independent on Sunday*, have entered the Sunday quality newspaper market. So five papers instead of three are now fighting for slices of a cake that is much smaller. When there is a recession, moreover, fewer jobs are advertised and fewer homes and cars are sold – and recruitment, property and motors are the three biggest earners of advertising revenue for *The Sunday Times*, the market leader in all three. "We are fighting for business," says Walsh. "If we sat back and waited for the phone to ring, we would wait all day."

Wednesday is the watershed of the advertising week when Walsh takes serious stock. To meet the budget this week he has to get 289 columns of advertising. On the same week last year he sold 11 full-page ads and 16 38×6s – ads that are 38cm high and six columns wide. Among the advertisers then, but who are not advertising this week, were the British Medical Association, the British Airports Authority, Blue Arrow, BET and British Gas.

Some ads, for big car manufacturers such as Ford, Renault and Volvo, are booked on an annual contract. Others have been booked weeks ahead, all three sites for colour, for instance. On Monday Walsh was told by his team that they were hopeful of getting ads from such clients as Whitbread, British Midland Airways, Nationwide Anglia, Olivetti and the Halifax. So by today the department has sold eight full pages, but it still has three to sell (minimum cost £36,000, rising to £44,000 in the main news section) as well as ads for another 11 positions.

Most ads are booked by the big advertising agencies and there are sales groups under Walsh – financial, fashion, travel, motors and so on – who pitch the advantages of using *The Sunday Times*, which has nearly 4 million affluent readers, to the agencies. Yet the competition is now so fierce that an advertiser can get an ad which costs £44,000 for one insertion in *The Sunday Times* into four papers – *Independent on Sunday*, *Sunday Correspondent*, *Observer* and *Guardian* – for the same price, make four "hits" and cover 35 per cent of the population. So Walsh's staff is armed with statistics on the unique readership strengths of *The Sunday Times* so that they can make aggressive pitches to the agencies.

With all the rival papers discounting the cost of ads, they have to work hard. "If we relied on the phone ringing, we would sit here all day," says Walsh. "We could fill *The Sunday Times* without question if we dealt at the same rates as the competition – but we are not in the business of philanthropy."

The advertising department fills an open-plan floor running the full length of the main building at Wapping. About 200 staff work on this floor, which resembles the New York Stock Exchange. Advertising staff are rallied to new heights of enthusiasm every day. There are daily target briefings every morning. Outside Walsh's office there are boards on the walls telling the staff how many ads they still have to get to meet their targets. There are roars of excitement and applause when a sale is clinched. "Sales people are thespians at heart," he says.

One of Walsh's responses to the advertising recession is to draw up lists of tactical ideas to tempt advertisers on topical issues. It will soon be summer so his team is pitching for summer advertising: summer pharmaceuticals (why not cure your hay fever?), summer drinks, the World Cup, Wimbledon, summer sales, summer books and student banking for the period after the A-level results are published in mid-August.

The response to the recession from the advertising agencies is ruthless. They exploit the competition between the five Sunday quality papers by keeping them waiting until Friday. That is when Sunday newspaper ad managers are desperate to fill the empty spaces (and oh, how the journalists hope they won't) and meet their budgets. That is when the agencies come on the line and try to sell their ads at prices that are much cheaper than the ratecard.

Some ads are sold at a premium – the front page, the first right-hand page, the first motoring ad. Other advertisers have prejudices – for instance, they don't want to be in Sport (a common theme for all newspapers). Yet Walsh has already had one success this week, in persuading TWA to put a full-page ad in the Travel section instead of News. Now there is another: one of his team has persuaded British Coal to increase the size of their ad from a 38×6 to a full page. Only 11 more ads to sell; and with the mad cow disease controversy in full flow the Meat Marketing Commission has just asked for a full page in *The Times*. Now Walsh wants to know if they want an ad in *The Sunday Times* too. The chase is on.

As Walsh worries whether he can meet his budget, Roberts is presenting the editorial budget. Rupert Murdoch, whose main headquarters is now in New York, is devoting this day to inspecting the budgets of all his British newspaper titles – *The Times*, *Sun*, *News of the World* and *Today* as well as *The Sunday Times*. The meeting with Roberts lasts four hours and his proposals are scrutinised by 20 of the top bosses at News International, including the directors of advertising, circulation and promotions.

It is a difficult year. There have to be cuts. The debate is over who suffers most. But Roberts's oversight of editorial costs has given *The Sunday Times* a good reputation for keeping to its budget. Murdoch wants to know when the paper plans to introduce individual contracts for the journalists and when the paper is due to start printing in colour. Then he inspects the budget for each section, starting with Style, Travel and Books. There is optimism about the paper – it has survived the dual onslaught of the *Sunday Correspondent* and the *Independent on Sunday* with its market leadership intact, and advertising bookings for the autumn are promising. The budget is approved but with cuts of £300,000. Roberts is highly satisfied.

James Adams meanwhile has been learning some of the difficulties of Roberts' job. The editor has been on the phone. Why has Marie Colvin, the Middle East correspondent, written an article for *The Times* about the time she spent

Walsh: "We are not in the business of philanthropy." The advertising department chase their budget target.

Aileen Ballantyne

Aged 37. Started career on *The Scotsman* in 1976 before moving to the *Guardian* as a reporter in 1979. She eventually became medical correspondent and moved to *The Sunday Times* in 1989.

with Yasser Arafat while making a documentary for the BBC? Why wasn't the article in *The Sunday Times*? "I called her," says Adams, "and it turned out that she had offered the article to Tony Rennell who had turned it down. I then spoke to Rennell who said he thought it was unsuitable for the Arts pages and offered it to Bob Tyrer for features. He turned it down saying that Colvin couldn't write. This tactless response has succeeded in upsetting both the writer and the editor. Bob is a talented editor and an intelligent man but needs to lighten up."

As Roberts was defending the budget to Rupert Murdoch, the staff of *The Sunday Times* was still spending. Nawrat wants a picture from the Atlantic to go with his story on the finishing stages of the Whitbread Round the World Yacht Race. The question is whether the paper wants – equally whether the budget can stand – a picture taken from a plane or a helicopter. Nawrat does want the picture and Aidan Sullivan, the picture editor, goes to consult Bambridge: is it OK by him to spend the money? Nawrat also wants Sullivan to send a photographer to Taunton to do a special portrait of the cricketer Jimmy Cook, rather than rely lazily on the usual corny picture of him batting. He also commissions a picture of Linda Keogh, the 400 metre runner in training. That will go with a story about her that has been suggested by Cliff Temple, the athletics correspondent.

Meanwhile David Hughes and Andrew Grice are working the House of Commons. Hughes is loitering in the lobby, where journalists meet politicians but on the off-the-record terms. He talks to MPs and ministers in the search for story ideas. The Commons terrace is open for the summer, which makes MPs much more accessible, and his talks continue late into the evening.

Grice is making good progress on following through the Labour policy review. On Monday he had rung Credit Suisse Boston, the investment bank, and fed them his latest information from the review. He was hoping they would analyse the estimated impact of the proposals on taxation on incomes to give him a story for Saturday that the daily papers would not have had the time or the inclination to get. Today they have rung him with the first figures. Now he is talking to members of the Shadow Cabinet and Labour officials to get more details of yesterday's meeting.

For Alex Butler it is the most boring day of the week – a day spent making sure that the subs who work on Saturdays get paid, arranging the rota for the next few weeks, and subbing the gardening, motoring and property pages. "They are three pages that can take a day and a half to complete," he says. "It's incredible. We can do 60 pages on a Saturday but these three pages are like a visit to a dentist. Pictures never arrive on time, ad shapes invariably change, the pages are often shifted from one section to another, requiring all the headlines to be done again." Stoically he starts reading the gardening copy.

By Wednesday afternoon Dorothy Ravenswood, the letters editor, also has a pretty good idea of the main subjects from the previous Sunday's paper that have upset, infuriated or pleased the readers. She meets me to decide which subjects should be highlighted on the Letters page. So far this week the main subjects exercising readers are mad cow disease (13 letters), Eton (with 12) and dentists (9). They are reacting to statements by Professor Richard Lacey on reducing the production of beef, a mocking article on Eton's celebrations of its 450th anniversary by writer Kate Saunders, and a column by Walter Ellis about his continuing fright when visiting the dentist. Ravenswood, who has dealt with readers' letters for several years, is not surprised by the dentists' angry reaction. "They always get very passionate when they are criticised – they are next to schoolteachers and doctors," she says.

Meanwhile two reporters have suddenly scented stories. Aileen Ballantyne, the medical correspondent, has been reading one of the many specialist medical journals that land on her desk every week but her news sense has been alerted by five lines on cancer trials: "There is also the suggestion from a study with 200 volunteers that tamoxifen, which was not anti-oestrogenic in no-breast tissues, may be a possible agent for the prevention of breast cancer."

"That was the sum total," says Ballantyne, a cool, unflustered Scot who joined *The Sunday Times* from the *Guardian* and has produced medical stories almost weekly. "But it reminded me of a speculative piece I had seen in another specialist journal last year. Ian Fentiman, a leading cancer specialist at Guy's Hospital in London, was interested in using tamoxifen as a potential preventive treatment for breast cancer – a disease which affects one in 12 women in the United Kingdom and kills 15,000 every year. If someone, somewhere, had tried this drug on 200 healthy women, and the trade press were picking up on it as a real possibility for prevention, this was clearly more than one doctor's pipedream."

She rings Fentiman and gets enough detail to convince her that the story has legs. "His excitement at the prospect of tamoxifen as treatment was evident." He has stressed, however, that she ought to talk to Trevor Powles, a breast cancer specialist at the Royal Marsden Hospital, but doesn't have his home number. That call will be made tomorrow.

Although the Bush Commission on Lockerbie has been given saturation treatment in the daily papers, David Leppard, an Insight reporter, is trying to satisfy the editor's demand for a fresh Sunday story. Leppard has spent months on the Lockerbie trail and is now convinced he has a decent new angle. A few weeks ago he had visited Germany to meet a well-informed contact. They spent five hours swapping information, and Leppard learnt that Hafez Dalkamoni, a leading Palestinian terrorist and the key suspect, was being visited by Sammy Sarkis, a mysterious Syrian lawyer who had been linked to hostage deals. His new angle is an investigation of Sarkis. Now he has three days to prove that Sarkis had indeed visited Dalkamoni in his high-security German prison cell and that Sarkis has been linked to hostage deals.

One of the jobs of the executive editor is to absorb pain. All the jobs that bore the editor or that he simply has not the time to handle himself land on Bambridge's desk, just as all the journalists with a moan or a complaint tend to go first to him. This is going to be one of those afternoons. The first to arrive is Walter Ellis, a mild-mannered Ulsterman recruited from the *Sunday Telegraph*, an excellent writer who has recently been given his own column. Ellis has read in *Private Eye* that Bryan Appleyard, recently recruited from the *Independent* to

David Leppard

Deputy editor, Insight. Aged 30, an Oxford graduate with a PhD in English Literature. Starting as a freelance, joined *The Times* Diary in 1986 and moved to *The Sunday Times* where he was crime reporter before joining Insight. His *On the Trail of Terror: The Inside Story of the Lockerbie Investigation* was published in July 1991 by Cape.

write a weekly column, is being paid £80,000 a year. If that is true, he tells Bambridge, he deserves a lot more money. Bambridge wearily points out that this is a lousy pay claim. The story in *Private Eye* is almost certainly untrue and anyway he is Walter Ellis and not Bryan Appleyard and we all believe in the market. He says he is going to write to the editor. "Fine," thinks Bambridge. "He'll only say what I say and he won't thank you. I prove right on all counts."

Now Bambridge turns to another complaint, this time from Nick Hayes, editor of Granada's *World in Action*. He has taken exception to an article by Stuart Wavell about one of the programmes, was unhappy with the response and has made a complaint to the Press Council. Bambridge now has the job of organising the paper's reply. It involves a lot of work checking the original story, assessing the seriousness of the complaint, talking to the reporter and drafting a reply. Occasionally there is a "trial" before 12 members of the Press Council, where both sides put their case, so the tenor of the paper's response is vital. Bambridge probably deals with at least ten such complaints a year, involving hours of work.

After her morning interview Valerie Grove has lunched at the *Sunday Telegraph* with her husband and colleagues, picked up two of her daughters from school at 3.10, driven them home by 4 pm and is now on her way to Euston to catch the 5.10 train to Birmingham for her second interview of the day with Dr Swire.

After his Savoy lunch Eglin has had a good and busy afternoon. In Los Angeles Philip Robinson has discovered that the Italian businessman Giancarlo Paretti, the former Savoy waiter who wants to take over MGM, faces an end-of-the-week deadline to come up with the money. One deadline has already been postponed. He also tells Eglin that Price Waterhouse, the international accountants, have just lost a sexual discrimination case against a senior woman employee. They are charged with sexual stereotyping, will have to pay heavy damages and have been told to make her a partner. "A good story," he says. "What happens next?"

Other good business stories are also rolling in. "Ove Arup are stepping up pressure on the Channel Tunnel rail link. They have a plan to route it east of the proposed line, which would be cheaper and less damaging to the environment. They want to tell us how their plan is shaping. There is also a story about who is talking to Dan Air about buying it – and is Rank going to bid for Mecca? Imbucon International are about to publish a big report on the pay of top managers in Europe. I have tried to get them to give us a leak – but they won't.

"Arthur Andersen have also rung. They are quite interested in helping to revive an award we once had for the most respected companies in Britain. It was a great success last time but the polling of hundreds of people in the City and business to establish the winners cost £35,000."

Now he is off for dinner with a gathering of steel industry executives, "not the most exciting of evenings".

After his night away in Dublin, and an afternoon making calls to stockbrokers and bankers in Ireland about Larry Goodman, City editor Jeff Randall faces another night out. "I'm feeling absolutely knackered and should really go home," he says, "but I've got a dinner with the chairman of a major construction group. A call to Mrs Randall to explain that I'll be late again. 'When are you going to find time for Lucy (our 16-month-old daughter)?' she asks. Good question. I mumble some nonsense about taking her out at the weekend and hang up feeling very guilty.''

Michael Williams is back from his day in Belfast and is not feeling Randall's guilt, although there is a thought-provoking irony about his day in Ulster when he makes a check call to the newsdesk. "An IRA bomb has exploded near Wembley Stadium. Should we treat it as a big story? asks the newsdesk. No, I say. It's a sad fact that a Wednesday IRA bomb that kills nobody rates for nothing in Sunday's news schedules."

Penny Perrick, the fiction editor, is also off to dinner. May is the period of the publishers' mid-season slump – most major titles are clustered around March to April or September to October, although some thoughtful publishers are slipping in an important American author, such as Mordecai Richler or Ellen Gilchrist, so that attention can be devoted to them before the distraction of the potential Booker shortlist titles in the autumn.

Today she has skimmed through ten novels before sending them out for review. "I need a constant supply of novels as others need cigarettes or Mars bars," she says. One of her tactics is match-making, trying to find marriages made in heaven between reviewers and novels. Since her lead reviewers, Peter Kemp, Shena Mackay, John Melmoth and Paul Golding, all have different tastes, it is not too difficult. "Among the novels I kept back for myself was *Dying Young* by Marti Leimbach, an American in her twenties. It's a first novel about a 33-year-old man dying of leuk-

emia. Amazingly it manages to be funny as well as very moving, definitely a lead review."

By chance her dinner is with Clare Alexander of Viking, a sister company of Hamish Hamilton, the British publisher of Leimbach's novel. Alexander admires the book but thinks it carries a whiff of the American creative writing course. "Too many young writers, she feels, are force-fed on the likes of Raymond Carver and copy the habits of the great before they have found a voice of their own. My own view is that the creative writing course, at its best, turns a key in the lock and unleashes a lot of dormant talent. One of our best novelists, Ian McEwan, whose *The Innocent* was published last week to great acclaim, is a product of a creative course. Long may they flourish."

As Perrick enjoys her dinner, James Blitz is busy at his typewriter in the Moscow office. His afternoon was spent making several fruitless calls to try to get a picture of the dating agency wanted by the London picture desk to go with his story. A colleague at Reuters eventually agreed to do it – but tomorrow morning. He then told the dating agency that he was coming round, only to be told they could not guarantee any women would be there. Irina has got his tickets for Latvia but he is still worried that if he is in Latvia when Yeltsin is elected he will miss all the colour of the Moscow story. After calling Witherow, he decides to go to Riga anyway. Now he is typing an article which he does not finish until 1 am.

Margarette Driscoll in Monte Carlo, meanwhile, is still waiting to hear from Gabriela Mayer. She waited in the hotel, then went back to the house and left a message, then waited in vain throughout the

Valerie Grove

Writer of weekly Valerie Grove Interview. Aged 45. A Cambridge graduate, she spent 19 years on the *Evening Standard*, where she was a feature writer and literary editor. Now writes the main interview of the week as well as contributing to other sections of the paper.

evening at the hotel. At 10 pm she is still waiting.

After arriving in Birmingham Valerie Grove has been more fortunate. Hers was a splendid evening. "Dr Swire's house turns out to be a lovely, remote old farmhouse overlooking a valley and the distant Malvern hills. We walk over the area he has planted with trees in memory of his lost daughter Flora: it is now called Flora's wood. He is the classic family doctor figure – tall and lean, Scottish, blue-eyed, calm, utterly dependable, and now utterly obsessed about getting something done to prevent another Lockerbie. He wears a badge: Pan Am 103 – The Truth Must Be Told. Inside the house we talk for three hours with his wife Jane, a teacher of religious studies. It is a real family house: old books, old portraits, piano, good, well-worn furniture – but it has lost its eldest daughter, who was truly beautiful (I see the photographs) and clever and creative and fun. Both parents are stricken and changed for ever but the mother's face lights up and rejuvenates when she talks of Flora. There is no consolation."

After this obviously moving interview, Grove caught the last train home and arrived at Euston at ten minutes past midnight. It has been a long day.

Yet it is Iain Johnstone in Cannes who has had the most glamorous evening, albeit after a hectic day. It started when he was woken by a call from BBC Wales asking him to talk on their morning show about the festival. Then it was movies, movies, movies. "The best performance by an actor in a leading role goes to Alexander Walker of the *Evening Standard* who berates Ken Loach at his press conference for his anti-British bias in *Hidden Agenda*. I thought the film was

quite tightly made and predict that it will win a prize. I'm right."

His evening started on the yacht of Jennifer and Roger Wingate who own the Curzon cinemas and several London theatres. "They're a tremendous couple, genuinely interested in the arts and prepared to lose money if their hearts are in a project," says Johnstone. "We repair to a portside restaurant for dinner – this is beginning to sound like

The result of a busy
week for Johnstone.

Iain Johnstone

Film Critic. Aged 48. Appointed
in 1983 by Andrew Neil, he was
presenter of *Film '83* and *Film '84*
on television, is chairman of
Screenplay on BBC radio and a
frequent broadcaster about the
cinema. His book *Cannes: The
Novel* was published in the week
this book was written. What most
upsets him is being told he has
the best job in Britain: "It happens
every day. If the people who
make that comment had to sit
through most recent films it's not a
comment they would make."

The result of a splendid evening for Grove.

Jennifer's Diary – with Victoria
Mather of GQ, her husband
Johnny, Mark Shivas, the drama
boss of the BBC, and Don Bennetts
from Australia who first came to
Cannes with Mark 23 years ago and
first took me there when I devised
the BBC's *Film '71*."

As Johnstone enjoys his dinner in
the South of France, Andrew Grice
is recording a triumph – he has been
handed a leaked copy of the Labour
policy review. All his talks have
proved worthwhile. "Mission ac-
complished," he says with a grin.
Nawrat has been watching Ireland
draw with Finland in a pre-World
Cup match. Scotland, who are in
England's group, have lost to
Egypt. How humiliating. He makes
a note: World Cup – with three
weeks to go, jitters set in on the
home front. That will be on his
newslist tomorrow.

New sections to beat off
the opposition.

Marketing

One of the main jobs of the modern editor is to "market" his paper – to define its image, select its niche in the marketplace (is it a paper for the upmarket ABC1 social classes or a tabloid for the C2DEs?), polish its brand image and then go out with his marketing director to sell the paper and its merits to millions of readers. An editor has to know about trends in sales and trends in readership. Are his readers owners of Mercedes and BMWs or Ford Orions and Vauxhall Cavaliers? Do they own one home, two homes or rent a council flat? Do they holiday in Tuscany or the Costa del Sol? On the answers will depend the paper's appeal to different categories of advertiser and reader – and how editors perceive the editorial identity of their papers.

Readers of *The Sunday Times* are predominantly ABC1s with children, who live in big homes, drive big cars, earn big salaries and enjoy foreign holidays. They are interested in politics, business, the arts, books and travel – which is one reason why the paper caters to their interests with so many dedicated sections which can be supported with advertising, since the readers are attractive to advertisers of jobs, homes, motors and travel.

Up to £5 million a year was being spent on marketing *The Sunday Times* after its move to Wapping in 1986 – and even in 1990–91, during the recession, £2 million a year was still being spent on wooing new readers to the paper and persuading existing readers to remain loyal.

Advertising campaigns work. When *The Sunday Times* serialised Kitty Kelley's unofficial biography of Nancy Reagan in the spring of 1991, and advertised the serial on television, sales rose by more than 40,000. Sceptics suggest that many advertising campaigns win promiscuous readers who switch between papers according to each new attraction. The main aim of marketing is to make the new readers stick with the paper.

After the Wapping revolution of 1986, sales of *The Sunday Times* were hit by the unpopularity of the "Murdoch press" after his sacking of more than 5,000 printers. "Murdoch" newspapers were reviled by those who believed he had acted too ruthlessly, even though subsequently it was universally acknowledged that the move to Wapping transformed the fortunes of the British national press.

Graham King, a cheerful, imperturbable Australian marketing expert, who had worked for Rupert Murdoch since he acquired his first Australian paper, was called to England to stop the rot. King knew how to exploit television. He was the marketing man who started *Sun* Bingo and saw the paper's sales soar upwards to 4 million. Now *The Sunday Times* was added to his portfolio of responsibilities.

King, who is no longer with the company and has been succeeded by his deputy, Alison Morris, also an Australian, was the biggest spender at News International. At one time he masterminded a £25 million budget for television promotion of the five titles. He was a master of bold, brash marketing strategies. One publisher was shocked when he brooded on how to get some "sex" into George Bernard Shaw when the paper was serialising the Michael Holroyd biography and he was thinking about how to promote it. Yet his occasional brashness belied the inner man. He was a writer of novels and a collector of antiquarian books. He decided that the strategy for *The Sunday Times* was to build on its strengths.

He started by studying the readers and meeting them in small focus groups where they were asked to study the paper and offer comments. Neil was invited along, too, to discover just what a catholic bunch they were. Neil was quite shocked, according to King. What emerged strongly from the meetings was the readers' thirst for knowledge about the arts and books and sports, particularly from so big a paper with such high aspirations. "It was clear that if we put a sugar coating on knowledge, more readers would buy the paper," says King.

That sugar coating – or added value, as it is described in the marketing trade – amounted to a series of major book serialisations, reader offers and part-works which readers had to buy for up to six weeks. "We thought of niche markets such as car enthusiasts, students, children or holidaymakers and focused a lot of activity into individually-tailored marketing exercises," says King.

Among them were the health series *Lifeplan*, *Examplan* for GCSE students, a *Handbook of Wine*, the *A–Z of Preventive Medicine*, the *Young Person's Guide to the Orchestra* and *The Taste of Italy*. Atlases and collections of maps were equally popular. There were also special promotions for children – who then demanded that their parents bought the paper for several weeks. Series on stamps, ghosts, seaside beaches, supported by wallcharts or stickers, were all successful. Editorially, the paper also responded with new Books and Travel sections.

King's campaign started in 1987 to coincide with the 25th anniversary of *The Sunday Times Magazine* and the launch of *Lifeplan*. It was an instant success. Sales rose by 350,000 to a peak of nearly 1.4 million. With television promotion it is easy to hit peaks. It is more difficult to lift sales on to a plateau. That was why the promotions had to follow thick and fast. An atlas part-work boosted sales by 200,000, a serialisation of a Richard Burton biography by 30,000. By 1988 King's strategy was working. It was also helped by a "generic" television campaign on The Perfect Sunday, showing a typical Home Counties family of mother, father, two children and statutory labrador sharing out the sections of the paper as the aroma of roast beef wafted through the sitting-room, sales were on a plateau of over 1.3 million.

The newspaper market is never easy, however. Suddenly it was announced that two new Sunday papers were being launched and that one of their prime targets was *The Sunday Times*. The senior editors took a weekend break themselves and went into retreat in the hills above Nice in the South of France to consider how to react to the competition.

The best idea that emerged was the *Funday Times*, a children's comic, added as an extra section, which was launched shortly before the *Sunday Correspondent* and was an instant success. So was an offer of weekend breaks, in which readers had to collect tokens during the first six weeks of the *Sunday Correspondent*. More than 100,000 responded. The Style section was also launched as an added attraction of the paper.

Within four months there was new competition from the *Independent on Sunday*, which was launched in January 1990. "Given that many of our readers will try the *Independent* anyway, our strategy should be to try to keep them with *The Sunday Times*," King said in a memo to the editor. "We should force them to think of the *Independent* as a second buy and not a substitute. Bridging their launch with promotable material must be our top priority. We must pay close attention to February 11th and 18th, a sensitive period when many

who have given the *Independent* a trial will be making up their minds about their future Sunday paper. What do we have to run during this period?"

King offered a part-work, the *A–Z of Classic Cars*, another offer of spring weekend breaks and the launch of the Funday Times Club, which quickly attracted more than 100,000 members. Editorially the paper responded with the memoirs of Boris Yeltsin, the challenger of Gorbachev, a series on Megatrends for the Nineties, a special opinion poll on the monarchy, and the results of a long news investigation of the Liverpool militant Derek Hatton, all timed to combat the launch of the *Independent on Sunday*.

The outcome of the biggest battle in the Sunday quality market for 30 years was that the *Sunday Correspondent* failed and the *Independent on Sunday* was incorporated within 18 months into a seven-day newspaper. *The Sunday Times* survived with only a relatively small drop in circulation and continued to outsell the combined circulation of its two main rivals. A significant element of that success was due to marketing.

According to King, the best marketing strategy works on two levels – a campaign consisting of generic advertising to keep readers favourably disposed (The Perfect Sunday), supported by tactical advertisements to prompt readers to go out and buy the paper for the special offers, part-works or serialisations. "It's a great effort to walk to the newsagents on a Sunday morning," he says. King's job was to persuade them to make that walk.

"The history of News International, particularly the *Sun* and the *News of the World*, has been that their fortunes are almost directly related to the fortunes of television," King says. "We have ridden piggy-back on the television audience – but it looks as if we have now reached saturation point and we are searching for other ways of promoting papers, including greater home delivery."

As the colour magazine and the Business section were added and *The Sunday Times* became a four-section paper, that success continued throughout the sixties, with sales rising to more than 1.5 million in 1967 when William Manchester's *Death of a President*, the story of President John F. Kennedy, was serialised. Since then it has never slipped below 1.1 million, whatever the new competition has thrown at it.

How to catch new young readers.

Sales rose by 40,000 when Kitty Kelley's book on Nancy Reagan was serialised.

Thursday

"A serious book review in The Sunday Times is just as important as writing an academic book. Surely the money the nation feeds into universities should be fed back? A book review feeds the cultured life of the nation."

At home and abroad, with edition deadlines now looming tonight, tomorrow and Saturday, the stress level is rising. Few casual words provoke more stress than the instruction: Be funny. Being funny is usually quite hard work, as Iain Johnstone is discovering in Cannes as he strives to meet the demand from Kate Carr for his Style review of the film festival. He has been up since seven for the morning screening – "you have to be there by eight to be sure of a seat" – and is now working on the less glamorous part of his job in his hotel room.

A few miles away in Monte Carlo Margarette Driscoll is still waiting to meet Gabriela Mayer; but in Manila an impatient Jon Swain, who needs to get his story by tomorrow night, is on the move. He has hired a car and has decided to drive to Angeles City, next to Clarke airbase, to try to get to the bottom of

the murder of the two US servicemen. Now he is talking to a former mayor, Neto Muceno, who escaped an assassination attempt two years ago.

"Today he takes no chances, surrounding himself with guns and guard dogs and driving an armour-plated car. I discover in this and other conversations that the Philippines four decades after independence still has not been able to forge a national identity. It still feels a deep dependency on the US. Today the most potent symbol of this unattained nationalism is the bases. There is a fierce inferiority complex towards Americans. The humiliation is complete with hundreds of thousands of the Filipino workforce working outside the Philippines in other South-East Asian countries or the Arab States. It is tragic but a Filipino *amah* can earn more in Hong Kong to support her family than a Harvard-trained economics lecturer at Manila University."

Aileen Ballantyne, with two days to get her story about a potential cure for breast cancer, is trying to reach Trevor Powles at the Royal Marsden; but he is out and won't be back until this afternoon, when he is seeing patients. "My heart sank," she says. Professor Fentiman is out also, as is Professor Michael Baum, who heads Britain's main breast cancer research committee. He too won't be back until the afternoon. When Rosemary Collins, who is starting to prepare her newslist for the 11.30 editor's conference, asks the strength of the story, Ballantyne cannot yet tell her. Collins still puts the story on her list.

Sleuth David Leppard, hunting Sammy Sarkis, is chasing his Lockerbie story. Already he has checked *The Sunday Times* cuttings library and the Wapping database and the Press Association library in Fleet Street. Nothing. He rang Reuters in Cyprus and spoke to their Beirut expert. She had never heard of Sarkis. Next he rang Marie Colvin, *The Sunday Times* Middle East correspondent, in Paris. She has checked *Le Monde* library. Still nothing. Nor is there any trace of him in Washington – and defence correspondent James Adams, who has checked with his intelligence sources, cannot trace Sarkis either. Leppard is beginning to wonder whether he exists.

The section heads are now preparing for the editor's 11.30 conference, the most important of the week. This is when firm decisions start to be made about the major features and news reports. Only one of the ideas that Bob Tyrer, editor of the News Review section, put forward on Tuesday as suggestions for Focuses has survived. The Romanian elections and hysteria over

The end of the chase: Collins checks Ballantyne's story so far.

paedophilia were both rejected. Now he is suggesting "The best show in town – the Marcos/Khashoggi trial in new York" as the entertaining Focus and either the hunt for the IRA bombers, who have struck again, or an idiot's guide to mad cow disease for the main serious Focus. He taps into his screen:

The hunt for the bombers – is the MoD complacent, is there any protection?

Mad cow disease – is anyone to blame? Inside the feed factories. Is there a burger danger? Meat sales slump.

News gathering for Sunday has now started in earnest and Michael Williams has been talking to John Witherow, foreign editor, and Collins. "Foreign tends to be easier – fine writing about faraway places produced by some of Fleet Street's best correspondents," says Williams. "Home is infinitely tougher. Here *The Sunday Times* is jostling elbow-to-elbow with every other national paper every day of the week. How do we out-scoop them on Sunday?"

Witherow leads his foreign list with the Romanian elections, the pressures on Gorbachev from the Baltics, the army and Boris Yeltsin, and moves over the British hostages in Beirut:

Romania:	Can it survive democracy?
Soviet Union:	Gorbachev under pressure. The women desperate to leave.
Hostages:	Did a doctor see Waite and how ill was he?
America:	New York on brink of race riots?
Philippines:	US defines its role in South-East Asia.
France:	Now the Jews flee France for Israel.

On the home front Rosemary Collins is keen on the stories from Ballantyne and Leppard and the Insight special. She too starts typing her list:

"A moving story of human error, which makes a two-page News Focus special report."

Page 1
Exclusive: Germany and Syria in secret negotiations over Lockerbie suspect in bid to free German hostages.
Revealed: How British taxpayers' millions are spent on subsidising high-tar tobacco which is dumped on the Third World.
Britain to join ERM this autumn.
The medical breakthrough which could lead to the end of breast cancer.

Then she proposes stories for the other seven news pages.

At the Business section Roger Eglin is sticking with his two main stories of Tuesday – Philips in crisis

③

8.26
The 737-400 hits the M1 embankment at
132 mph and slews across to the opposite bank

④ The plane broke up, fatally injuring 47 people.
Rescue workers carried 79 survivors from the wreckage

Bob Collier

TO DIE!'

● continued from page 14

airfield, which meant the Boeing had dropped just below the glide path for landing on the runway.

DESMOND recalls the terror among the passengers, none of whom had any idea of what might happen but feared the worst.

"Everyone was praying. We were losing height fast, going down, down. I looked out of the window and I could see the lights of a town. I heard the throttle roar and then there was a beautiful hum of the engines. Then the hum turned into a death rattle again. It was as though the good engine was fighting it out against the bad. A grating sound became very prominent and then there was silence. Just silence."

Eight seconds before impact, the passengers were told by Hunt that the plane

flow out of my body and I was filled with this sensation of utter loneliness. I could smell kerosene and thought: 'Oh God, we're going to burn.' I knew what I was going to do: when the whoosh of fire swept through I was going to inhale it, fill up my lungs and become part of it. I wanted to die quickly.

In front of Desmond, a woman, lying in a seat which had sheared from its mounting, was screaming for her son. Desmond remembers telling her: "Quiet now, your boy has gone to be with Jesus."

A passing motorist, Graham Pearson from Hull, was among the first on the scene. He climbed into the fuselage to help survivors. Desmond remembered it: "He said to me, 'Hello, my name's Graham, what's yours?' It was so normal, like meeting a guy in a supermarket. He made a

was carried out it seemed as if I was being raised up by a procession of monks who were chanting for me to live. I felt as if I were about to leave my body.

"When I reached the hospital, I remember five people diving on me, cutting my clothes off. For the first time I sensed these were people who could cope. I relaxed, put my trust in them and fell unconscious."

IN ALL, 47 people died at Kegworth. Many others were injured, some grievously. Desmond spent 11 weeks recuperating at Musgrave Park hospital, Belfast, in the orthopaedic wing where his wife had worked as a senior house officer.

His injuries have reduced his height by an inch and a half and he walks with a stick in considerable pain. He has resumed his studies

husband Brian, 52, a British Telecom engineer. They wanted the answer to a single question: why was the wrong engine shut down? They left knowing it would never be answered.

The couple's daughter, Karin, and son-in-law, David Campbell, both constables in the RUC, were among the dead of Kegworth. They were returning from a weekend break in London. By coincidence, the Johnstons were waiting at Belfast airport to catch the return flight of BD 092 to London for a business trip when they learnt of the crash.

A week ago, the Johnstons inspected the wreckage of the Boeing 737 during a visit to the Department of Transport's Air Accident Investigation branch headquarters at Farnborough, Hampshire, organised for survivors and relatives of the dead.

and the contrast between Marks and Spencer and Storehouse. At the Arts section Tony Rennell is staying with Glyndebourne and the Rolling Stones; but after his triumph at Montreux he has put a profile of Rowan Atkinson down for the Arts page 3.

Now they troop in to meet Andrew Neil, the banter outside his office as they await his summons concealing the very real tension within. When Neil is dissatisfied with a list he lets his assistant editors know, often in savage terms.

"How's his blood sugar level this morning?" one of them asks Marie Jackson, his personal assistant.

Ever contrary, Neil starts today

with Style instead of the Review and asks about the state of the article on Garbo. "It's a good tragic read," says Rennell. Is fashion getting a good show, can you see the clothes as well as the models? Neil asks. What's the angle? It's what to wear for the posh events of the summer season, says Rennell. That's a great idea, says Neil, but that is what it's got to be. Style is also suggesting an inside page combining the Cannes festival with an article about the history of haircuts. Neil dismisses the idea of an article on hair as too marginal. "Give me good pictures and a good read from Cannes."

Now he turns to Tyrer and instantly dismisses a two-page Focus on the IRA. "There is nothing to say. It ain't going to make a spread. Cover it we must, but not as a Focus." His heart also sinks at a two-page Focus on mad cow disease. "It's the story of the week," insists Bambridge, who is supported by Michael Williams. It is also going to run on into next week and the row has now spread to Germany and America, he says.

Still unconvinced, Neil asks about the state of play on Lockerbie. Collins tells him that the story is that the West Germans have been talking to the man behind the bombing with a view to exchanging him for western hostages. It's a good story but Neil is sceptical that it is worth 4,000 words across two pages.

Williams suggests the M1 air crash. The main pilot, Captain Kevin Hunt, is due to speak tomorrow at the inquest into what happened at Kegworth and a moving story of human error is emerging. It could be presented as an Anatomy of an Air Crash, using the actual words of the two pilots. Neil is enthusiastic at last. "That's Focus 1. It will work by being a cracking read." Now his mind is ticking over. Why not get comment from an aviation expert: was it pilot error? He turns to Michael Jones, the political editor, whose judgement he respects. "It's a good story, Mr Jones?" Jones agrees: "A cracking story." There is suddenly so much enthusiasm that it becomes the two-page Focus spread, the main news feature of the week. Mad cow disease, Neil decides, should be the Focus 1 – but with no cheap shots at John Gummer, the minister at the centre of the row.

Neil turns to the Insight story. As he is told that the European Community pays £600 million in subsidies to Greek farmers to grow

tobacco that is then dumped on the Third World, he is outraged. He suggests that Insight also tries to find out how much the EEC spends on anti-smoking propaganda. "That could go across the top of page one," he comments. The main cornerstones of the front sections of the paper are beginning to be laid.

Norman Stone, professor of modern history at Oxford, who writes the main political column, is at the conference today and Neil asks him what subject he is planning to tackle. Stone wants to take a "gentle amble" through the mad world of agricultural protectionism. "That's the cartel that must be bust in the nineties, just as oil was in the eighties," he says, adding that each American cow gets more subsidy than an American university student.

The weekly left-wing column is written by Robert Harris, whose waspish and elegant pen all too often outrages the predominantly Tory readers of *The Sunday Times*, never more so than when he suggested that Mrs Thatcher was perhaps clinically mad. Against his name today is written his subject this week: Labour should be taken seriously. It is an opportunity for some gentle banter from the editor. "Haven't we read this before, Bob?" What interests him, says Harris, is why, although Labour is so far ahead in the opinion polls, the "chattering classes" still do not support it. It is also worth exploring why Labour has taken its fight so much on to Conservative ground. Neil agrees.

Half an hour has by now been spent on the Review section and attention turns to the foreign list. There is a short discussion about Gorbachev and the plight of the Lebanese hostages and Neil notes a few other items: Gorbachev's upcoming tour of America, the race trial in New York and the de Klerk meeting with Thatcher on Saturday. Witherow is congratulated on a good list.

Neil starts the discussion of the home news list with a scoop of his own. ITN, he says, has resolved the issue that was ripping it apart – the question whether Trevor MacDonald or Julia Somerville should say Good Evening at the start of *News at Ten*. (The quarrel over who should take precedence has been a running story in the national tabloids.) Somerville and MacDonald are going to take it in turns and will now be able to appear together, he says with a mocking smile to show that this is a trivial but entertaining story. Nevertheless the newsdesk should have some fun with it and it will leaven the news pages.

His attention turns to the IRA. The story of the latest bombing has to be covered, but how can it still be made news by Sunday? After a short discussion he suggests that it is tackled by investigating what the government is saying – is it officially admitted that there is now an IRA bombing campaign on the mainland? – and the background to the campaign: why has the IRA made this decision?

There are 23 items on the newslist and only a few can be discussed. What most interests Neil are the new income tax proposals from Labour contained in the policy review. There must be a table on how its proposals will affect incomes, he insists: "That's right up our readers' street." He is told that Grice has obtained the document and can deliver. He checks on the progress of *Maiden*.

Has Collins got the story on London beggars? She has. Begging is now turning to robbing, she says.

There is a short discussion on the state of Labour in London. The newslist proposes a story on why Labour may lose London in a general election. "I know that and that's not the angle," says Neil. Surely it should be why London may sink Labour. He checks on the state of an oil slick threatening the Devon coast. He likes Aileen Ballantyne's story about a cure for breast cancer.

Now he wants to know what the paper proposes to do about the decision to close the Ravenscraig steel plant in Scotland. Was the decision by Malcolm Rifkind, the Scottish Secretary of State, right? he asks Eglin. It was. So how are we going to handle it? Neil asks, sensing the sort of political and economic story with a Scottish angle that metropolitan papers tend to ignore, which really gets his hackles rising. He starts giving directions. We need to check on what went on in Cabinet and how it was handled by Rifkind. There must be a contribution from the Business section and colour from Scotland. The story is clearly shaping in his mind: Motherwell, the steel town with a mill that should never have gone there, a disaster typical of the politically-motivated regulatory policies of the sixties and seventies. This was Harold Wilson's smelting mill, similar to his decision to put British Leyland at Speke or Macmillan's decision to put Rootes at Linwood.

It is 12.30 and Neil turns to Business, where he spots a story on the newslist that the government's enterprise initiative is in the melting pot and under review by Nicholas Ridley, then trade and industry secretary. The advertisements which had been flooding television screens were a waste of time, says Neil. What did they cost, how many retired businessmen were used as consultants? "We ought to expose it."

Eglin mentions as potential front

Helen Hawkins

Chief sub-editor of Arts, Style and Travel. Aged 40. She is a graduate of Kent and Colorado Universities with a PhD in Comparative Literature. Hawkins joined *The Sunday Times* as a sub-editor in 1987 and is now deputy Arts editor. Before that she worked on a variety of magazines, including *Computing, Media Week, Broadcast* and the *Architects' Journal.*

page "basements" (entertaining light stories to leaven the heavy diet of solid business news) either a story that the Chicago Mercantile Exchange is launching classes in ethics or the story about sexual stereotyping at Price Waterhouse. What's your splash? asks Neil. Eglin suggests the economy and the state of the stock market, where there is a new surge of optimism. "It's doesn't grab me. I prefer something I know about," says Neil. Eglin has to find a new lead.

On to the Arts. Neil makes one major change. Rennell has commissioned a caricature of Rowan Atkinson from Gerald Scarfe. It's brilliant, he says. That decides the issue. Neil decrees that Atkinson should be the main article on the front. "He's so funny, so popular," and relegates the future of Glyndebourne to page three. Sammy Davis junior has died, so has Jim Henson, creator of the Muppets, and a new series of *Spitting Image* is being launched. The jazz critic is writing on Sammy Davis, why not get Fluck and Law, who make the *Spitting Image* puppets, to write about the Muppets, suggests Neil.

The Sports list is always last and always gets the least attention. After the end of the football season and in the few weeks before the World Cup, Wimbledon and the test matches, it is a quiet period of the year. Sport hopes to lead on the Whitbread race (but on Scotland against Poland in the pre-World Cup match in the Scottish edition) and draws the editor's attention to the Oxford–Cambridge athletics meeting where Roger Bannister's last record may be broken.

"That's it," says Neil. "We're not in bad shape." It is 12.40 and he is off to lunch with Ian Vallance, the chairman of British Telecom, accompanied by Andrew Lorenz.

Elsewhere in the office it has also been a busy morning, for none more so than Helen Hawkins. Today she is concentrating on Style and Travel, which go to bed tonight, and she will not finish work until 10 pm. As well as subbing and rewriting copy herself, with the help of a team of sub-editors, she has to supervise the flow of copy and approve the final pages for all three sections, meeting the strict production deadlines, as well as liaising with the section editors and the design department to make sure that what ends up on the pages is what they each intended.

"I also have to keep a mental eye on what the section editors will want on the pages – content, layout, pictures and headlines," she says. "If my desk doesn't get it right, they will want to make changes when we can least afford the time, when the pages are in proof form and we are involved in the early stages of other pages, or ready to go home. One bad hold-up and the delicate balance of the week's work can be thrown out."

That "delicate balance" has been under threat all week. Earlier on Travel was waiting for its pictures to be flown in from Iceland. When they finally arrived yesterday they were not worth the wait. "Design managed to use them to best effect but this involved two cut-outs and more waiting for the pictures to be shot, brought back upstairs to Design for cutting out and finally put in the page. The Iceland copy had been subbed and cleaned up last week but the Travel front was still a day behind schedule. Luckily nobody wanted any significant changes to it once the final proofs were eventually circulated and it was ready for press at the normal time."

Style has also had a difficult

week. It is trying out a new columnist, who may or may not work out, there are two weak articles for the food and drink slot – and the late decision to go for Garbo. At 7.30 last night, Rennell discovered that the Americans wanted $8,000 for the Garbo pictures. A normal fee for such pictures would be $500. That was too much, so even now, with deadlines only hours away, the picture desk is still hunting suitable photographs.

Hawkins's problems are mounting by the hour. Three columnists are attending funerals, which means that their copy will be late. Valerie Grove has just rung in to say that her article on Laura Ashley has been wiped out on her home computer by a power cut, which means that she is having to start it again from scratch. Hawkins is way behind: the only copy in her queue

at the moment are the food articles and nobody knows yet whether they are even going into the paper.

Grove had been working all morning at home on her Laura Ashley article when disaster struck. "At 1.50 I was almost there when, horror, the screen went blank, every electrical thing in the house went off – a power cut, in Highgate, in 1990! Seven phone calls later, amidst mounting fury and perspiring desperation, I reach the engineers who say they may not be able to put it right until late in the evening. Sit and snivellingly start to rewrite it from scratch by hand. After three pages, lo and behold, the screen lights up – and there is the story as it had been at about 11 am when I had last saved it. Lesson: save more frequently." She eventually phoned it to Hawkins at 6 pm.

How a page is made: first the design and then the finished pages.

Another chief sub has had a harassing morning. Alex Butler has decided that the Property page does not work. Now it is being redesigned and all the sub-editing will have to be done again. He has also had a memo from Gordon Beckett, the design editor, addressed to "Alec" Butler, an obvious source of irritation to a punctilious sub. It tells him that headlines are no longer to be "squeezed" to fit. A command on the office computers can shrink the size of headlines when they do not quite fit into one, two or three columns. It works but a specialist eye can notice that the appearance of the type is different.

"Typical designer, never written a headline in his bloody life," Butler reflects with irritation. "I tinker with the idea of letting him write ten headlines for pages 2 and 3 in 15 minutes on a Saturday when we are up against the deadline. There is a rumour going round that all this fuss is about a page one headline which was dreadfully squeezed by the backbench (where Fallon, Bambridge and Williams write the page 1 headlines). Subs are too lowly to write headlines for page 1. I have a firm rule that only revise subs are allowed to squeeze headlines and then only sparingly. As usual the footsoldiers pay for their generals' mistakes."

Nor has James Blitz in Moscow had a good start to his day. His plane for Riga leaves at 12 noon, which gives him only two hours to start to send his pictures of Soviet dating agencies back to London – but his driver has rung to say he is sick. Blitz hails a taxi and gets to Reuters by 10.30 and accompanies the photographer to the dating agency. "He'll never find it if I don't go with him as all Soviet flats are hard to get into," says Blitz. When they arrived there were lots of wo-men, mostly wearing hardly anything. Blitz then took the film and raced to the office hoping that his taxi driver could take it to the airport. The driver has disappeared.

Since he now has to leave for Riga, Blitz takes the film with him to hand to British Airways at the airport. Another frustration: the BA office is shut. He gives the film back to the taxi driver, asking him to take it back to his office, meanwhile praying that he will do so and not sell it on the black market. At 2.30 he finally catches his flight.

James Adams has spent the morning learning still more about the job he is taking over from Peter Roberts. One of his first jobs will be to introduce personal contracts for all the staff, as Rupert Murdoch mentioned at the budget meeting yesterday with Roberts. "They are due to be issued in two weeks and are certain to be a nightmare as every journalist will want to discuss their own problems, fears and salaries," says Adams. "When the contracts go out the journalists will be offered a 5 per cent cash bonus for signing and Andrew also wants to correct some anomalies on pay, so we need some extra cash beyond the budget." He has been to see the finance director and asked for an extra £50,000. He wasn't pleased, however, to hear staff discussed as "items".

One other spat from yesterday – the editor's anger over Marie Colvin writing for *The Times* – has also ended amicably. Neil has faxed a letter to Colvin congratulating her on her film and apologising for not running her story and copied it to Rennell and Tyrer, so that they get the message. "Rennell came storming in a few minutes later complete with his well-known heart-attack flush," says Adams. "I explained the criticism was aimed at Bob

Tyrer and not at him and all was well."

Sports editor Chris Nawrat is also an angry man. He has missed the editor's conference to go to the launch of Superstadia, which claims to solve the problems of modernising stadiums in Britain. The sub within the soul of journalists will always come out. Not only is Nawrat distrustful of the hype, he is worried by the name: "The plural of stadium is stadiums not stadia," he says. Now he has wasted three hours on a slide show with music and uninformative speeches by self-important people. "There was no question and answer and afterwards they tried to herd an entire theatre of people into a small bar. If this consortium was running Hillsborough the same disaster would have occurred."

Meanwhile in Monte Carlo Driscoll has at last heard from her quarry, but it hasn't done much to lift her spirits. "Yes, she did want to see us, she said, but no, we couldn't come to Milan. She was not busy that evening but when we offered to buy her dinner, she refused. In any case, she said, she might not stay there. She was thinking of perhaps going to Lugano. A further game of cat and mouse and all extremely frustrating. If we set off for Milan, would she still be there? Was she in Milan at all? Finally she said that perhaps we should meet next week in Merano in northern Italy. I relayed all this to the office. If I stayed in Monte Carlo I might be waiting around for days, even then not knowing whether she would decide to do the interview or not. At 2 pm it was decided I should go back to London." Now, after three wasted days, she is on her way to Nice airport.

Along the coast at Cannes, Johnstone is making progress and has decided to ring his new chum Gloria Hunniford to try out his funny lines. "I'm beginning to get addicted to these phone calls," he says. "I want Gloria to ring me whenever I go abroad." They just pass muster. He rings the office to dictate his copy and rushes off to see the new Fellini film.

At the House of Commons it is the busiest day of the political week. With Prime Minister's questions, the weekly meetings of backbenchers from both sides of the House, the business statement for the following week and journalists' briefings from the Tories and Labour, David Hughes finds Thursday the best afternoon to be in the lobby. He is also due to interview John Gummer, who has been photographed during the week feeding his daughter Cordelia a beefburger to allay fears about mad cow disease. Gummer tells Hughes that was the only way the public would believe what he was saying. Apart from mad cow disease, Hughes also slips in some questions about European Community subsidies for tobacco growers for background to the Insight investigation.

Andrew Grice is still working on the Labour policy review. He has failed to sell an analytical article to Bob Tyrer for the Review section because both Brian Walden and Robert Harris are dealing with Labour in their columns and Tyrer is wary of overkill. Grice has now sold the story to the newsdesk. Now that Credit Suisse have given him early figures on the cost of the Labour proposals, he is feeding their results to Labour frontbenchers and economic advisers. Armed with their reactions, he calls Credit Suisse again to ask them to re-run the figures through the computer to take account of Labour objections.

Penny Perrick is concentrating today on *The Sunday Times*/Hay-on-Wye Festival of Literature, which starts next week. She organises the festival and is facing the usual catastrophes associated with such an event when so many speakers are booked to appear. Dennis Potter, the playwright, is ill and the novelist A. S. Byatt has broken a tooth. "Ludovic Kennedy has changed publishers several times in his career and it is challenging to say the least trying to track down every title of his that is still in print for him to sign after his talk in the festival theatre."

The festival is one of the most enjoyable events of the year for Perrick who also masterminds *The Sunday Times* Literary Banquet every spring. Trying to organise writers and publishers *en masse*, however, is like trying to pick up Jello, she says. She makes another mental note: "Our star guest is Arthur Miller, not only talented but photogenic as well. Must remember to tell photographer that his left side is the prettier."

For Susan Crosland, who writes a column about her very feminine insights into news items of the week, Thursday afternoon is the watershed of the week. The die is now cast: she has got to sit down to write. She can delay no longer.

Eglin and Bambridge have now made an offer to Andrew Davidson, the man they interviewed yesterday. They are not surprised when he turns them down. He points out that he will have to give up his company car to join *The Sunday Times*. "We are very strict about cars, but every other newspaper seems to give cars to everyone," says Bambridge. Bambridge, a former editor of the Business section, returns to his office to work on a strategy for the future of the Business section, which has been requested as a priority by the editor. "I can't put it off any longer." Eglin, setting his reporters to work on the Ravenscraig story, is delighted by Paddy Masters' article on Gwendoline Lamb and he loves the headline: "Shorn Lamb bites Man."

The Insight team, meanwhile, is chasing the Third World tobacco story. Nick Rufford, the editor, has spoken to stringers in Italy and Greece, who are now trying to trace farmers who have been getting the fat payments from Brussels. He has also been talking to officials in Brussels, as well as European MPs. At any one time Insight is pursuing several story leads. As one team works on tobacco, Chris Blackhurst, for instance, is investigating allegations of tax avoidance on capital gains, amounting possibly to £5 billion a year. It involves placing assets in an off-shore trust before they are sold and thus avoiding capital gains tax. He is working this week on finding examples of millionaires who have benefited.

The beauty of an Insight investigation, says Rufford, is that it doesn't just tell you what happens in a scandal, it also shows you how it happens. That is why he is tracing the tobacco chain from Italy to Brussels and then onwards to Africa. Even now he is awaiting a letter from British American Tobacco's lawyers – but against that there have been letters from former BAT employees explaining what really happens. "A perfect Insight," he adds, "should be a good read on a serious issue. There should be human beings involved, victims and villains. It should shock and entertain, read like a detective novel – and get questions asked in the House of Commons."

For David Leppard, that detec-

Susan Crosland

Having sworn nothing, absolutely nothing, could induce me to write a weekly column, I enjoy doing it. Procrastination is ruled out, which is a relief as procrastination makes one feel uneasy.

I am told it's harder to write 850 words about four subjects than to write 1,200 about one. As I make a speciality of unexpected allusions, my head has become a basket of miscellaneous information. (Yes, I have a proper steel filing cabinet as well.)

Reason has triumphed over the initial fear that I would run out of subjects: if all these newspapers can produce myriad stories each week, there have to be at least four which interest me – though I may not find them until eve of deadline.

But a terrible price is paid: reading newspapers no longer is fun. Who but a freak like me would go through seven newspapers on weekdays – scavenging and mugging up new subjects – and nine newspapers on the day of rest?

And my Yoga teacher disapproves of combining my body exercises with Radio 4. Yet *World At One* can be invaluable: politicians are strangely unguarded in the things they say on radio.

Then there is my evening life. When another guest at a dinner party is a Cabinet minister, for instance, he may get nervous: "Is this conversation going to appear in your column?" My general rule of thumb is to ring him in the morning and say: "Can we hold that conversation again, please?"

Alternatively, especially when it is dinner *à deux*, I will ask the other person if he happens to have a piece of paper and a pen handy, as what he is saying is so interesting I might like to use it one day. Normally his vanity is greater than his discretion, and he hands me his elegant little Cartier memo pad to scribble alongside my plate of *feuilletée de langouste*.

Thursday afternoon is a relief: the die is cast. Unless my life is in crisis, I write the first draft late Thursday and then rewrite and cut on Friday morning. I envy writers who "never change a word", producing their brilliant copy at the first go.

Telephone calls from the subs on Friday afternoon are surprisingly agreeable, for the subs bear an uncanny resemblance to real human beings. One or two of the lawyers are something else. Okay, so what I have written may be actionable, but when

the person I have insulted (for instance a criminal) is never going to sue, why do the lawyers have to be so robotlike? Occasionally the editor has to be brought in to adjudicate: the editor rules.

By Friday evening the column is behind me. Heaven. Saturday papers need to be scanned at the most. That's heaven too. And then CLONK. Through my letter-box drops a large thick envelope from *The Sunday Times*: readers' letters on last week's column. Yarggghhhh. Being a well-brought-up journalist I answer letters addressed personally to me (unless they are unacceptably abusive). If you find answering letters a chore, never mention gun licenses or Israel in your column. Gun lobbyists and anti-Zionists will write back a second time.

Finally comes Sunday. Were I not a freak, I would enjoy my Sunday treat. As it is, I look bleakly at this mound of nine newspapers, tied in a special bundle by the newsagent, which lies in wait outside my door. I rarely get a charge out of anyone's column, my own included. For I've moved on psychologically to the coming week. What next?

Insight

Insight is the most famous byline in *The Sunday Times*, a hallmark for the campaigning investigative journalism that was pioneered by the paper in the sixties. The campaigning tradition still flourishes under Insight editor Nick Rufford and his team of four reporters. Among the most notable investigations made by the paper under Andrew Neil's editorship have been:

ARTHUR Scargill's efforts to raise money from Libya's Colonel Gadaffi during the miners' strike in 1984.
THE French government's funding of the bombing of the Rainbow Warrior in 1985.
THE full details of Israel's secret nuclear bomb factory in 1986.
THE links between the Prime Minister of the Bahamas and the drug trade, again in 1986.
NAMING the senior industrialists most responsible for polluting Britain's rivers in 1989.
THE exposure of how Asil Nadir siphoned off money from Polly Peck in 1990.
THE revelation of the web of local government corruption in Liverpool in 1991 which led to arrests and charges.

Andrew Neil pointed out in 1991 that within the past year *Sunday Times* investigations had resulted in the arrest of nine people, including the well-known politician Derek Hatton and the chief executives of NCP and Polly Peck, two of Britain's biggest companies.

Hostages may be swapped for Lockerbie bomb suspect

INSIGHT

WEST German police have held secret talks with the man believed to have masterminded the Lockerbie bombing, to discuss the possibility of exchanging him for Western hostages.

Records of a prison interview obtained by The Sunday Times show that the Germans ed to Hafez... another suspect who, police believe, carried the bomb around Europe before packing it in a suitcase that was put on to an Air Malta flight to Frankfurt. From there it was transferred, unaccompanied, to Pan Am Flight 103 bound for New York via London.

Dalkamoni is already charged with attempted murder in two attacks on American troop trains in West Germany. He has confessed to the lesser charge of possessing weapons which carries a lengthy sentence. According to the inter...

European subsidies for 'killer' tobacco exports

INSIGHT

THOUSANDS of tonnes of high-tar tobacco are being shipped to the Third World under a European Community scheme that is costing British taxpayers more than £100m a year in subsidies, and the community as a whole £740m.

The trade, which has been condemned by the World Health Organisation, is expected to increase sharply in coming years following main EC producers) has a high tar content, and sales are already falling fast as the West becomes more health conscious.

The unsold tobacco is being exported at knock-down prices subsidised by the EC, or taken into intervention and stored in EC warehouses. There, it forms part of the European tobacco mountain that has more than doubled in the last five years, by European taxpayers.

As markets in Europe are blocked, even more of the highly addictive tobacco will be exported to the Third World, which the giant cigarette companies see as their fastest growing market.

Dr Roberto Masironi, head of the Tobacco Or Health programme at the WHO headquarters in Geneva, said: "It is totally unacceptable, against all ethics, for the...

tive novel is proving hard to write. After his frustrating morning he has tracked down four West German defence lawyers who had acted for Dalkamoni while he was held in prison. "One pleaded client privilege and said he could not comment, but three confirmed that Sarkis was seeing Dalkamoni. One even claimed he had resigned because of interference from Sarkis. He told me Dalkamoni had been boasting he would be exchanged for hostages in the Lebanon. He also told me there had been meetings between German officials and their Syrian counterparts over Dalkamoni's future. This was very exciting – but was it true?" He starts his phone calls again.

At 6.30 Helen Hawkins is facing at least another five hours' work. The travel pages are completed except for one illustration of a bird but that won't arrive for at least an hour. Style obviously won't meet its deadlines. Valerie Grove's copy on Laura Ashley has just arrived, the Garbo pictures (obtained now at a reasonable price) arrived only half an hour ago, the editor has seen the new column and decided that it does not work. Nor did he like the fashion page. He wanted bigger pictures. What's more, the compositors who paste up the pages are now working on *The Times* and won't get back to work on the Style pages until 9 am. "I'm afraid the editor has been poking his nose in," says Rennell. It now looks as if the pages will not be finished until 3 am.

John Walsh and Harrie Ritchie, however, are now signing off all their 16 pages and starting to think about their next edition and what will keep the editor happy. They know already what their lead review will be – a review by John Carey of a new biography of A. A. Milne. Carey, Merton Professor of English Literature at Oxford, is the chief book reviewer, selects the books that he himself will review, writes 26 reviews a year, each 1,200 words long, and almost always makes the front page. His is a powerful position in British publishing – a good review by Carey will help to sell a book, a damaging one will stunt its sale. In his study at Oxford he is now starting to write on *A. A. Milne: His Life* by Ann Thwaite, a major biography of the author of the Winnie the Pooh stories. It runs to 546 pages and is published by Faber at £17.50.

When Carey prepares a review he does not simply read the book. He reads around the subject. As an Oxford professor he is fortunate – he has the Bodleian, one of the world's greatest libraries, nearby and can plumb its riches for material about his subject. Over the past few days he has studied Milne's plays, which he had never read, as well as a collected edition of his early journalism. He has read Thwaites's biography in his college study in the evenings, making notes as he went along. When he started to write a week ago, his notes covered two pages.

For an Oxford professor, as for a junior reporter, the job of writing a review has the same journalistic imperative. The first paragraph is all-important. That, for Carey, is the hardest, most vital part. "It is what decides whether the reader carries on reading your review or decides to turn the page. This week his review came quickly and he soon found an arresting first sentence:

A. A. Milne's most famous stories are about a stuffed toy, and in many ways he resembled one himself. He had virtually no interest in literature, art, music, travel or ideas generally. The great writers of the modern period seemingly left him cold. Despite his success as a children's author, he was not even, he declared, particularly interested in children – a verdict endorsed by his son Christopher Robin.

The review proceeded in stages. He wrote part of it, then moved on to other jobs because he finds that he works best when he does a review in stages. It was on his screen for at least two days, as he played around with it, before he was satisfied on Monday. It arrived with Walsh today and he and Ritchie have already thought up a witty headline: Now We Are Sick.

Carey shares the aim of all journalists which is to be read. "The review must be a readable, interesting piece of writing, which gives a fair impression of what the book says. It has got to be decisive: it should tell readers whether they should buy the book or not. My verdict on the Milne was No. *Sunday Times* readers do not have a lot of time so they need to know quickly what I think of a book. I have to be interesting and lively without being patronising."

Carey swiftly dismisses any suggestion that Oxford professors should not be involved in journalism. A serious book review in *The Sunday Times* is just as important as writing an academic book, he argues. Surely the money the nation feeds into universities should be fed back – by a professor of English as much as a science professor who invents things that make it easier for us to live. A book review feeds the

Aidan Sullivan

Picture editor. Aged 34. After freelancing as a photographer in London, joined the *Mail on Sunday* and spent six years travelling the world, including stints in Afghanistan, the Far East, the Middle East and India. Became deputy picture editor and joined *The Sunday Times* in same position until promoted. Thrill of the job is steering a good picture into the paper through the genesis of an idea, briefing photographers, selecting contacts and helping to lay out the page.

cultural life of the nation. What a "desolatingly arid" prospect if universities were not meant to do that.

Reviewing books also helps his teaching, Carey says. It makes him read books, particularly twentieth-century books, that he would not otherwise read. Indeed many of the books he has read for *The Sunday Times* have influenced his next book, on intellectuals and the masses in the twentieth century.

Carey has finished his work for next week – but this week's deadlines are drawing closer. Bob Tyrer is delivering the Review front – the Chinese student leader Li Lu's story of the Tiananmen Square uprising – to Butler for its final editing now that it has been approved by the editor, and Michael Williams is holding his 7 pm Thursday news conference. With him are Rosemary Collins, Greg Hadfield, her deputy, and Aidan Sullivan, the picture editor, and now is when they start making preliminary decisions on which stories should go on which news pages. Since national dailies will be published on Friday and Saturday, they have to do a lot of second-guessing about which of their stories will still seem new by Sunday morning. Mad cow disease is proving hard going, with the reporter telling Collins that there is no new angle. Williams is impatient with that. "Technically he is correct – but Sunday newspapers have their own way round conventional news values. What, I say, will happen to shoppers in Tesco's and Sainsbury's on Saturday? At least there's the start of a story that the dailies can't get at. I tell them to get on with it."

Collins has selected her early candidates for the front page – the Insight scoop on Lockerbie; Insight on Third World tobacco; a prediction by David Smith, economics editor, that Britain will join the

European Exchange Rate Mechanism in the autumn; Aileen Ballantyne's story of the breakthrough that could cure breast cancer; and, as a lightener, the story of a classic car collector who is thinking of suing the auctioneers after a £1 mil-

"What have you got for the front page?" Williams checks the news list with Collins.

lion Jaguar with the same chassis number as his own has been offered for sale at a Monaco auction.

Williams wonders whether the ERM story will survive until Saturday. Collins assures him it will. He worries about breast cancer. There have been so many reports of cures. Ballantyne should be very careful. Have there been any victims of the new drug? If the story is to make the front page it will need to be very positive. He likes the classic car story but prefers the ITN scoop as the basement for the front. "The great conundrum: who says Hello on *News at Ten*," he muses with an ironic smile.

Collins is offering a report with pictures on seals for the back page. White seal pups are being caught and fattened before being killed so that hunters from Russia and Norway make more money, she says. Sullivan adds that he has very moving pictures. So what are the alternatives? Williams asks. The story about beggars is dismissed as too downbeat and manufactured for so prominent a page as the back. Two other thoughts crop up – the story of Tracy Edwards and the crew of the *Maiden*. They are due off Cornwall by Saturday and their race would make a stirring report, especially if Sullivan can get pictures from the Atlantic. There is also the oil slick in Devon.

Is a news conference really necessary two days before the News section goes to press? It is crucial, says Williams. On a Thursday night he can steer the newsdesk towards or away from stories. "The only way to get a good newslist is to analyse constantly what the newsdesk is offering and never to take any item at face value." There is undoubtedly always a temptation to oversell stories at the conference to gain the editor's approval. Williams has to make sure subsequently that the stories will be good enough to go in the paper and survive the editor's scrutiny. Otherwise he is faced by the nightmare of blank pages with no stories good enough to fill them. Although it is still only Thursday, eight reporters work in the office until 10 pm.

One is Aileen Ballantyne, who has eventually got through to Trevor Powles, who had been seeing patients all afternoon – most inconvenient for a busy journalist,

says Ballantyne with a sardonic smile. "He told me he now had more than 400 women in his two-year research project. He spoke of his anxieties, earlier on in the trial, about giving any drug to healthy women, and of the problems he had getting enough money to do the research. I asked if he could arrange for me to speak to one or two of the women on the trial. Who were these women who were sufficiently worried about developing cancer that they were willing to take a drug when they were perfectly healthy?"

As Ballantyne phoned more cancer experts, she discovered why none of them had been at their offices this morning. They had all been discussing Powles's study at a meeting of the United Kingdom Co-ordinating Committee on Cancer Research. As she spoke to them, she discovered a consensus: for the first time with cancer, a drug was to be given to thousands of healthy people in a £3.5 million trial sponsored by the main cancer charities. It is a big vote of confidence in the potential of the treatment and it looks as though she has got on to a strong story.

"But there was a nagging doubt. Giving drugs to healthy people can hardly be sound medicine, I thought. Drug stories, in particular, need to be treated with extreme caution. It is important not to raise false hopes or give prominence to developments which owe more to their commercial value than their potential human benefits. I treat such claims with enormous scepticism."

There are, however, several crucial points which make this development different, she believes. The patent on tamoxifen had run out years ago, so this was not a trial sponsored and marketed by a drug company but a 20-year-old drug, used effectively by thousands of women throughout the world, to help prevent the cancer spreading further. The trial was also being recommended by the main breast cancer experts in Britain. They too had their doubts, but Powles had shown that tamoxifen could work and his colleagues had judged that his research was worth backing.

Ballantyne was still not satisfied. She wanted another independent view. She phones Richard Peto, one of the world's leading medical statisticians and director of the Imperial Cancer Research Fund's cancer unit. "It emerges that he has been one of the scheme's main critics for months, but something has changed his mind. Powles's study had shown that in healthy women tamoxifen reduced cholesterol levels by an average of 20 per cent. It took a statistician to tell them what that means in terms of a risk benefit analysis. Peto concluded that Powles's results meant that the long-term chance of developing heart disease for women are likely to be cut in half if they take tamoxifen. That was the finding that tipped the balance and caused the experts to back the trial." Her patient work has got her to the story and she will resume her calls tomorrow.

City editor Jeff Randall is working late in the office after a busy day. At 11 am he was meeting a mole in a Fleet Street wine bar who had tipped him off about a secret break-up bid for Scottish and Newcastle Breweries. Then he lunched at the Howard Hotel with Sir Lawrie Magnus of the merchant bank Samuel Montagu and Philip Gee, chairman of Amber Day, the menswear retailer. "Both are terrific for City gossip and I leave with a few more hints about what might be going on next week."

According to Randall, the difference between weekday and Sunday financial journalism is that Sunday journalists have nothing to report on from Saturday. "Our job is to be predictive – to tell the readers what is going to happen next week. It makes the job a lot harder and means that good contacts are all the more precious. Next week's news is the most elusive quarry of all." Now he is settling down to write 1,500 words about Larry Goodman and finishes at 10.30. "My wife, who is a saint, knows that Thursdays and Fridays are always late nights, so I don't bother to call her before going home."

John Peter, the drama critic, is at the premiere of Sir Peter Hall's production of Ibsen's *The Wild Duck*. It is his fourth night at the theatre this week. On Monday in London he was reviewing a David Lan play on Zimbabwe, on Tuesday in Birmingham for *The Writing Game* by David Lodge, and back in London last night for *Vanilla* by Jane Stanton Hitchcock, starring Joanna Lumley. On Friday last week he was at Watford for *Tartuffe*. He has agreed with the Arts editor that he will sum up four of the plays, each in about 200 words, in one review, and do a longer, considered review of *The Wild Duck*.

Peter, a master of English style, prepares thoroughly, usually spending his weekends reading for homework any classical plays that he is about to review. He never reads new plays beforehand, however, because he believes it is fairer to the playwright and the actors to see a new play fresh on stage without any preconceptions. "Classics have been done before so it is fair to judge them in the knowledge of the text, previous productions and performing traditions, but you introduce an element of prejudice if

John Peter

Drama critic. Aged 52, he arrived in England, unable to speak English, as a refugee from the Hungarian revolution in 1956. He went to Lincoln College, Oxford, eight months later, read English for his degree and then did a postgraduate thesis on Elizabethan and Jacobean drama. After working for *The Times Educational Supplement*, he joined *The Sunday Times* as an assistant editor of the Arts and Books pages and was appointed drama critic by Andrew Neil. "I write about the only major art form which cannot be properly appreciated in any kind of reproduction," he says. "It's live and the text is only a jumping board."

you read a new play before reviewing it, because you are not the director.''

Although he estimates that he has seen at least 30 *Hamlets* and 20 to 30 of *Macbeth*, *Othello*, *Twelfth Night* and *The Tempest*, Peter is never bored. ''The text has a life of its own – it is like something that can be galvanised by each new production into electricity. Each new cast gives a classic play a different electricity – it comes to life in a different way, although that is obviously truer of the great plays because they have more to say. I don't really understand why but it is a curious fact that although there is more than one way of playing a great play, the more restricted the ways of playing a play are, the less interesting it is to see a third or fourth time. I certainly find that true of George Bernard Shaw – *St Joan*, for instance – Somerset Maugham, Galsworthy or, say, Granville Barker. I can admire them but they have so much less to say than William Shakespeare. There seems to be something almost inexhaustible about hearing and seeing the great texts being acted.''

Unlike ordinary theatregoers, the drama critic cannot switch off if he is not enjoying himself. As Peter points out, a reviewer is always called to account. ''If you believe that a cast is rising to a challenge, you cannot let your attention flag.'' He admits, however, to a streak of exhibitionism in his enjoyment of the job. ''I like to feel that readers read my review and want to know what I have said so that they know whether they want to see a play or not – and why. You certainly feel chuffed when you hear that a reader has been to a play because of what you have written.''

Thousands of miles away the drama is going on in the streets instead of on the stage. Blitz has arrived in Riga and succeeded in arranging an interview tomorrow with the head of the Russian nationalist movement. Now he is at the Latvian parliament but nothing is going on. He has, however, met an American who is working in the parliament and who has given him a good briefing on the political situation. He is worried that he has not got enough information to file to London tomorrow. He phones the Moscow office, only to discover that the film he left at lunchtime is still there. Fortunately the defence correspondent of *The Times* is in Moscow on a visit with Tom King, the Secretary of State for Defence. He agrees to take the film back to Wapping. Now, before going to bed, Blitz has to dictate his report on dating agencies. He is able to get through quickly. ''That's rare.''

At 10 pm in Angeles, Swain is touring the city after his talks with officials during the day. ''The bars, nightclubs and massage parlours should be flooded with off-duty American servicemen each of whom spend on average $50 a night on booze and women – but since the murders the ambience of the red light district, named after General MacArthur, has become funereal. In this ghostly atmosphere security has been stepped up in the form of tough-looking soldiers in full combat fatigues manning the gates of the huge airbase complex, checking identity cards. He decides to return to Manila. ''There are still many people I need to talk to if I am to try to excite interest in the Philippines in a British audience whose main pre-occupation is the poll tax and eastern Europe.''

After the frustration of Monte Carlo, Margarette Driscoll has arrived home at 9 pm, when the

How to pinpoint the pain of Ibsen's walking wounded

JOHN PETER applauds Peter Hall's new production of **The Wild Duck**

Greatness in the theatre is often a matter of small things: a sound, a gesture, or the look on an actor's face. As the curtain rises on Peter Hall's production of **The Wild Duck** (Phoenix), we hear the sudden flutter of birds' wings. This is more than just symbolism in sound. The effect is both realistic and eerie, like the whole play. Hall is signalling that we are about to enter two worlds: one where people give parties, run photographic studios and munch bread and butter; and one where they babble of moral imperatives, act out fantasies and mutilate their souls. In the last scene, as Hedvig's dead body is carried out, Gregers Werle (David Threlfall) sits stunned, self-knowledge breaking through his illusions of moral grandeur, and shivers two or three times with shock and disbelief. This is one of those unforgettable moments when you know that you are in Ibsen country: this is a dramatist who knew better than anyone except Shakespeare that moral retribution is strict in his arrest.

Hall's production is full of such passages, and, as they follow one another, the great play stretches its wings and takes command. This was Ibsen's first play to be greeted by his contemporaries with incomprehension. Then, once people had cottoned on to the play, some of the criticism read like shopkeepers' inventories: whom, for instance, did the duck represent, Hedvig or old Ekdal? – and so on. This production reveals the futility of such hunt-the-clue symbolism. One way or another, everyone here is wounded or crippled. The moment Threlfall's Gregers comes on, you can see that he is, morally speaking, loitering with intent. Shambling, hirsute and slightly sinister, he looks like a cross between John the Baptist and the Demon King, or an out-of-work Old Testament prophet posing as a psychiatric social worker. He has an iron diffidence which can be lethal in debate; and he waves away his father's cigar smoke as if it physically represented the old man's moral pretensions.

Alex Jennings's Hjalmar is full of lugubrious complacency: one of those people who watch themselves having emotions, preferably in public, and, like all such people, ignore or misinterpret the emotions of others. Temperamentally, Jennings pitches him between premature middle age and a slightly spinsterish fastidiousness. Hjalmar is clearly terribly fond of himself. But the important thing is that these two young men are deeply alike. Self-pity and righteousness are essential ingredients of their characters. Both are moral exhibitionists and, therefore, eager to be described and analysed. Note how intently Gregers listens when Dr Relling (a masterful, acid etching by Terence Rigby) brutally takes him apart.

Ibsen's point, and Hall and his actors bring this out with the force of a revelation, is that Gregers and Hjalmar are both destroyers. Gregers's conspiratorial cunning and his crude, psychological manipulations are just as deadly as Hjalmar's ludicrous pride because both are based on a ghastly ignorance of life. Ibsen's younger contemporary, Nietzsche, once described the dramatist as a typical old maid and berated him for not being able to liberate himself from the illusion of morality. This hostile bluster embodies a profound, if unintended, compliment. Ibsen knew perfectly well that people were earth-bound and needed compromises to sustain them. For him, there was no such thing as pure morality: it was an applied science. And Hall's production brings out with sombre, meticulous care the sense of tenacity and simple loyalties of ordinary life.

Nichola McAuliffe's Gina, a sad, brave, battered woman, has learnt to be both submissive and cajoling; observe how she bustles with humble efficiency, tidying away Hjalmar's coffee cup while he blathers on about moral laws. Maria Miles, a young, serious and prodigiously talented actress, plays Hedvig as a very real young girl, fragile but purposeful, almost stubborn. There is nothing charming or sentimental in this performance: it is a portrait of innocence suffused with intelligence, which is why her Hedvig becomes, as it should, the moral fulcrum of the argument.

Is The Wild Duck a comedy? I haven't actually read what Hall had to say about this before the opening, but personally I think the play is funny in the way King Lear is funny: it makes you laugh painfully at the sight of small, untidy people driving themselves helplessly into large, bloody conflicts. Hall transfixes such moments with iron precision. Hjalmar sits in the depths of self-pity eating bits of cold meat; and old Lieutenant Ekdal (a pitiless portrayal of broken dignity by Lionel Jeffries) potters about grandly and pathetically like a cross between the Holy Roman Emperor and a tramp. It's like laughter in hell.

Deadline midnight: the performance from Peter.

phone rings. It's the office. Collins wants her to go now to report on the oil slick in Devon that is threatening marine life and polluting beaches. "Unpack one bag, pack another," says Driscoll with resignation.

At the subbing end of the paper Butler and Hawkins are still at work. Butler has had to wait for the Li Lu pages to be designed before he can start to sub them. They were late and he managed to finish only one by 9.55 when he leaves. For Hawkins, it is "wading through mud" time as she and her subs deal with the delaying effects of all the decisions that have changed the contents and the layout of the Style pages. Rennell, for instance, changed his mind at 4 pm about which of the food articles to use, when both had been edited and headlined and were in the page. She has, however, managed to edit the weekly review by Marina Vaizey, the art critic, as well as to scheme two of the Arts pages for Friday. By 10.30 her work is done – but one of her subs, who checks the pages as the compositors work on them, does not leave until 1.15 am, and is due back at 10 am.

After his day tracking Sarkis, Leppard has returned home depressed. He is now reading the Bush Commission Report in bed. "I fell asleep and dreamt of Palestinians conspiring over a bomb suitcase in Malta, where I have always believed the bomb was loaded on board for a connecting flight to Frankfurt."

After *The Wild Duck*, Peter has returned to his Islington home and written his review in longhand. "Greatness in the theatre is often a matter of small things: a sound, a gesture, or the look on an actor's face," he wrote. "As the curtain rises on Peter Hall's production of *The Wild Duck* at the Phoenix, we hear the sudden flutter of birds' wings. This is more than just symbolism in sound. The effect is both realistic and eerie, like the whole play. Hall is signalling that we are about to enter two worlds: one where people give parties, run photographic studios and munch bread and butter; and one where they babble of moral imperatives, act out fantasies and mutilate their souls."

Those who decry journalism should try to write so well as that at midnight.

In Cannes, Iain Johnstone is reflecting that he would have been better off giving himself more time to write his article on Cannes than going to see the new Fellini. When he gets back to his hotel at midnight, there is an urgent message: Ring *The Sunday Times*. "I do. 'Can you tell me what day the festival ends?' the Style sub asks. That's all." Silly – but necessary – questions like that is also what journalism is about.

Godfrey Smith

From the time when Harry Evans first suggested I should write a column on our resumption after the year's stoppage, until today, ten years later, no one has told me what to write or what not to write. This is both a blessing and a facer: obviously it's good to be left alone; but you could get lonely on such a solo trip. Fortunately I don't, because from the early days I got into a rambling, discursive, undisciplined, but, to me at any rate, always diverting dialogue with my readers which is still unrolling.

Like most columnists, I am at one level always working. I don't deny that it's an agreeable form of work, but it's not quite like being off-duty. An idea for the column may crop up anywhere and any time. For example, this last week one of my strongest runners has been the debate about which is the world's worst airport. This had its origins in a grisly journey I had from Naples to Gatwick recently. Another last week was the origin of the word Henry to describe a drink of orange juice and lemonade. That arose from a chance conversation with Martin Hall, landlord of our justly famed village pub, the Horse and Groom. The real Henry called me last week – delighted to have given what looks like being a new word to the language. Although a lot of publishers send me books which yield stories, I should be fighting with one arm behind my back if I didn't go up to London often. Three young daughters open up dimensions to stop me getting too blimpish.

Living just off the Portobello Road in London is a terrific plus; with its vivid social and ethnic mix, it's to me the new Latin Quarter of London. I get quite a lot of invitations to events like the Grosvenor House Antiques Fair, which normally yield copy; and am often asked to judge contests like the Royal Watercolour Society's annual exhibition or the Young Waiter of the Year Award. If I meet another ST man on the same story, as happened when I found Russell Harty was a fellow judge, I always give way on the grounds that it's usually their only topic of the week, whereas I can never get all mine in. A glance through the files of readers' letters over ten years now reveals the weird eclecticism and eccentricity of subjects we've discussed. Thus under the letter M, picked at random, I find files on (among others) Machen, Edward;

Memorable Poetry since 1950; Men writers who understand women; Mid-Hants railway; Mille Miglia; Millihelen; Mills, John; Missed Abroad (by readers in foreign parts); Misprints; and Monocles.

I suppose our biggest correspondence was over the most beautiful word in the language. I got the idea for this from a diary entry by James Agate, who remains an object lesson to all those of us who aspire to the exigent column form. Seven out of ten taking up the challenge were women; the oldest – at any rate to declare herself – 91; the youngest five. Melody and velvet tied for the top spot. Almost as fertile was the correspondence about the Tingle Quotient – a term devised by a reader to describe the frisson given by certain passages of music. It was described by one lady as a shudder from shoulder to thigh; but whatever you might make of that, it was a deeply religious piece of music, Bach's *St Matthew Passion*, that came top, though pressed hard by Richard Strauss's *Der Rosenkavalier*. Elgar was hearteningly popular too! There was a diverting sub-issue – the TCQ or Toe-curling Quotient dreamed up by one reader to describe the most awful piece of music of all. Here Dora Bryan's incomparable rendering of *All I Want for Christmas is a Beatle* carried off the palm, though *In a Monastery Garden* whistled

by Ronnie Ronalde was a strong runner.

I give a bottle of champagne as a prize when genuine intellectual effort is involved and it is no doubt this that gives me the Champagne Charlie image. If you study my copy carefully, though, you'll see I'm at pains not to celebrate expensive things; on the contrary, we've had a lot of fun discussing how cheaply you can dress for a big occasion by getting your dress at Oxfam or why it is you can eat so much more cheaply in France than here.

Each Friday at around 7 am I sit down at my Tandy 200 and knock out 4248 bytes on it – not a byte less, not a byte more. I know it'll fit exactly. Then there is silence from the office till next Thursday morning when a large parcel of mail comes up from Wapping, which I spend the morning opening and reading. There is no end to the random information readers want: "my boss heard these lines in an after-dinner speech. He thought it was Kipling but I can't find it. Can you help?" (This time yes – but it's not always so easy.) Such arcane queries may provide copy, they may not; but they seem to me a modest subscription fee to pay for access to the collective wisdom, prejudices and predilections of surely one of the most intelligent and responsive readerships a man could ask.

Friday

"On the occasion when I can't make up my mind, democracy never helps. It's much better when I know what I want and insist on a decision," says Neil. "So I take the decision myself."

Around the world the adrenalin is rising. Most of the paper will be put to bed tonight. Today the deadlines are real and the paper engages top gear and starts early.

At 7 am in Riga the phone wakes James Blitz. Still bleary-eyed, the Moscow correspondent listens patiently as the head of the Russian nationalists harangues him about an "abominable" article his predecessor wrote about him last year. Blitz argues for 20 minutes but fails to persuade the nationalist to agree to an interview. "Even my mother didn't recognise me after that piece, you bastard. Get lost." It's not a good start to a day that won't end until midnight.

The phone rang for news reporter Margarette Driscoll at 6.30 – and by 7.30 she is also already at work. Yesterday it was Monte Carlo and a failed mission. Today it is Devon. She is hoping for better luck and is now driving west with photographer Mark Ellidge to report on the oil slick threatening the South Hams coastline.

At 8 am the sun is blazing down on the fabled Côte d'Azur, and Iain Johnstone in Cannes, after filing his Style report on the film festival yesterday, is now settling down to write the 1,500 words of his weekly film review. "Columns from festivals are always difficult, describing films that nobody at home will ever see," he says. Nevertheless *Hidden Agenda* gives him a crisp start and Clint Eastwood a recognisable finish; and David Evans, the deputy Arts editor, has extended his deadline until noon.

At 8.30, after not getting home until 1 am, Valerie Grove is at her desk, where she will sit until exactly 6.15 pm when she has to leave to take over from her nanny. That sets her own personal deadline. Today she has been given 165 cm for her interview, the biggest space she has ever had to fill. It is no problem, though. "Dr Swire is so enthralling and has so much to say. It is a moving story."

At 8.45 James Adams is enduring a session in the gym before another meeting to discuss personal contracts for the journalists. With Peter Roberts, he is meeting Tudor Hopkins, director of human resources, and lawyers. "I truly hate lawyers," says Adams. "At every discussion I have ever had with them they have either been cowards or wimps or both. At the very least, as this morning, issues that appear simple become complicated. But to be fair they have a better understanding of the complexities of employment legislation than I do and I would get the paper into serious problems without their guidance. The sheer scale of the managing editor's job is proving so vast that it is very difficult to comprehend it all."

At Wapping, where the Style, Travel and Books sections are now thundering off the presses – you can hear the hum in the newsroom – this is the longest day. After arriving between 8.30 and 10 am, most executives and reporters won't see daylight again – and many, as they munch lunch and supper at their desks, will envy Blitz, Driscoll and Johnstone their life on the road. They will work until midnight, and some, particularly the staff of the Arts and Business sections, will work until 3 am. It is a gruelling regime, the work ethic is paramount and the pace is set from the top by an editor who rarely leaves on Friday nights before midnight. There is a taunt for those who leave at 10 pm, after a 12-hour day: "Going home early tonight?"

Most journalists cannot really start writing until their adrenalin is set going by a deadline. Since the three sections that go to press today cannot be printed until the printing of *The Times* and the *Sun* has finished at about 4 am on Saturday, some of the deadlines are not until 2 am. So, many reporters don't start writing until after 6 pm, hoping that every extra phone call will yield an even better news story.

The early Saturday morning deadlines allow the business reporters to read the early editions of the Saturday papers and make sure that what they write is not stale and out of date. It is rarely a problem since the big City companies tend to leak stories to the Sunday papers because they are read more thoroughly than the dailies.

It is going to be a day of anxiety, stress and tension all the way for the section editors. That is why they are all in early and there is not the usual gossip and chat before they start work. Aidan Sullivan, the picture editor, needs pictures of the Tiananmen Square uprising for the News Review front, has despatched Ellidge to Devon, is trying to arrange a flight over the Atlantic to get pictures of Tracy Edwards and the crew of the *Maiden*, and is now planning how to cover the de Klerk–Thatcher meeting in London tomorrow. Roger Eglin is contemplating how on earth he is going to get 11 pages finished by midnight; and Helen Hawkins knows that she will not even receive two of her reviews until after midnight.

Still worried that his Lockerbie story may not stand up, David Leppard has also arrived earlier than usual. He is in luck. "At 10.10 the phone rang. It was a contact in Geneva who had checked Sarkis with his intelligence sources. Sarkis had been linked by them to Robert Polhill, the American hostage released after 39 months in captivity. He had

Jon Swain

Jon Swain is the Far East correspondent of *The Sunday Times* and is based in Hong Kong. His career as a foreign correspondent began in Paris with Agence France-Presse, the French news agency, which he joined after a short spell in the French Foreign Legion and learning journalism in London and the provinces. At the beginning of 1970 AFP posted him as a war correspondent to Vietnam and Cambodia where he lived until the end of the war, witnessing, in April 1975, the Khmer Rouge takeover of Cambodia and its horrific aftermath. Swain joined the staff of *The Sunday Times* in 1975 and then lived in Thailand. He has won several British press awards for his reporting at home and abroad. He was portrayed in the Oscar-winning film *The Killing Fields*, and in 1976 was kidnapped and held captive for three months by guerrillas in Ethiopia. Swain is 42 and is married, with a nine-year-old daughter.

also been linked to the release of the US hostages in the American embassy in Tehran in 1981 and to two French hostages."

Leppard is on a winning run. He rings a contact in Wiesbaden in West Germany, who confirms that Sarkis is an international commercial lawyer who conducted negotiations between Syrian companies and the US State Department. Now he knows that he has the right man. He tells Rufford and Collins. The story goes to the top of the newslist.

Aileen Ballantyne is also winning. She has heard from Trevor Powles, who has contacted a patient on the trial who is willing to be interviewed. This is a small triumph in itself. "Doctors are notoriously cautious about approaching patients and asking them to be interviewed by the press," she explains. "Some, including Powles, are even more cautious. To ensure that his patient felt under no pressure whatsoever to do an interview with us, she was contacted not by him but another doctor. For the doctor, giving out patients' names is an understandable problem. For the journalist it can make all the difference between a good readable story that people can readily understand and a dull rather academic piece. In a medical story, which often contains highly complex detail, it is all the more crucial to explain the detail by telling the story through one individual."

When she calls Katie Warder, the patient who has been alerted by Powles, her call is expected. Warder explains that all the women on the trial had mothers or sisters who had suffered from breast cancer. "Just imagine the benefits for future generations if we can actually prevent this disease," says Warder. "It kills thousands every year." Ballantyne caught her just as she

was going out, but she agreed to be photographed at her home in Kent. A picture catches the reader's eye and the small photograph of Warder made all the difference to the way Ballantyne's story looked on Sunday.

All Ballantyne has to do is to write the story. It has, however, demonstrated a journalistic principle, she says. "Getting a good story is 90 per cent hard graft and 10 per cent luck. Spotting those few lines in that journal, just as the country's main experts were making their decision on this important trial, was where the luck came in. But if we had not been able to stand the story up, as happens all too often, we would have dropped it. However much graft, effort and grind were involved, we would not have run the story."

Now she waits to see if it will make the front page.

With some of the foreign pages due to be made up tonight, Jon Swain is at a joint US–Philippines press briefing on the air bases talks. "The US negotiating strategy is in strong hands. It is masterminded by Richard Armitage, a former deputy assistant secretary of defence. Armitage pumps iron, has a footballer's physique and is a tough-talking Vietnam war veteran with a chequered record in counter-insurgency. 'If you ask us to leave, leave we shall as expeditiously as possible and with our pride intact,' he tells the Filipinos.

"His Filipino counterpart, Raul Manglapus, is if anything a still more extraordinary man. A left-leaning orator with only one eye, Manglapus has immense dignity. He has weathered an extraordinary life that has taken him from Japanese water torture in the war to all-night jazz sessions with the king of Thailand."

Radio odyssey sinks in farce

by Simon Worrall, Taipei, and Jon Swain, Hong Kong

THE odyssey of the Goddess of Democracy, the French radio ship which set off as a beacon of democracy to the Chinese masses, ended in farce last week, its bills unpaid, its crew on the verge of mutiny and the transmitter impounded by customs.

The former British ocean survey ship, sponsored by French news organisations, had hoped to be on the air by now, beaming a mixture of Senegalese pop music and speeches by leading Chinese dissidents into mainland China. But on Friday it was gathering barnacles in a harbour on the northern tip of Taiwan, the credibility of its mission in tatters.

It turned out that Taiwan, once the sworn enemy of the communist regime in Peking, was less than enthusiastic about the mission to democratise China over the airwaves. The arrival of the Goddess coincided with efforts by Taipei to build diplomatic and commercial bridges to the mainland. It seemed a pity to see all this jeopardised by a boatload of French campaigners and journalists.

On Friday, the organisers blasted Taiwan for going back on "secret agreements" to help them, which Taiwanese officials deny existed. "Taiwan made us understand that some people are afraid of freedom and don't keep their word," said Jean François Bizot, one of the sponsors of the project, adding the vessel would go to Japan instead in a last-ditch effort to salvage the mission.

It could be that Taiwan had

lowest close in five months.

This weekend, as the organisers gloomily pondered their options, the ship looked increasingly forlorn. Most of the journalists who had been covering the voyage from its beginnings had long since flown home. Typhoon Marian had begun lashing the decks and tempers aboard were flaring. There was little talk of democracy or braving the wrath of the hardliners in Peking.

It was a far cry from the enthusiasm with which the expedition was launched in the French port of La Rochelle nine months ago in association with a movement for exiled Chinese dissidents.

From the start, the organisers lost no opportunity in generating publicity to raise funds. At one point, while the ship was heading through the Indian Ocean to Singapore, it lost radio contact for several days. Organisers floated the possibility that the ship might have run into trouble. In fact, it had gone off the air because of interference from an electrical storm.

Excitement had been running high during the ship's long journey. There were reports that it had been shadowed by Chinese vessels and buzzed by Libyan jets, and by the time it reached Singapore the organisers had begun to believe their own propaganda about the risk posed by China. An atmosphere of paranoia set in.

According to one report last week, separate meals were requested for the captain and his number two in case Peking tried to poison the officers. A request was made for divers to check the hull, and the organisers asked for powerful fire-fighting h⸻

Swain worked hard on his story but it was spiked. This one got in, however, after a 2 am phone call.

After the briefing Swain watches more demonstrations against the bases. Banner-waving students are surrounded by police in riot gear. He manages to talk to one of the leaders before returning to his hotel to call the office.

All the main columnists in the News Review are now finishing their columns, which are due in by midday so that they can be edited, set into type and pasted up in their pages by midnight. As one of them myself, I have a great respect for columnists. Columns may seem effortless but they conceal a lot of very hard work – and when one is finished you immediately wonder what to write about next week. The next morning you also wish you had written your column differently as new thoughts occur to you, but too late. Newspapers can succeed or fail by the quality of their columnists and *The Sunday Times* has more than most. Whether they amuse, provoke, entertain or inform, columns are usually the best-read bits of their papers, their comments savoured by readers long after they have forgotten the news. That is why the best columnists are assiduously courted and cosseted by editors and handsomely paid. It is hard work living up to a reputation week after week.

The subject Robert Harris has chosen this week is why the Labour Party, in spite of the reformist policies demonstrated in its new policy document, is still failing to get the credit it deserves. As the left-of-centre columnist, says Harris, the subject seemed obvious. He has lunched with Frances Morrell, a former Labour Party policy adviser, and spoken to Peter Mandelson, head of communications at the Labour Party. Most of his ideas are formed over lunches or in conversation. He is not a member of the parliamentary lobby and visits the Commons rarely, although he was previously political editor of *The Observer*. "My job is to think not to report." That, today, is an attack on the chattering classes who won't acknowledge Labour's intellectual revolution, which he argues is equivalent in scale to that which swept through the Conservatives in the mid-1970s.

He reads all the papers every day and thinks about what he is going to write for most of the week, usually settling on his subject by Wednesday or the Thursday editorial conference. Then he makes calls on Thursday, writes on Friday morning and delivers his column at 1 pm. The column is "great fun", mainly because he is usually out-of-step politically with the paper. "Writing against the grain gives an edge to what you write, and because I don't have the burden of being the main column and having to be balanced, I can be a gadfly, often unexpectedly. On Lithuania I was advocating the right-wing argument."

Harris agrees that a weekly column can be a strain. "You're so exposed. You're only as good as last week's column and each week you venture out into new territory. My column last week was my 62nd. It's easy for most journalists to knock off five or ten columns, but when you get to 40 it's quite difficult to avoid repeating yourself." He enjoys writing for *The Sunday Times*, even though he disagrees with most of its political views. "I made a deal that I could write what I like. When I get worked up, I really let fly but the paper has stuck by the deal and I have been well treated by Andrew Neil. I'm also conscious of an enormous readership. People I've never met, even Tory MPs, tell me they have read it, even though they disagree with me."

Friday is also the morning when Gerald Scarfe, the most scathing caricaturist in Britain, has to finish his weekly cartoon. This week he

Robert Harris

Political columnist. Aged 44. A former president of the Cambridge Union, he started his career with the BBC, where he was a reporter on *Newsnight* and *Panorama*, before becoming political editor of the *Observer*, which he left to join *The Sunday Times*. Author of several books, including, *Gotcha!*, on the media and the Falklands conflict, and *Selling Hitler*, the story of the Hitler Diaries fiasco, filmed for independent television in 1991. His most recent book was the bestseller *Good and Faithful Servant*, an interim biography of Sir Bernard Ingham, Margaret Thatcher's Press secretary.

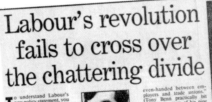

Labour's revolution fails to cross over the chattering divide

Neil Kinnock has won the working class but not yet the intelligentsia or the media, writes **ROBERT HARRIS**

Shock of the new: Benn talks rightly of revisionism but the message is not getting through

has also been asked to do a caricature of Rowan Atkinson for the
Arts pages. Often it can take hours
before Scarfe gets the idea for a
drawing that clicks.

Today the ideas have come
quickly as he worked in his Chelsea
studio. John Major, the chancellor,
is drawn astride an aeroplane
named inflation. It is plunging out
of control and the joystick has come
off in his hands. It is captioned:
"Major Disaster". He found that
his first drawing of Rowan Atkinson also worked.

"I can almost tell when I draw the
first line on the paper whether the
caricature will work," Scarfe says.
"The difficulty with actors is usually
that they have no persona of their
own. They are the roles they play. I
did Rowan as a rubbery figure
whose limbs were tying themselves
in knots. It was an effort to get to
the character of the man rather than
of the parts he plays. It is much less
difficult to portray the characters of
politicians. I love turning them into
animals. I like transmogrification –
turning Mrs Thatcher into a cow to
make a comment on mad cow disease, for instance.

His cartoons, often wounding
and upsetting to some readers,
arise, he says, either from a sense of
political injustice or from his view
of what fools we all are. "We are all
fallible and I like to point to the
fallibility of the leaders who set
themselves up as beacons in our
world. My role is to be the court
jester, to say, 'Hang on a minute. It
may not be quite like that.'"

Meetings with the editor start
shortly after 11. The first is to discuss the leading article, which this
week is to be a broadside at the
effect of Labour's new tax policies
on middle income voters. Then
there is a debate about whether *The*

Scarfe's ideas come quickly this week. John
Major astride an aeroplane. Rowan
Atkinson as a rubbery figure.

Sunday Times should buy the
memoirs of George Blake, the British traitor now living in Moscow.
They are due to be published in the
autumn and are on offer to *The
Sunday Times* for serialisation.
Should the paper be associated with
a traitor? Will he get the money?
Will it be a story worth reading?
Since *The Sunday Times* got first to
Kim Philby, shouldn't it also be first
with Blake? Ivan Fallon and Tony
Bambridge are strongly against the
idea and believe that there is no
longer any interest in the memoirs
of spies. The debate is not resolved
today – later Andrew Neil does buy

the memoirs, but with a stipulation that no money goes to Blake and that the interviews with him are by Phillip Knightley, a former *Sunday Times* journalist who has specialised in hunting spies and who is unlikely to be hoodwinked by Blake.

In Moscow Blitz's morning has continued as frustratingly as it started. At 9, refusing to be put off by the robust call at 7, he set off to the office of the nationalist leader. He is met by a "colossus" of a secretary who refuses to let him in. "You're totally discredited," she says. He has nevertheless waited for half an hour before leaving. Now it looks as though he will be unable to interview the most vital person for his story.

Then his luck changes. He bumps into a British journalist and persuades him to try to interview the man. He takes Blitz's tape-recorder with him and succeeds in getting an interview. But the verdict is still the same: "Boy, that chap hates your guts." Now he is hanging around the parliament building and getting interviews, before driving round the town to check on the panic buying of food and petrol by Russians fearful of an economic blockade from Moscow.

Alex Butler arrives at 12.07 (it is typical of such a stickler for details to be so accurate). With the help of four "casual" subs, hired by the shift, his main job today is to sub the News Review section, although he will also push through some of the Saturday news pages. "All copy for the Review and News sections has to go through to the editor after it leaves the subs," he says. "It's my job to chase after Bob Tyrer and his team in an attempt to get the section off by around midnight, which would then give us a couple of hours to sub up, revise and send down-stairs some overnight pages for the News section, which greatly helps the Saturday operation. That is the idea. I am told that Andrew shouted at Bob Tyrer at Thursday's conference, telling him to make sure his section is off on time. Andrew insists it was a stern talking to with no shouting!"

The day doesn't start well for Butler. "As usual the one page we completed overnight has to be re-made as the Review section has cocked up the ad shapes. The Review section is a joy to work on as the copy is invariably good but the subbing must be careful. I hate having late copy for this section as it cannot be rushed and it requires the very best of subs. We need another hefty hike in interest rates. Every time the building societies put up their rates, top-notch subs ring up offering their services for shifts. In times of low rates they don't need the work."

Now, at 12.30, it is time for the third main editorial conference of the week, focused today on the two news sections. It is decision time, when the editor has to commit himself to his choices of the two main Focus articles. Today there is a new story on the agenda. Christian Brando, son of Marlon, has been in court in Los Angeles pleading not guilty to the murder of his half-sister's lover in Brando's own home. But is it a big enough story, however entertaining, to justify 2,500 words in one of the paper's main slots?

The debate goes back and forth. The story of the Kegworth air crash has good words and pictures and is a good read, says Bob Tyrer, the Focus editor. Should Brando be substituted for mad cow disease? asks the editor. Mad cow disease followed by the air crash is certainly a heavy diet – but isn't the Brando story too slight? The mood of the conference is swinging in favour of Brando. But what to do about mad cows? If it becomes a news story, says Neil, it still must be done properly, as a major event of the week.

Michael Jones, the political editor, intervenes. Do we really care about Christian Brando? Surely food is a big issue for readers? But the first Focus is supposed to be a light, entertaining read, says Tyrer. Do they really want to read about sheep's brains?

So what are the other big news stories? Neil asks. Michael Williams runs through the list: Lockerbie, the tobacco scandal, a cure for breast cancer, beggars in London, the Devon oil spill. Neil has constantly been checking the news on Sky Television and he suddenly notices that the market is improving. He interrupts Williams to ask Jones what's on his agenda. He says he is working up a report about the state of the economy and what the government is planning for the autumn.

Williams resumes and runs through the rest of his list: the IRA (not a major read, says Neil), seal pups (terrific pictures, he says), workaholics, the imminent arrival of the *Maiden* in the Whitbread race and the new Labour Party manifesto (that will need a lot of space and tables, says Neil). Attention switches to the BBC for the *One o'Clock News*, then back again to the Focuses. Neil decides on the air crash for the centre spread. "Let's make it a ripping yarn, a thrilling read." Meanwhile Tyrer will work on both Brando and mad cows for the Focus 1.

Neil turns to Roger Eglin. "What's your splash, Rog?" Eglin says it will be the state of the market. "But that's what the FT will do." Ivan Fallon backs Eglin.

There has to be a market story. Eglin insists that the Exchange Rate Mechanism is going to be a big story the following week and that his splash will be forward-looking. Neil is still unconvinced. "Give me a people or a company story – a company I've heard of."

Eglin suggests a story on British and Commonwealth, the big financial company which is heading into trouble. "That's a bit Ruritanian tea leaves," says Neil. "You've got to do better than that. You've got a lot of work to do. Find something I want to read."

As the conference breaks up, one of its members mutters bitterly: "I hate that man at times."

Neil, now settling down for the long slog to midnight, is happier. "There's a lot of good stuff. If we really are going to enter EMS, we've got a good Sunday political splash. The Insight story on the tobacco scandal will create a lot of interest and Labour's tax policies will be a strong interest for our readers."

He is also reflecting on decision-making. "On the occasions when I can't quite make up my mind, democracy never helps. It's much better when I know what I want and insist on a decision. Otherwise everybody tries to second-guess me. So I take the decisions myself. It's a constant balancing act. If we were the FT or *The Times*, the decision on Focuses would be easy – mad cows and the air crash. Since we are a mix of the FT and the *Daily Mail* we've got to think about Brando as well as issues of public policy."

At 2.45 pm a meeting is occurring in Downing Street that is never reported. It is the meeting of the ten members of the Sunday lobby, the political journalists for the Sunday papers. They sit with Bernard Ingham, the Prime Minister's press secretary, and discuss the state of the nation. He also briefs them on upcoming government announcements. The lobby can also ask their own questions. What they write will be attributed to "Downing Street sources" or "government sources". It is never attributed to Ingham. That is the way the lobby works. Some of what he hears today will appear on Sunday in reports by David Hughes.

As David Hughes walked into Number Ten, Margarette Driscoll and Mark Ellidge were arriving at Mothecombe in South Devon. Driscoll is now slithering around over the oily sand and tar-strewn rocks and interviewing workmen clearing up the tons of dead seaweed. As she tries to piece together how the accident happened she will talk during the afternoon to the RSPCA, the Devon Wildlife Trust and council officials at the emergency centre, all of whom have different points of view on what went wrong and how to clear up the damage.

Meanwhile, as Iain Johnstone in Cannes tries to catch up on the sleep he has missed during a hectic week with an afternoon nap, Ian Coxon and Simon Taylor, the executives responsible for the editorial production of the paper, are haggling with the advertising department over the positioning of advertisements. They are presented with a small dummy of the paper, showing where the ads have been placed. Then they negotiate to juggle them round the paper to suit editorial requirements. Some cannot be moved, the advertiser has booked the first or second right-hand page or, as is the case today, there is an advertisement with a cut-out coupon that has to be on a right hand page so that the scissors can get to it.

They tell the advertising department that it cannot have a big ad on the centre spread, where it will spoil the effect of the big feature on the Kegworth air crash and limit the display that can be given to pictures. They also argue over the placing of classified advertising. Neil gets very upset if, say, property ads are split between two sections, making them difficult for readers to find, and Coxon and Taylor are constantly juggling to get the right fit. Today there is so much property advertising that it won't fit into the Arts section, and overseas property has spilled into the Business section. The editor won't allow it. Taylor swings into action.

On the newsdesk Michael Williams is reflecting that there are more news pages than stories to fill them. He had been hoping to steer the editor against the Brando Focus so he could grab the story for the news pages – but failed. As another ploy he has persuaded John Witherow, the foreign editor, to yield the story of the seal pups so that he can use it to fill the home news pages. "It's simple," says Williams. "We'll ring up Greenpeace, get them to say the treatment of the pups is scandalous, and we've got a story." He thinks he has now got enough at least to fill the first edition tomorrow. As Saturday stories arrive, he can then junk the weaker items.

When Williams wants a picture to go with a news story, it is to Aidan Sullivan that he will turn tomorrow. That is why the picture editor is now ensuring that he has every story covered. He has staked out de Klerk's London hotel and organised pictures from Moscow and Paris for foreign news pages. Pictures are coming from Italy to go with Insight on tobacco and from Rotterdam for the Rolling Stones concert. The oil slick is covered and he is now researching for the M1 air crash story.

His most difficult job, however, is organising aerial pictures of the Whitbread yacht race, whose leading boats are still 800 miles from the Solent. He has rung Rothmans, sponsors of the leading yacht *Steinlager 2*, but they cannot help. Nor can the navy or the fishing ministry. Sullivan is now trying to hire a plane which can fly 800 miles and back and also checking with other Sunday papers to see if they wish to share the costs.

At 2.45 a big Arts story breaks. The buyer of a Renoir and a Van Gogh for £100 million has been revealed as Ryoei Saito, the Japanese business tycoon. Five of the eight most expensive paintings ever sold are now owned by Japanese. It is an obvious story for the Arts section, where one of the main articles is about the prices the two pictures fetched. Now it has been overtaken, and since it goes to press tonight, the Arts section won't be able to add anything to what is in tomorrow's national dailies. The editor decides it should be treated as a news story, allowing another 24 hours to assemble a better report. Now, hours from the deadline for the section, Tony Rennell has a big hole in one of his main pages – and a big problem. So has Marina Vaizey, the art critic, whose original article is now spiked and who sits down to write 1,100 words on Phillip King, the British sculptor, to fill the blank page. She files it via a modem from her home to Wapping at 7 pm, while pictures of King's work are biked over from the gallery where his work is on display.

After his earlier roasting from the editor, Roger Eglin has been determined to find a new splash. Even when he was being lashed by

Neil, he knew he had a story about Saatchis, the big advertising agency, but was worried that it might appear in the Saturday papers. So he didn't mention it. At 4.30, however, he senses that the Saatchi story is going to keep for Sunday. The agency has decided to sue eight of its staff who have set up a rival agency. It's a story that has got what the editor wants – a name that is instantly recognisable and a story spiced with intrigue and revenge. It is also a scoop. He races to the editor's office, checks that he is on his own and not surrounded by colleagues playing to the gallery, and sells it to him. Neil is delighted.

Satisfied with the Business Focus on Philips, he turns to the City Focus on Marks & Spencer. It is a tightly-written piece by Margaret Park about why its results are so much better than those of its High Street rivals. There is, however, one problem. "Pictures of Lord Rayner, the chairman, and Rick Greenbury, the chief executive, are an important part of the display but they don't appear in the text."

Margaret Park says they refused to talk to her – a lordly M & S press officer says everybody who wanted an interview booked up a month ago. So much for waiting to see if M & S's results were newsworthy.

"It's a pity Margaret didn't say sooner. We could have mounted a high-level counterblast at M & S. Instead I vow bitterly to cancel my next buying of a shirt and get Margaret to write Rayner and Greenbury into the story. The headline isn't easy. I want something that encapsulates how M & S has overcome poor retail trading as well as its rivals. Bingo! There it is two-thirds of the way down the story. An analyst at Shearson has said that it's really M & S and the rest. M & S and the rest – and it fits!"

On the Sports desk Chris Nawrat, his deputy Nick Pitt and Chris Campling, a casual sub, are in the middle of shifting 10,000 words of copy, as well as headlines and captions.

"This is the day that guarantees that Saturday will work," says Nawrat. "All the files for every moving story, including rewrites, for all planned editions are set up. Thus, when the copy arrives, it is inserted into the appropriate file and the sub simply writes headlines and captions. The files are constructed so that all stories fit to the line in whatever shape and are a single piece of bromide. This means everything fits and goes into the page at high speed. We also set up sheets for each page, which are given to Carolyn Wigoder, our secretary. When every writer rings in tomorrow, she will give them their wordage, deadline, catchline and time of rewrite. We also establish on another file what time pages go, which change on which edition, and what stories are expected to change or be updated. These are then typeset, photocopied and distributed to the production executives, printers and senior Saturday staff. The system works wonderfully well – unless you make an error. Then the entire army will follow you into the abyss."

Penny Perrick, the fiction editor, is still working on *The Sunday Times*/Hay-on-Wye Festival of Literature. This afternoon she is meeting Alice Thomas Ellis, the novelist, John Stuart Roberts, head of BBC TV in Wales, and Peter Florence, the festival director, to nominate the winner of the £5,000 John Evelyn Hughes prize awarded by the Development Board for Rural Wales. "Asked a year ago to lay down the conditions for this prize, I said airily that it should be a work of fiction or non-fiction with a rural theme. Since then I've had to compare a factual book about circles that appear in fields with a volume of poetry, an autobiography with a novel, a selection of letters with a book of photographs. I am grateful to the other two judges for still speaking to me after landing them this impossible task. The meeting is at the Poetry Society in Earl's Court Square. Because it is none too pleasant sitting in a large bare room, we reach a decision quickly: George O'Brien's book of his early life, *The Village of Longing and Dancehall Days*.

"We are all it seems suckers for nostalgia and the book is delightful in a seductive Irish way that appeals not only to me but to the two Welsh judges. George O'Brien, who was taught English at university by Germaine Greer, is also scheduled to make an appearance at the Hay Festival. There is a 'family' feel about English literature which I find very pleasing."

With the judging over, Perrick is off to Paris for the weekend with the rest of the staff of the Books section.

At 6.15 sharp, with her interview written, Valerie Grove leaves the office. Since her husband is still at work at the *Sunday Telegraph*, she has to relieve her nanny, who has caught the 7.30 train home to Essex every Friday for the past 14 years. "The ritual is: get home, take nanny to Archway station, stop off at Becky's the newsagent's for *Evening Standard* and sweeties for each child. The price comes to £3.60, just to rot their teeth," says Grove. "The working week is now over and a mothering weekend begins. But at 11.40 I ring the features sub in a sudden panic. Could he have a certain paragraph lawyered? It is very hard to get the piece out of one's head and it seems a long time till Sunday. I always need another hour – just one more hour."

So does the advertising department, but its week is over too. There is no business to be got after 5 pm on a Friday afternoon when the rest of the world is anxious to get home for the weekend. Pamela Hamilton Dick, classified advertising manager for *The Times* and *The Sunday Times*, is counting columns. Has she met the budget? The 1989 advertising recession has started and the answer is No. Almost the first sign of a recession is a slump in ads for homes and cars and jobs. Hamilton Dick is one of the first to know that 18 per cent interest rates are biting into family budgets.

She points out that classified is the only form of advertising where there is proof that it succeeds or fails. If you sell a lot of jars of Nescafé, it may be because it was advertised; it may be simply because millions want to drink coffee. Yet if you advertise your home and get 20 responses, your ad has worked.

One of her jobs now that the economy is slumping is to think up new categories of advertising. Until quite recently there were always at least four pages of motoring ads in *The Sunday Times*. Now the BMWs and the Audis are not being put up for sale. So she has introduced Classic and Performance Cars categories to win new trade. The inducement to advertise was three free lines to advertise for a saddle for a 1934 Humber motor cycle or a spare wheel for a 1970 Bugatti. It worked and has been the most successful new category ever introduced.

The Sunday Times is one of the most successful papers in Britain in attracting classified ads, the small personal ads for cars, holiday cottages and homes placed by individual readers. A week ago there were 3,670 separate ads in the paper accounting for about 60 per cent of advertising revenue and worth £1 million a week. That is why Hamilton Dick oversees seven field managers and 140 sales staff. It is a tough life as a tele-ad salesperson, competing for business against the *Daily Telegraph*, *Financial Times*, *Observer* and all the other papers or magazines, such as *Country Life* which is strong for property advertising. So their sights are constantly lifted to still higher targets by Hamilton Dick and her senior managers.

"*The Sunday Times* has always been the leader for motors – but too many advertisers are down-sizing and tightening budgets due to hard times," says one classified staff bulletin. "Remember to pitch, that a smaller ad gets smaller amounts of calls. Business to Business needs just 1.5 columns to reach its weekly target. Keep Going – You Can Do It."

Each tele-ad salesperson is given a weekly target and then starts making phone calls. According to Hamilton Dick, you have only eight seconds to capture a potential advertiser's interest. Once that is achieved, the job is to close the deal. One tactic is the testimonial. Did you know that one estate agent got 300 replies to an ad in *The Sunday Times* last week? Or you may ring an advertiser who used a rival paper and say: "Congratulations! You almost got it right – but surely you should have used *The Sunday Times*, where you would have reached another million readers for the same price?"

She doesn't believe in the hard sell. If you persuade an advertiser to buy an advertisement that they don't really want, it rebounds on the paper's reputation. The policy is to put the facts persuasively – say, *The Sunday Times* has more ABC1 women readers or more readers earning £40,000 a year with two cars – and to allow advertisers to make their own choices.

With the advertising market in its worst state for 15 years, according to Hamilton Dick, other papers are discounting on their rates to get advertisers to make bookings. She says scornfully that one rival paper is almost giving away advertisements.

At News International, however, the policy is not to discount, although the present climate has dictated some "unusual flexibility" over rates. All the same, Hamilton Dick is pleased that she got £2,000 for a 10 × 3 column ad last week, when the main rival persuaded the same advertiser to take almost a full page – but for £750. What counts more than sheer columns is the yield per column inch. All salesmen are competitive and Hamilton Dick is as fiercely combative as any. She talks scathingly about another rival paper. "Is it really worthwhile to spend £5 to get three replies when by spending £86 in *The Sunday Times* you get 50?" she asks. Given the state of the market, she can be satisfied with her department's work. In April the *Daily Telegraph*, publishing six days a week, took 852 columns of classified. *The Sunday Times*, publishing only once a week, took 753, she says.

David Walsh is also satisfied with his week's work. At 5.30 he has just sold the last advertisement, a 20 × 2 on the op-ed page. Since Wednesday night he has sold three of the four full pages that were still open, to Nationwide, the Post Office (who were persuaded to double their money) and Teacher's. He reckons that *The Sunday Times* will have the biggest share of the advertising market this weekend and says he feels like the cat who got the cream. One coup that has particularly pleased him is that Fiat decided to use the Style section. They were persuaded that it was a section well read by women, who were a powerful influence on decisions to buy cars.

Altogether this Sunday there will be 146 display ads and 4,300 classified ads in *The Sunday Times*. So the cat has got the cream – but the recession has left its mark. Even though there are 576 columns of advertising this Sunday, volume is down by 16 per cent. The 134-page paper will therefore consist of 54 per cent of advertising against a target of 60 per cent. Four out of ten of the ads have been sold since Monday and there are 240 columns (at eight columns per page) of display ads.

Walsh, the cheerful Gazza of the ad department who relishes scoring goals, shakes a clenched fist to celebrate a good week. This is the attitude that inspires his staff. "You've got to lead from the front," he says. "You've got to be seen to be motivated and inspirational. It's no good looking crestfallen if you've failed to get an ad. You've got to keep enthusiastic and alive. Ultimately it's down to our salesmen who do the business – but they operate according to how we manage them and keep their enthusiasm infectious."

As the advertising department shuts up shop, the editorial department is now motoring on six cylinders in the period of peak activity of the week. It is time for the editor's 6.30 conference when dispositions start to be made for the news section. It is the worst moment of the week for Michael Williams. Will the editor be satisfied with his newslist? He is leading on three good stories tonight:

Britain to join the ERM in November as inflation falls.

Exclusive: Germany and Syria use Lockerbie bomb suspect as a bargaining chip in secret negotiations to free German hostages.

Revealed: How British taxpayers' millions are spent on subsidising high-tar tobacco which is dumped on the Third World – by Insight.

Classic car collector sues after his million pound Jaguar is offered for sale in Monaco auction. Will the real car – or the counterfeit – please stand up?

So it's a rosy scenario for the Tories, says Neil as he studies the first item, which means that the government would be able to cut interest rates. Jones says that there is now a strong political package – not only the rosy scenario but the Labour manifesto, suggesting £5 billion cuts in the defence budget and a neutral Germany – as well as its proposals on income tax. Neil is getting excited as he realises that Andrew Grice has got hold of the Labour manifesto that is not due to be released until next week. It could make a Focus.

He mentally files that story and checks through the rest of the list. He likes the Lockerbie and tobacco stories but is doubtful about classic cars. The Devon oil slick is scheduled for the back page. Are there good pictures? he asks. Ballantyne's story of the drug which could prevent breast cancer is down for page 3 but Neil suggests it could make the front. He pushes again for a much bigger story on Malcolm Rifkind, the Scottish Secretary of

State who has put himself out on a limb after his Ravenscraig decision. "As long as she's there, he's finished as a UK politician," he says.

Now it is back to politics. Grice has come in to the room and Neil asks how much of the Labour manifesto he has managed to get. "I've got the lot." Neil is still tempted to do a Focus on the Labour Party – but there are several alternatives. Tyrer argues for mad cows, Fallon suggests the Japanese businessman who has bought the Van Gogh. I suggest the arrival of the crew of the *Maiden* in the Whitbread race. Rosemary Collins points out that the *Maiden* is a story that will be read by every woman.

Neil's mind is suddenly made up and he raps out his decisions: *Maiden* as Focus 1, switch the big ad on page 4 and devote it to Labour, make mad cows a big news story, put Rifkind on page 10, and Brando and Van Gogh on a foreign page. Thatcher's meeting with de Klerk and the events in Lithuania remain as candidates for the front. He checks the Business front page with Eglin. Williams can stop sweating: he pronounces that the news seems in pretty good shape, especially with the EMS, Lockerbie and tobacco stories for the front. Once again, though, he reminds Williams that he wants a strong story on Scotland and Rifkind.

Alone in his office afterwards, he thinks aloud about the effects of the Wapping revolution. Four years earlier the sort of decisions he has just made would not have been possible. Now he can still decide what should be the Focus 1 at 7.30 on a Friday night, knowing that the production system can cope with up-to-the-minute news decisions.

He is also happy with the balance that is emerging between all the

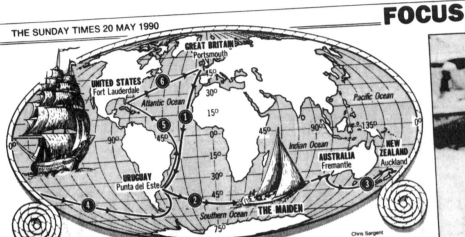

THE SUNDAY TIMES 20 MAY 1990

Chris Sargent

MAIDEN'S RETURN

On Friday morning, Maiden, the first Whitbread round-the-world yacht crewed entirely by women, is due to sail past Southampton's dockhead to the sound of cheers and champagne corks popping. **TIM MADGE** and **MAURICE CHITTENDEN** report on the closing stages of her epic voyage

IN FREEZING temperatures, Dawn Riley, 26, captain of the watch, prepared to steer through the grey seas of the north Atlantic last night searching for a heavy wind to carry the crew of the yacht Maiden home to Britain.

After 32,000 miles, the first all-woman team to crew a yacht in the Whitbread round-the-world race are only days from completing their feat of endurance.

Below deck the talk is of stepping ashore later this week, of romantic reunions and of at last abandoning a constant diet of freeze-dried food for a binge of hamburgers, ice cream and cold beer.

wrote in the ship's log: "With icebergs looming up and the wind changing, the constant drizzle and rain and freezing water . . . we have all decided that hell is not fire and brimstone; hell is here."

The Whitbread is the stuff of nightmares. There is no yacht race like it, covering such vast distances over such a long period. Edwards took part as a cook last time, and was determined to be her own captain on the present race with the first all-woman crew.

Fulfilling that ambition meant embarking on a four-year battle for sponsorship in the race,

ahead. I just hope if there are any out there they show up this time. We did have a full moon last night which helped, but of course it meant we were all bloody freezing.

This evening we came across a fishing fleet and they told us they were in a search pattern for a man overboard. They presumed he was dead but they were going to continue to search until dark. It felt worse for us I think because we have seen death on the Whitbread this time [Tony Phillips was washed overboard from Creightons Naturally in the Southern Ocean]. It seemed almost a desecration

sea ahead. That was a very brave act because of the cold. It was also very, very foggy — visibility was down to 100ft at times. Because the wind has been going up and down it has meant that we have had to do many sail changes, which has tired everybody out.

Wednesday May 16
46°32''N 39°38''W

We got so close to Rucanor at one point in the night that they asked if we would like to come over for breakfast. But the wind dropped again this morning and they zoomed off.

Thursday May 17
46°50''N 35°59''W

lost the wind this

Friday night: the paper starts to come together — a News Focus and three of the section front pages are now completed.

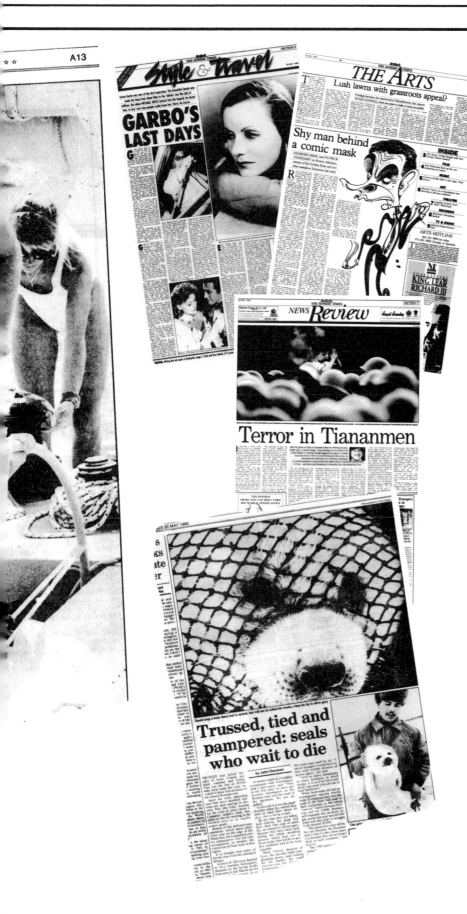

different sections of the paper. That is why he is delighted with the contrasts given by Greta Garbo front for Style (show business), the Rowan Atkinson front of the Arts section and the moving photograph on the News Review front illustrating the story of Li Lu, the Chinese student revolutionary leader at Tiananmen Square, a strong political read. Now he has got a potential mix for the front page of a major domestic political scoop, a tobacco scandal and an international Insight investigation.

With the conference over, the newsdesk can kill the stories that the editor doesn't want and direct the reporters to the stories he is keen on. Many will now work until at least 2 am. For Williams it is the start of the most interesting period of his week. "All the other sections of the paper have gone to press or are on their way. All that remains now is the news. Sixteen pages and they're my responsibility to fill.

"With four rival quality papers to beat, we knew the newslist wasn't good enough. Now Aidan Sullivan has rescued us from our despair with the set of pictures of seal cubs trapped by the Russians – cruel, but it's news. I buy them instantly. Later in the evening I am rescued by another tragedy – a Soviet magazine reports that two cosmonauts are stranded on a broken-down space station. 'Trapped in space', a large explanatory diagram will make it the perfect Sunday story."

Meanwhile the newsdesk is scanning the first editions of the morning papers. Tonight they can relax. There are no scoops. Aileen Ballantyne arrives at the newsdesk to tell Collins that she has managed to talk to Katie Warder about her role in the tamoxifen pilot study. That gives her story the lift it needs to get on to the front page. Driscoll rings

ations. How-
arried man with two   The survey by Mark Frank-   married man with two children   now and pay
Full details, page 4

Drug offers new hope against breast cancer

A DRUG that could prevent breast cancer has been pioneered by British doctors and is to be offered to thousands of women.

Experts believe it is the best hope for eradicating the cancer short of a cure, still thought to be 10 years away. If proved safe, all women will be offered the drug in the form of a daily pill.

The decision to offer the treatment widely was taken at a confidential meeting of leading cancer specialists last week, and marks a new approach to the disease, which affects one woman in 12 and kills 15,000 a year in the United Kingdom.

The move coincides with

by Aileen Ballantyne, Medical Correspondent

the death this week of the British-born actress Jill Ireland, 53, after a six-year battle against breast cancer.

A five-year scheme involving 30,000 women will assess the extent of protection against breast cancer offered by the drug, tamoxifen, to healthy women.

The drug is already used to prevent the spread of breast cancer in women who have the disease. It appears to work by "switching off" oestrogen-dependent cancer cells in the breast. Doctors realised just over two years ago that it might also prevent healthy

women getting cancer, and launched a small pilot experiment. No toxic side effects have so far been detected.

Dr Trevor Powles, a breast cancer specialist at the Royal Marsden hospital in London, who has pioneered the drug as a treatment, said: "There is a real possiblity that we will be able to prevent a substantial number of women from getting breast cancer."

Powles estimates that taking the drug could reduce the average lifetime risk of getting breast cancer from one in 12 to as low as one in 60.

In the past few weeks

Powles's team, which has given the drug to more than 400 healthy women, has discovered that far from causing any significant negative side effects, tamoxifen reduces cholesterol by an average of 20%, greatly reducing the risk of heart disease.

Among those taking part in the Royal Marsden pilot study is Katie Warder, 43, whose mother had breast cancer. "Just imagine the benefits for future generations if we can actually prevent this disease," said Warder, who lives with her husband and two sons in Biddenden, Kent. "It kills thousands every year."

None of the women on the pilot scheme knows whether

Katie Warder: welcomes drug trial

the pill she takes every day is tamoxifen or a placebo to test the drug's effectiveness. Nor will the thousands more about to be asked to take part.

The £4.5m tamoxifen programme is expected to be funded jointly by the Imperial Cancer Research Fund and the Cancer Research Campaign.

Ballantyne gets her front page scoop.

from her hotel in Brixham to say she is writing her copy. She eventually files at 11.30 pm.

The final stages of the week for the Business section occur after 9.30 when Wall Street closes and they get the first edition of the FT. The two events are important. They know the news that will dominate the American and British papers on Saturday and can ensure that their stories will still be fresh by Sunday morning. They are also still making and receiving calls. Many of their best scoops have come from calls made late on Friday night when the men from the City have started to relax or want to stage-manage scoops that will set the City talking on Monday morning.

Against its main rivals, the Business section works under a big handicap: it is the only one that goes to press on Saturday morning, which means that their rivals have all Saturday to try to beat them. But they boast that in the four years

since they moved to Wapping they have never been significantly scooped.

The most influential column in the Business section is by Ivan Fallon, who has been writing about the City for 20 years. He is on first name terms with all the big chairmen and City personalities, and what he writes matters. They all read him. At six tonight several of his calls have still not been made.

"I need to talk to Saatchi, which is once again in the news, and make a call. The brothers aren't there but Jeremy Sinclair, formerly number three, returns my call. I am two minutes into it when Charles Saatchi calls me from his car. I cut Sinclair off and take the Saatchi call. We spend half an hour going through the company's problems and the solutions he sees to them. Later I check with Bill Muirhead, head of the Saatchi agency in London.

"Then I call Bob Maxwell about

a story that he is going to buy into BSB. Ernest Saunders rings from a callbox at Waterloo station. He has kept notes of all the main events of the Guinness trial all week and we discuss how it has gone. He wants to discuss with me next week, he says, whether he should or should not go into the witness box himself, 'the most important decision of my life'. We agree to meet. I call a number of people in the market and several old friends whose views I respect. David Fuller [Fallon's guru] is as usual succinct and clear.

"After the 6.30 conference I tackle the profile, which needs far more work than I had anticipated, and it is 9.30 by the time I return to my column. Having talked to Charles Saatchi, Jeremy Sinclair and Bill Muirhead I feel there is a story on Saatchi I want to do. Saunders and the lawyers have given me some interesting material on Guinness, I want to write about Maxwell, and I have to write about the markets, so I have several items too many. Canary Wharf and a piece on the property market drop off.

Farewell to market's frolic

IT IS extraordinary how little it takes to change sentiment in the City. Last week the ostensible catalyst was a perfectly innocuous interview with John Major in Thursday's Wall Street Journal where he asserted that "Britain is a pretty convinced European" (whatever that means), and made it clear "that the Thatcher government is backing away from its ideological opposition to a central European banking authority".

"Backing away"? I read very little new into that. The market, however, decided it was dramatic and the FT-SE index blazed up 63.3 points, the biggest rise since November 1987 and the pound gained three pfennigs.

Then, on Thursday, the chancellor addressed the Confederation of British Industry dinner, repeated his determination to join the system, and the next morning the market lost all interest after another early burst. Deep in the analysts' room, somebody must have calculated that entry into the exchange rate mechanism, with the tough anti-inflationary discipline this will bring, is not that marvellous.

Yet it has been a fascinating few weeks for the markets, reflecting in London a widening belief that Margaret Thatcher's fortunes reached their low on May 3, the Heseltine challenge has faltered, and the Tories will get back next time.

The news from abroad was cheering too. Wall Street rose 63 points in a single day and has been hitting new highs, Tokyo has steadied and, most important, bond markets around the world have staged a rally from their miserable levels three weeks ago. That is the best news the markets have had for some time.

But is it enough? I consulted my guru David Fuller who reckons the London market is now as overbought as it was oversold at the end of April. In other words, the end of this happy few weeks is nigh — he reckons it peaked on Friday. Wall Street's rise is not being confirmed by the broader-based indices, and the rise in bond markets has not...

which will probably run to Whitsun. The most interesting witness last week was perhaps Alan Scrine, the veteran company secretary, who confirmed that meetings of the new non-executives had been held without his knowledge, and not always properly minuted.

One witness last week raised a number of eyebrows among the legal profession: David Donaldson, one of the two Trade and Industry department inspectors who carried out the inquiry into Guinness. We have already had the speedy reading of transcripts of what the various defendants said to the inspectors, and Donaldson explained the powers of the inspectors — which exceed those of the police.

In any ordinary criminal investigation, an accused person has

VIEWPOINT by **IVAN FALLON**

the right to remain silent. DTI inspectors on the other hand can compel a person to answer their questions — and have him sent to jail if he doesn't. It is one thing for those responses to find their way into a DTI report, but rather another for them to be used as evidence in a criminal court.

● *Guinness trial, page 18*

SAATCHI PARTINGS

WHEN Charles Saatchi heard of the latest defections from his Charlotte Street agency last week, he exclaimed: "But who are they? I've never heard of them." Although technically the five who left were called "directors", in an advertising agency, *everybody* is a director. Clients don't like dealing with anything less. At Charlotte Street there are — or were — 9⁵...in a London...

executive, Robert Louis-Dreyfus, seem to have found a working relationship which suits all three: Maurice is the chairman, counselling and advising, and keeping his hands off the day-to-day running of the business; Louis-Dreyfus is the chief executive who is fully in charge, but refers to Maurice; and Charles, as ever, is just there, doing what he has always done — which is quite indefinable but nonetheless vital.

Below these three the ranks have thinned dramatically as Louis-Dreyfus has applied the knife. Charlie Scott is getting control of the finances, much to the relief of the brothers. Within a fortnight I expect the Hay consultancy to have been sold, and by the end of the year Saatchi will be trimmed back to a company making around a third of the profits it did at its peak, but nonetheless fighting its way out of debt, defections and crises.

The attitude of the brothers is very much along the lines: we made some big mistakes, we deserve to be kicked, but we've handed the running of the company over to a very able manager. The problem is that the publicity is still so adverse that it can be self-fulfilling.

MAXWELL ON AIR

IN A memorable appearance on the Wogan show last week, Robert Maxwell announced he would decide this weekend on whether he should bid for Alan Bond's stake in British Satellite Broadcasting. It would, he said, be a "real tough one" for him.

When I rang to ask how his pondering was going, he said he would now make his decision tomorrow. The Bond stake, 36% at one stage, has been diluted down to 26% but is still by far the largest. At the end of the month another rights issue will dilute it again, unless the new owner subscribes.

Maxwell is in the market for 20%...the maximum allowed...Bond paid...

Another influential column from Fallon.

"By 10.30 I have an early copy of Saturday's *Financial Times*, plus *The Times*, and I go through these in some detail. By 11.30 I am done. I read through the stories in the Business subs queue and then go down to the Business section to look at the front page scheme. I leave about midnight and ring in again at 1.15 in case there are any final queries on my column and to check that Wall Street hasn't gone crazy in the final hours. All is well."

For City editor Jeff Randall, Friday is madness. "The phone goes all day. Every lead, every half-lead is chased. This week is poor for news and I'm hustling all the City team for that elusive scoop. In between calls I decide what stocks we must analyse in our Contago column and in the odd semi-quiet moment I try to write it.

"Facing one of the weakest news pages for many weeks, I make a final call at around 7 pm to a contact at the Midland Bank. Bingo. As if by divine intervention, I'm on to something. Senior executives in the banks are expressing private doubts about the Midland's merger with Hongkong and Shanghai Bank. There's our splash."

In the Insight office David Leppard is now settling down to write the story that is at the top of the newslist. He has rung the German Foreign Office, as well as the German prosecutor's office. Neither has denied his Sarkis story. "I regarded that as significant – but it wasn't until 9.30 when I sat down to write that the truth dawned on me with a blinding flash. In my files, from long ago, I had a German police record of an interview with Dalkamoni.

"The transcript made it quite clear that two senior German police officers had asked Dalkamoni a series of questions about his attitude to a possible hostage exchange. The questions had nothing to do with the criminal investigation into his alleged terrorist acts. They could only be designed with one purpose in mind. Dalkamoni told them that if he was sentenced for ten years or more his backers in Damascus would 'then do something for my release'. The Germans had been given the signal they wanted. They had solicited an offer of a hostage exchange. They would undoubtedly convict Dalkamoni for the crimes he had committed – but if they wanted their hostages back they were being offered the opportunity of doing so by releasing him early." He starts writing.

Wherever you look now there are journalists with different problems. As he looked through the TV listings, Tony Rennell discovered that they list a cricket match at Wembley and the 50th anniversary of Churchill's "election", neither of which can be correct and both of which need checking. It is the sort of inaccuracy, he says, that can so easily slip in and persuade finicky readers that newspapers cannot be trusted.

Eglin is in trouble with the lawyers on the Saatchi story. "It's a good story," says Bambridge, "but if we print it and no writs are issued, we'll be swinging in the wind. We have to get a reaction. It is now 11 pm and Rufus Olins (the advertising reporter) is pessimistic – but he dashes off. Eventually he tracks one of the breakaways to a restaurant and gets the necessary 'absolute rubbish' quote."

Bob Tyrer has now cleared every article in the News Review and has switched his attention to the Focus on the Kegworth air crash. It will be a long read of about 4,000 words and he has to ensure that it looks attractive on the page so that readers are tempted to stop and read it; then that it is written so that they carry on reading. A Focus needs a dramatic headline, strong pictures and must be a good Sunday read. The two main stories are being written by Richard Ellis and Richard Caseby, two experienced reporters, Walter Ellis is editing their copy, and now Tyrer is looking for good pictures of the crash. It is nearly midnight. That is plenty to be going on with – and there is also the *Maiden* Focus still to be organised.

At 11.30 the three Business subs are working on the front and back pages of the section and the front page is being designed, while Eglin reads every word of every story on the front page. Some are not up to scratch and he starts to edit them into shape. Production editors Coxon and Taylor are down in the composing room, where at 11.45 there are still 29 pages unfinished.

Helen Hawkins has finished six of the eight Arts pages and is now waiting for the reviews from the Coliseum and the Rolling Stones concert in Amsterdam so that she can put the section to bed. Opera critic Paul Driver has been to the English National Opera world première of *Clarissa* by Robin Holloway and is writing his review on a Tandy in the Coliseum press office. His is the sort of work that makes you admire journalism. Within minutes of the curtain, he has to write 750 words within 75 minutes for an audience of highly critical readers. Tonight he was not able to start until 10.50 – but his copy arrives before 1 am.

When Robert Sandall files from Rotterdam on the Stones concert shortly afterwards, after rushing from the Feyenoord stadium, Hawkins is nearing the end of her week. Since Sandall has dictated his

Paul Driver, Music Critic

It seems such a glamorous job being a critic. Yet Paul Driver's week ended at midnight, sitting in the press office of the Coliseum, writing a review within half an hour of the production and sending it to the office from his Tandy. He didn't finish until 1 am.

That was exceptional, particularly for a Sunday paper critic. Yet even in a normal week he probably attends at least three or four events, usually operas and often away from London. Normally, however, he would start to write his review on a Thursday, not at midnight on Friday.

Driver always tries to find a theme so that there is a unity to his review, even if his week has been devoted to two new operas. Two weeks ago he was writing about two Finnish composers. Next week it will be two Danish composers. He makes his own selection of the music he will write about, selecting the events which will help to make a readable review.

Does he get bored with listening to so much music? Yes, indeed, and certainly with Mozart. "I don't want to see *Cosi fan tutte* for a long time, as well as most early music before Verdi. I go occasionally to see if I still hate it."

Driver composed music as a teenager, plays the piano, and studied music at Oxford, but doesn't believe you need to be a musician to write about it. "Music should speak for itself. As Shaw showed, it is more important to be a good writer than a good musician."

Driver is fortunate in that he rarely has to dictate his reviews over the telephone with the risk of the copytaker in the office mishearing. The classic mistake, he says, occurred to Joan Chissell of *The Times* when she reviewed *Dido and Aeneas*. "When I am laid to earth," she dictated. Her review appeared in the paper the next morning. It said: "When I am laid enough."

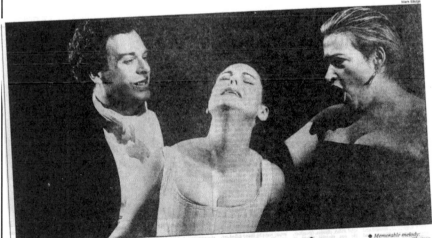

Memorable melody: Vivian Tierney as Clarissa, centre, in David Pountney's production at the Coliseum

A heroine for our time

PAUL DRIVER applauds English National Opera's stunning Clarissa

review to a copytaker at Wapping, she calls him back to check queries. "Exhausted and slightly queasy from a diet of crisps, cocktail gherkins and geriatric cheese left from our buffet lunch," she says, "I then muster one last burst of energy to find a Stones headline idea that hadn't been done to death and which also fitted the shape available." It has to be two lines across three columns. She hits on "Satanic majesties who can still strut their stuff". Her pages are finally finished at 2 am.

Back in the newsroom Williams and Witherow are deciding what to put into the seven news pages that are prepared on Friday night so that Saturday gets off to a flying start. Driscoll's story from Devon is at present scheduled for the back page, where it can be illustrated by Ellidge's pictures. They stand over a drawing board with Gordon Beckett, the design editor, and decide which two or three stories should go on each page, striving to keep the subjects varied and to obtain a change of pace between serious and entertaining stories.

Many stories from foreign stringers are rewritten by the foreign news editor but staff copy usually goes straight in. The home reporters, meanwhile, are going through their stories with Rosemary Collins, who will often suggest new angles or new first paragraphs that will arrest the readers' attention and satisfy Williams, who likes to keep the news stories lively.

Even after midnight many reporters are still busy. Tony Bambridge is checking every table in the Business section to make sure it is accurate. Phil Green, the graphic design editor, is still working on the illustration for the Kegworth Focus, while Tyrer is starting to design the two pages on which the story will be

---

THE SUNDAY TIMES 20 MAY 1990

IN CONCERT: *The Stones rock Rotterdam*

Satanic majesties who can still strut their stuff

Don't write off the Rolling Stones, says ROBERT SANDALL

It would be easy, but very wrong, to conclude that at this stage in their 27-year career the Rolling Stones are simply trading their mythical reputation for cash. Steel Wheels, their last album, was only a modest hit with the fans. Steel Wheels, The Tour, on the other hand, was widely reported as the most profitable rock and roll outing ever. As it made its triumphal way around America and Japan last autumn, gross profits of $60m to $100m were talked up to the point where the Stones came to seem like nothing more than an exercise in creative accountancy.

This is not so much unfair as completely beside the point. The reason why 3m people paid to see the Steel Wheels tour and why another 2m have stumped up for its European counterpart — redesigned and renamed Urban Jungle — is that the Stones live are still a breathtakingly, perhaps uniquely, effective stadium act.

The crowd of 50,000 who filled the Feyenoord football ground in Rotterdam on Friday night, for the inaugural night of a 37-date European tour, witnessed an event which was part rock concert, part rude kinetic junk sculpture and part *son et lumière* spectacle. The songs, even the new ones, may have stayed pretty much the same, but not since the glory days of the early 1970s have they been played with such raw conviction; and never perhaps have they been put across with more theatrical abandon.

Indeed, the stage set — and its associated stunts — is such a strikingly designed affair that there are several points at which it steals the show. As a wall of flares flamed and the familiar lurching chord slash of Start Me Up heralded the concert's 8.30-sharp start, it was hard to make out who was doing what. Only Jagger, flouncing about like a distressed fowl in a frock coat at the front of the stage, stood out beneath the vast panoply of scaffolding, cantilevered walkways and corrugated Dayglo flats which comprise the Urban Jungle set.

Essentially this is a modification and a scaling down of the Steel Wheels techno-baroque fantasy. Mark Fisher's last design recreated a steel mill. This one is, according to Fisher's own eloquent assessment, "based on an industrial folly, a huge decaying building which might once have been a generating station, corroding in a fluorescent jungle of mutant foliage".

The relevance of this vision of a post-industrial apocalypse to songs as firmly rooted in the Stones' past as Ruby Tuesday, Tumbling Dice and Bitch wasn't immediately apparent. But by the time a couple of 60ft-tall inflatable dolls wobbled into view to illustrate the sleazy subject matter of Honky Tonk Women, it was getting dark. All over the scaffolding lights began to blink, then blaze. Jagger, already on his fourth of a dozen costume changes, somehow found his way onto a platform at the top of the 100ft-high stage structure to sing Sympathy for the Devil. The Urban Jungle idea was looking more and more like a vast illuminated adventure playground.

There were more visual gimmicks to come. Four inflatable dogs ballooned unexpectedly from in front of the speakers at the side of the stage during Street Fighting Man. An aerial firework display abruptly exploded around the ground after the inevitable final encore of Jumping Jack Flash.

But the real strength of the show lay less in these larky cosmetic devices than in the underlying sense of purpose and commitment to the musical performance. On their last European tour in 1982, the Stones played it fast and loose, like a scruffy bar band made good. They knew we knew the

One last burst of energy finds a headline that fits.

emed to feel that y adventurous done to these old send a crowd . The music to y contrast, is as nged as the stage

nes' regular key-, Chuck Leavell, fore Friday's con-2 tour was a lot of didn't have any-he determination aration that we

The inclusion of a horn section and three black backing vocalists are the most obvious signs that this time the Stones have been doing their homework. As a result, the songs which rely on more than slambam guitar routines — numbers such as You Can't Always Get What You Want and Harlem Shuffle — have had their subtle dynamics and hypnotic rhythmic sway miraculously restored. But the hired hands can only take part of the credit for this return to form. The

five Stones themselves are plainly trying harder than ever to live up to their distinguished name.

Even Ronnie Wood, a man who has often in the past exuded the genial redundancy of a gatecrasher at a party, made some decisive solo interventions. Keith Richards was quite audibly off the bourbon. And the Stones rhythm section of Bill Wyman and Charlie Watts never drifted, as they can do, into automatic pilot.

Most impressive and

surprising of all was the Stones' keenness to showcase new material. No group presently functioning has a bigger or better back catalogue to fall back on, yet nearly a quarter of this show's 26 numbers were new songs taken from the Steel Wheels album.

Jagger himself remarked on the eve of the Urban Jungle tour that "a rock show which goes on after two hours has got me itching to leave. My attention's bad at a rock show." Where stadium rock is con-

● *Mick Jagger and Ronnie Wood on stage in Rotterdam*

cerned, I couldn't agree more. And the greatest compliment I can pay this superbly presented package is to observe that two and a half hours in the open air has never passed so quickly

The Rolling Stones' Urban Jungle Tour plays Wembley Stadium, London July 4, 5, 6, 7, 13 and 14; Hampden Park, Glasgow July 9; Maine Road, Manchester July 20-21.

The file from Riga: will the Lithuanians tear up their declaration of independence?

Blitz's reward: "there's nothing like seeing your story in print."

two pages on which the story will be published. Michael Williams is unhappy about the balance of his news pages. They all seem to be about victims and he thinks he will juggle them in the morning. Now he is ensuring that a reporter is at work on the Soviet astronauts and a report on how they will be rescued.

James Blitz has just filed his report from his hotel in Riga. It was a difficult story to judge. The news from Moscow that the Lithuanian Prime Minister is to meet Gorbachev has worried him. Will the Lithuanians tear up their declaration of independence when they

Face to face: James Baker, the US Secretary of State, and Mikhail Gorbachev at pre-summit talks aimed at reducing nuclear weapons, in Moscow yesterday

Russia's military bridles as Lithuania flouts Gorbachev

by James Blitz
Riga

AS LITHUANIA ruled out abandoning its break from the Soviet Union yesterday, an ominous warning was sounded in its sister republic of Latvia that the drive for independence could lead to civil war.

Kazimiera Prunskiene, the Lithuanian prime minister, said she had refused to suspend the declaration of independence during talks with Mikhail Gorbachev.

It was yet another blow to the Soviet leader, who has

threatened further sanctions against Lithuania if it does not bow to his command. The situation could soon get critical, with energy supplies due to run out at any time.

Suddenly, however, Lithuania seemed the least of Gorbachev's problems. Far more alarming for the Soviet leader are the first signs of civil strife in neighbouring Latvia, where pro-Moscow demonstrators tried to storm the parliament building.

Latvia, which has a much

bigger Russian population than Lithuania, has moved more cautiously than its neighbour, but that did not stop one former army officer, Igor Lopatin, yesterday warning that the movement to secede must stop or be crushed. It was not an idle threat, and it is one that could plunge the rebel republic into civil war.

As leader of the Russians in Latvia, Lopatin commands massive support, and he warns that the republic could become the "Nagorno-Karabakh of the Baltics".

A third of the republic's population are Russian and in capital Riga, only 30% are

"the situation remains very serious. The demonstration which occurred on Tuesday may happen again. In Estonia, national guard units are already being formed to protect the nationalist government. This may be the beginning of civil war."

People in Riga are not as calm as the Lithuanians were last month. There is panic buying in Riga's main stores for fear that Gorbachev will impose an economic blockade on Latvia as he did on Lithuania.

At the Univer Mag department store, there was no pasta or meat on the normally well-stocked shelves. Sugar and salt were sold only when identity cards were shown to prove that customers were locals. "The panic is going to get serious. The food situation gets

country, and on Thursday he gave a rare interview to reporters at the Russian Federation Congress.

The effect was to suggest that Gorbachev was alarmed, quite apart from the fears he may have about whether the Communist party will split at the July congress.

Yet another headache is the possibility that Boris Yeltsin will be elected president of the Russian federation parliament in the next few days. It would be a huge blow to Gorbachev, giving Yeltsin a prominent platform from which to launch his assaults on the Soviet leader.

In addition, Gorbachev's economic reform programme, announced in March, has hit the rocks. Nikolai Ryzhkov, the prime minister, admitted as much last week when he meet tomorrow? "That would be a far bigger story than this. I think about driving down to Vilnius tomorrow but it's too risky. The city is closed to journalists and my taxi driver told me it was heavily covered by KBG men. But I must fly to Moscow tomorrow as I cannot possibly cover Vilnius from here. I get my tickets changed."

Swain in Manila has also telephoned his report from the Philippines after finding that the lines were so bad that he could not transmit direct from his computer. Now he has fallen asleep.

For Alex Butler it has not been as hard a Friday as usual – he even got the editor's leader at 6.30 and every column or feature for the News Review was down with the composing room by 11. "But they still struggle to get the section off. A shortage of compositors delays the pages and corrections take time getting through. Everything begins to drag. Meanwhile I press on with Saturday's paper and manage to get four pages down. It's not a great start but better than nothing."

The final spurt of activity of the day is in the composing room, where the pages are being pasted up ready for the press, supervised by Coxon and Taylor. One by one, whether for the News Review, Business, Arts or Scotland, the pages get subbed and headlined and are made up by the compositors, who are now not so busy working on *The Times*. Shortly after 2 am they are sent across to the presses, where they are also faxed to Scotland for the editions printed from Glasgow. The presses are still churning out the *Sun* and *The Times*.

One by one the staff have left, too; many will get only four hours sleep before they are back. Andrew Grice, deeply immersed in getting

the figures for the effects of Labour's tax policy accurate, thought of working through the night but decided to go home at 2 am – where he set his alarm for 6 am. Alex Butler finished at 2.35, when Bambridge, now back home in Surrey, is watching *Philadelphia Story* on the television with a whisky and a tuna sandwich. At 3 am only Tony Rennell, Roger Eglin, a few of his staff and Simon Taylor, the production editor, are still at work.

Suddenly there were no more changes they could make in the pursuit of perfection, even though Eglin wants to change a headline. The system has closed down for the night. Taylor goes to the canteen for a bacon sandwich and the rest go home. The presses churn out *The Times* and the *Sun* until 4 am. There is a brief rest. Then they switch to *The Sunday Times* – and the Review, Business, Arts and Appointments sections start printing. At Wapping over the weekend the presses never stop printing newspapers.

After reading every reporter's file, listening to the BBC, ITN, Sky News, reading the Press Association tapes and the early editions of the morning papers, Michael Williams is picking his way through the vans waiting to despatch *The Times* and the *Sun*. "I recall the 'God will provide' maxim of one of my former editors," he says. "I say a little prayer."

Even prayer may not help Jeff Randall, who left at 2.30. "As I crawl into bed at 3.20 my wife says: 'Randall. Let me see. I know the name but not the face.' I get the message."

James Blitz

Moscow correspondent. Aged 30. After graduating from St Andrews University with a first in modern history, Blitz read for a master's degree in Soviet Studies at St Antony's College, Oxford and then joined the BBC as a news trainee, where he became a producer. He then moved to the foreign desk of the *Financial Times* before joining *The Sunday Times* in January 1990. "The Soviet Union remains the most important story in the world," he says. "The political crunch is still to come. Will Gorbachev take this country on a giant leap towards the market? Or are the bureaucrats and the Communist Party bosses too powerful to let him?"

Michael Williams

Managing Editor, News. Aged 42. A graduate of Liverpool University, he worked for the *Liverpool Post*, *Birmingham Post* and *The Times* before joining *New Society*, where he became deputy editor. He was the first features editor of *Today* before joining *The Sunday Times* as deputy home news editor and then home news editor.

The Sunday Times Goes To War by Michael Williams

It's 4.30 am Sunday three weeks into the war. The foreign editor and I have been in the office for exactly 20 hours with barely a Scud in sight. The news, or rather lack of it, is amply conforming to the Murphy's law of Sunday newspapers: if it's news it won't happen on Saturday.

With only 50,000 copies left to run off the presses, Witherow and I debated whether to watch another hour of bored CNN reporters interviewing other bored CNN reporters on American breakfast TV, or to go home for some much needed sleep. But that wasn't accounting for Andrew Neil.

"Well," the editor said, rubbing his hands as he almost bounded into my office. "It's breakfast time in Baghdad. Saddam will just be getting up. Let's see what he's got in store for us."

It was Neil's irrepressibility that kept enthusiasm running high as week after week our colleagues on the dailies got all the action, and the gulf forces seemed to treat Sunday as a day of rest. Some reporters joked that Saddam was punishing Neil for his hawkish attitude before the war by making sure that the rival papers got all the scoops.

The pattern was set right at the beginning – exciting and frustrating alternately as we prayed for the big stories to fall into Sunday newspaper time.

Few really believed that war would break out that Thursday night as the UN deadline expired. After watching a confused edition of *Newsnight*, I prepared for bed firmly believing that Bush simply didn't have the guts, and that he'd hang on to the available compromises.

Then the telephone. Calls after 11.30 always have a particularly tense ring for news editors. It was Greg Hadfield, the deputy home editor and one of the sharpest-eyed newsmen on the paper. It had started, he said. What's more, it was running live on ITV.

It was now adrenalin time. Recalling a similar occasion, when a northern stringer rang to say he thought he'd heard on a local radio station that a jumbo jet had crashed on a Scottish town, I hit every number in turn.

John Witherow (foreign editor): "I've got the TV on, too."

Tony Bambridge (executive editor): "That's amazing."

The telephone of the defence correspondent, deep in his country retreat, gargled as only rural phones do. Eventually a sleepy James Adams answered.

"The war's broken out," I said.

"Don't believe it – you're joking." I held the phone against the television speaker as Peter Arnett ducked another hail of shells. "OK, I believe you – I'm on the flight to Washington in the morning."

Over in South Kensington Andrew Neil was on answerphone. Out at another high-powered function somewhere, I surmised. The reality, as I found out later, was touchingly different. Neil had taken a rare early night, switching off his bedside phone. But Gerry Malone, the Scottish editor and an old university friend who was staying overnight, had keen ears and heard the machine come on.

It was a night none of us would forget. But while daily paper staffs were throwing off pyjamas and speeding back to their offices we had to remain onlookers, knowing that it would be three days till we had our first bite at it.

We were well prepared, with some of the best reporters in place throughout the Middle East: Marie Colvin in Baghdad, Jon Swain and Richard Ellis in Saudi Arabia; Tony Allen-Mills in Jerusalem. We had a special war desk in Wapping, with cover round the clock, and even a special "war sub-editor", who had the knack of writing the best headlines in the office.

The Sunday Times had another special reason for wanting its coverage to be the best. Back in the summer, after the invasion of Kuwait, we had taken a tough line in predicting the likely consequences. "US ready to send 250,000 troops," we had written in a 72pt headline back on August 12. The following week, our splash said: "US on brink of war with Iraq."

Most of these early predictions turned out subsequently to be true. But at the time there was carping from other newspapers, who criticised us for being too gung-ho and too uncritical of the Americans. The sour note was most typically set by Matthew Symons, foreign editor of the *Independent*, who talked about copy that was "jauntily

FRIDAY 113

Neil visits the battlefield.

bellicose" and "hubristic bilge".

As it happened our first Sunday of the war was also the first day that threw up no real action news stories. The Americans and RAF bombers continued to pound Iraqi installations and the Israelis voted not to retaliate against Saddam's missile attacks.

At 3 am that night the office was fuller than I'd ever seen it. I counted six reporters, six sub-editors and several executives. Our pages were full of excellent colour and analysis. But where was the news?

At 4 am Ian Coxon, the production editor, rang me from the print works. Should we go for a special 6 am edition? "No," I remember saying glumly. "I don't think we've got any news."

By and large Saddam managed to dodge us for the next four weeks, and Norman Schwarzkopf, the American forces chief, didn't give us much help either. All the big landmarks of the war fell to our daily rivals.

The dailies got Saddam's first missile attack on Israel; the Iraqi "invasion" of Saudi Arabia and the ensuing battle of Khafji. They also got the other big stories: the parading of the captured RAF pilots on Iraqi television; Iraq's release of tonnes of crude oil into the Gulf waters; the Allies' recapture of the first piece of Iraq and the American hit on the civilian shelter in Baghdad in which more than 200 people died.

The other Sunday papers, luckily, fared substantially worse, and the quality of our "scoops of interpretation" from our two Washington men, James Adams and John Cassidy, allowed us regularly to give over two-thirds of our entire news coverage to the war.

But still we waited. After the first edition went to press on Saturday nights, Neil would take a group of his lieutenants to Orso's, a trendy Italian basement in Covent Garden, much loved by media people.

General Neil's table on a Saturday night, it was said, was the best place to be outside General Schwarzkopf's tent in Riyadh. The atmosphere was heightened by the fact that the West End was almost ghostly, deserted by Americans and suburban Londoners alike, fearful of a terrorist bomb.

At Orso's war strategy and editorial strategy fused as we dissected the other Sunday first editions over *spaghetti alla carbonara* and carafes of fizzy wine. Conversation was punctuated frequently by calls to Neil's mobile phone from the night editor back in the office, and with faxes, which sometimes arrived hotter and faster than the *fettucine*.

Eventually, section two of Murphy's law took control: you get a good Sunday newspaper story just at the moment when you have given up all hope of ever getting one. It happened in week six of the war.

Another frustrating day, I said to my wife as I read the headlines at 7 am, looking ahead to a 22-hour day in the office. It was becoming harder and harder as long Saturdays devastated weekends, with very little news in the paper to show for it.

"Threat of attack if Iraq does not begin to withdraw today," said the *Telegraph* that morning. "Dark stain on the sky foreshadows battle," said the *Independent*. Bush had given the Iraqis an ultimatum: that he would launch a land war unless Iraq withdrew from Kuwait within a week and stuck to UN resolutions, including the acceptance of UN economic sanctions and paying reparations for war damage.

Oh, that it were so clear! As I drove to the office through West End streets, wondrously clear of tourist buses and taxis, Brian Redhead on Radio 4 was busy pointing out that there was confusion about the midday deadline. Was it Washington time, London time or Riyadh time? Probably won't be in our time, I muttered to myself.

Matters were further complicated by the fact that Mikhail Gorbachev, beleaguered at home, seemed to have done a peace deal with Saddam that would be acceptable to the UN and give him some much needed world glory.

I parked the car thinking that Bush might have had the guts to start the bombing, but would he now dare to launch what was probably the biggest battle in history, with the Soviet Union and much of the Third World against him?

Whatever happened, it would all fall unhappily for our first edition, whose copy deadline was 5 pm and which went to the printer at six. If full-scale war did break out we would be unable to break it to our readers in the west country and Wales, whose papers would leave Wapping shortly after teatime.

Even with a big story in prospect, news editors always have to cover for the fact that it might never happen, and this is what preoccupied Witherow and me at our 9 am meeting that day. It is the editor's habit to ring from home at 10 am on Saturdays, and, even with the land war in prospect, I still needed a respectable standby menu to offer him for page 1.

I had some good home stories: Mrs Thatcher, we could reveal, was planning to stand down from her Finchley constituency as an MP; the former ICI chairman, Sir John Harvey-Jones, was to endorse the Labour Party; Sir Yehudi Menuhin was bitterly denouncing film maker Tony Palmer

for what he saw as a hostile biography. But it was clear that the Gulf had to dominate.

Here we had a couple of decent holding stories. Richard Ellis, in northern Saudi Arabia with the Desert Rats, had filed an excellent piece on how British troops were preparing for battle. And we had our war panel – a poll of 1,000 people, which had allowed us each week to take the temperature of public opinion. This week it had found that the public was almost unanimous in wanting Saddam to be brought to trial for war crimes.

But it wasn't enough for page 1. Witherow and I deferred judgement until breakfast time in Washington, when Adams and Cassidy would sniff around the State Department and the Pentagon.

By mid-morning Adams had a good line that the British 1st Armoured division would lead the assault into Kuwait, a story confirmed at midday by Neil, who had been told the same thing during a personal visit to Saudi earlier in the week. On the strength of this I asked the art department to start work on a map of the Gulf showing in detail how the invasion might happen.

This formed the rough shape of the paper at the lunchtime conference. Neil agreed that the Adams story would make a splash and took the graphic idea a stage further. "Why not," he said, "put the map across four columns on page 1 as an echo of the newspapers of the Second World War?"

I readily agreed to this as it would solve the problem of a lack of pictures if the land war did start, and would allow us quickly to update events through the night. There was further luck later in the afternoon: the Americans gave a briefing in Riyadh, saying that Saddam had let loose execution squads in Kuwait.

No matter whether this was Saddam's desperation or an over-enthusiastic American reading of tactics, one thing seemed sure: battle was about to commence. By teatime I was even happier as reports came in that American tanks had crossed the Iraqi border, allowing a splash headline: "American tanks smash into Iraq; Desert Rats to lead Kuwait attack." At 6 pm I passed the final news pages for press, secure in the knowledge that whatever happened later that night our farthest-flung readers would still get a taste of the action.

But by 8 pm I was fretting again and Neil was restless. There was no land war; no statement from Bush – merely some opaque

THE SUNDAY TIMES

Allies face long and bloody war; Bombing to last ten more days

America steps up B-52 blasting of Iraq's elite guards

Israel's military will not retaliat

Overwhelming support fo British role in attack on Ir

MORE EXOTIC...LE

THE SUNDAY TIMES

2AM: LAND WAR BEGINS
American tanks smash into Iraq; Desert Rats to lead Kuwait attack

Large number of Iraqi troops surrendering

Saddam lets loose execution squads

Which company would you buy your pension from?

Bayonets sharpened ready for final push

"Miracles of modern communications" – Gulf War front pages and one of the war's most evocative pictures.

discussions in the UN about the Gorbachev plan. It was a depressed group that trooped off to Orso's that night.

Still nothing at midnight. "Well," someone joked, "perhaps we'll be in at the ceasefire." We looked forward to another long, empty night, and discreet packs of cards started to appear on the subs' desk.

Then, shortly after 1 am, it happened.

"There's a flash on AP. The land war's started," shouted Vic Chapple, the night news editor. A seasoned hand who works for the *Sun* during the week, it was unlike Vic to get excited. But with 400,000 copies, a third of our circulation, to come off the presses, we had a real chance of making a mark.

Neil rang circulation to order a special 6 am war edition, which sales reps would take direct to newsagents in the London area, and *The Sunday Times* war machine glided effortlessly into action.

Neil and Witherow updated the stories; Ivan Fallon, the deputy editor, and I edited them and wrote the headlines.

Bush went on television to address the nation, and our reporter Tim Rayment had it down in shorthand and written up even

before the American news agencies. The newsdesk put a call through to the *News of the World* to discover, with some satisfaction, that all their senior executives had already gone home.

For the next three hours we updated edition after edition, with Britain still sleeping. As the last copy went to the printer at 5 am we had a front page devoted almost entirely to the story of that morning, under a heading in 72pt capitals: 2 AM: LAND WAR BEGINS. "Let the copy run," Neil had said. "Let the story tell itself." And so we did.

"A miracle of modern communications," I said to my wife, as I heard the newspaper that had almost raced me back from the office thump on to our doorstop at 7.30 am.

I had been home for barely 15 minutes. Here was the material representation of something which only hours before had been merely thoughts in the minds of military commanders in some far-off desert. Here it was: reported, analysed, printed, delivered and on our breakfast-table.

As I went to bed, listening to the dawn chorus, I wasn't sure that I couldn't hear gunfire somewhere in the far distance.

Saturday

"Thirty-one of the past thirty-six hours have been spent in the office. So why do I do it, with never a normal weekend, no Friday-night movies or Saturday dinner parties? My adrenalin gives me the answer – I'm addicted to it."

Today there are no tomorrows. Saturday is the climax of the week. As the first reporters and editors arrive shortly after 7 am, huge 20-ton lorries are rolling out of the plant to deliver seven sections of the paper to newsagents throughout Britain and the roar of the presses printing the sections that were put to bed five hours earlier can be heard all over Wapping. Although most of *The Sunday Times* is now printed or printing, nothing sets a newspaper's adrenalin rising so much as news. On Saturday *The Sunday Times* becomes a real, live newspaper throbbing with the tension and suppressed excitement that goes with reporting news as it happens against urgent deadlines.

It is also the most important day of the week. No matter how brilliant a paper's arts and book reviews, its articles on travel, style or business, its quality and character is defined by its selection and treatment of the news. What readers see first is the front page and the "splash", the report that the editor has decided is the most important of the week. The splash defines what the paper is about – and the front page is the paper's shop window.

A front page scoop, moreover, helps to sell the paper. It gets picked up on the television news bulletins and discussed on Sunday's early news bulletins. A scoop gets talked about and helps to sell extra copies. So does a big news story, though they are rare on a Saturday when neither the courts nor the Commons are sitting. Yet when there is a big Saturday news story Sunday papers sell many more copies. On the day after Hillsborough sales rose by more than 500,000.

On every other day of the week there is time to think and plan since there is no paper that night. Today the newsdesk acts like any other daily paper and must respond to the news, whatever it is, wherever it happens and even if it upsets all the well-laid plans made since Tuesday. Several stories that reporters have been working on since Tuesday will be killed in the next 16 hours.

After Rosemary Collins left at 2 am, the newsdesk was staffed throughout the night until she returned at 8 am. The night reporter has been busy. A 20-year-old English student, a woman, has been murdered in France, near the village of Moneteau, 80 miles southwest of Paris.

Staff photographer Bob Collier was rung at home at 5 am and told to set off for France immediately. After driving to the office to collect a wire machine so that he could transmit his pictures, he got to Heathrow by 7.20, only to be diverted to Blackbushe airport in Hampshire. Also rung at home, Michael Williams decided that a French stringer could be trusted to send back pictures from the murder. Aidan Sullivan has now decided he wants Collier to spend the day in search of Tracy Edwards and the *Maiden* crew.

It is already evident from the Reuter and Press Association news schedules that it is going to be a busy day.

Collins and John Witherow, the foreign news editor, are covered on all the major stories. James Blitz has flown back to Moscow from Vilnius this morning and is now covering both the Shevardnaze–Baker meeting and the stranded astronauts, with back-up from John Cassidy in New York, who is also filing on Mayor Dinkins. All the PA stories are also being covered by staff reporters. Now Witherow is reading reports filed overnight from the United States (on Marlon Brando), Tokyo and Taiwan before clearing them for the sub-editors.

After his muttered 2 am prayer for God to provide, Williams was up at 7 am, after three and a half hours sleep, and the Almighty had yet to respond. He was at the office by 8.30 and had to take the plunge and lay out some early news pages. "I chose to lead them on a row in the Tory party over the closure of the Ravenscraig steelworks and a story about the increase in professional beggars in London.

"I sound out the home, foreign and political editors on their agenda for the day. Now things are looking up. I like the story about enlightened companies trying to prevent their employees being workaholics (will the proprietor read it?). And the South African president is in London today to meet the Prime Minister, with a press conference nicely timed for 3 pm. When the editor rings from his car I am able to sound reassuring, even though I haven't a clue about what to lead page one with."

At 9.36 a report from the Press Association flashes on to Collins's screen:

The threat of further pollution on South Devon's beaches receded today as strong winds forced the oil slick floating off the coast out to sea. Devon County Council emergency planners said remnants of the slick were now ten miles offshore and heading south. Weather experts forecast that favourable winds would prevail throughout the day, raising hopes that the oil would disintegrate in choppy seas.

At her hotel in Brixham Margarette Driscoll, already disappointed this week after her Monte Carlo

Reuter World News Outlook at 7.30

Moscow: Baker confers with Shevardnaze in further attempt to clinch accord on long-range weapons.

Vilnius: Lithuanian parliament debates possible concessions in independence row with Moscow.

Moscow/New York: Possible developments on orbiting Soviet Mir station, whose two cosmonauts are reported to have been without reliable means of returning to earth since February.

Bucharest: Final preparations for Sunday's first free elections in Romania for more than 50 years.

New York: Mayor Dinkins appeals for calm after white youth accused of leading mob that killed black teenager is acquitted of murder in case that inflamed racial tensions.

Press Association schedule

The body of a 20-year old British student called Joanne Parish has been found in a river in France.

Mrs Thatcher is meeting President F. W. de Klerk at Chequers. He is expected to give her a detailed assessment of his reforms.

The campaign against British Steel's decision to close part of the Ravenscraig steel plant with the loss of 770 jobs gathers momentum with a meeting of industrialists, politicians and churchmen in Glasgow.

Butchers will be waiting anxiously to see the effect of the scare over "mad cow" disease on their weekend sales.

```
CATCH:ZOIL            VER:01        BY:PAWWC1;19/05,09:36      OPR:WIRE1 ;19/05,12:15
FG:                        EDN:       PG:           PDATE:                LBR:        MA:
MEMO:1 ENVIRONMENT OIL SUBSTITUTE                FR:WIRE1 ;19/05,12:18 STYL:
KEY:                                                HJ: 01              QUE:MACAR-STI
```

STORY FETCHED BY WIRE1 ON 19-MAY-90,12:10: NEW NAME IS ZPOIL-WIRE1-NWE
STORY FETCHED BY COLLIN ON 19-MAY-90,09:43: NEW NAME IS OILLEAD-NEWS-NWE

WINDS FORCE OIL SLICK OUT TO SEA
    By Mike Chilvers, Press Association
    The threat of further pollution on south Devon's beaches receded today as
strong winds forced the oil slick floating off the coast out to sea. [EM] caus
    Devon County Council emergency planners said remnants of the slick [EM] caus

          ...anker collided last Saturday [EM] were now 10 miles offshore

```
CATCH:ZPREST          VER:01                              ...throughout the
FG:                        EDN:       BY:PAWWC1;19/05,09:59   OPR:WIRE1 ;19/05,12:10
MEMO:1 AIR PRESTWICK       PG:            PDATE:               LBR:        MA:
KEY:                                      FR:WIRE1 ;19/05,12:18 STYL:
                                          HJ:157             QUE:MACAR-STI
```

SERVICES BOOST PLANNED FOR PRESTWICK AIRPORT
    By John Clark, Press Association
    A new airline plans to create an American-style hub airport at Prestwick on
Scotland's west coast.
    Emerald Air will link up with Icelandic Eagle Air to provide feeder
services to a number of British, Irish and European destinations in the hope of
attracting transatlantic services back to the airport.
    Several airlines have switched to Glasgow Airport following the
Government's decision to withdraw ... in Scotland.

```
CATCH:ZMAGUIRE        VER:01        BY:PAWWC1;19/05,10:39      OPR:WIRE1 ;19/05,12:11
FG:                        EDN:       PG:           PDATE:                LBR:        MA:
MEMO:1 INQUIRY GUILDFORD                          FR:WIRE1 ;19/05,12:18 STYL:
KEY:                                                HJ:940             QUE:MACAR-STI
```

(With pictures later)
BOMBS-CHARGE FAMILY ENTERS FINAL BATTLE TO CLEAR NAME
    By Grania Langdon-Down, Press Association
    The Maguire family, jailed in 1976 for allegedly running an IRA bomb
factory, are praying that Monday will mark the beginning of the end of their
long fight to prove their innocence.
    ... be listening closely as the first public hearing of the judicial
          ...begins in London.   ... two young sons, two relatives

```
CATCH:ZCOAL           VER:01        BY:PAWWC1;19/05,11:09      ... prosecution
FG:                        EDN:       PG:           PDATE:      OPR:WIRE1 ;19/05,12:15
MEMO:1 INDUSTRY MINERS SUBSTITUTE                 LBR:        MA:
KEY:                                 FR:WIRE1 ;19/05,12:18 STYL:
                                     HJ: 78             QUE:MACAR-STI
```

LABOUR TO QUESTION BRITISH COAL JOBS 'HIT LIST' CLAIMS
    By Amanda Brown, Press Association Energy Correspondent
    Labour will be demanding a Commons statement on Monday over the reports
that more than 10,000 miners jobs could be lost because of plans to clean up
power stations.
    The BBC says documents leaked to them reveal the jobs will be at risk
because the Government has broken a promise to install expensive flue-gas
desulphurisation clean-coal equipment at power stations.
    The EC is demanding major cuts in sulphur emissions to help combat the
acid rain problem.
    The plan ...

```
CATCH:ZSAVE           VER:01        BY:PAWWC1;19/05,11:47      OPR:WIRE1 ;19/05,12:15
FG:                        EDN:       PG:           PDATE:                LBR:        MA:
MEMO:1 ECONOMY SAVINGS                            FR:WIRE1 ;19/05,12:19 STYL:
KEY:                                                HJ:133             QUE:MACAR-STI
```

STORY FETCHED BY WIRE1 ON 19-MAY-90,11:55: NEW NAME IS PASAVE-WIRE1-NWE

(discloses in what? A report? Ask Keith pec)
EMBARGOED to 0030 Sunday May 20
WOMEN HANG ON TO THEIR CASH
    By Keith Manning, Press Association Married working women are emerging as
big savers, particularly since the introduction of independent taxation, it was
disclosed today.
    There was a ''very rapid response'' when independent taxation was
introduced in April, the latest monthly bulletin from National Savings reveals.
    A record #315.3 million was invested in NS Income Bonds in April, nearly
#54 million higher than the previous month, which was also a record figure.
    A further #6... ...to NS Investment Accounts, #13 million in
Capital B... ...e fourth issue of Index-linked

story failed to stand up, says she can feel the newsdesk's interest moving away from the story as fast as the oil is moving from the shore.

Aidan Sullivan is often a worried man on Saturdays, especially over the picture to offer the editor for the front page. This morning he is smiling. Staff photographer Jeremy Young managed to see de Klerk at 6.30 am and got himself an exclusive picture of the South African president looking over the Thames from his Chelsea Harbour hotel. Sullivan thinks he has solved the problem of the front page.

Collins is thinking that a Cabinet defence row or the Moscow arms talks could make the splash. Her other front page candidates are the French murder, the Soviet cosmonauts, Labour's income tax plans, and Aileen Ballantyne's story on a cure for breast cancer, which has now, after the death of Jill Ireland, become highly topical.

The editor has already been on the phone four times. He rang Collins to ask what was moving on the news front, then switched to Bob Tyrer to correct a mistake in his leader and to ask for changes in the design of the News Review front page (the pages are remade by the subs and "slipped" on the presses within 30 minutes). There was however a kickback for Alex Butler, who did not get home until 3.50 am. At 8.30 he was rung by Tyrer.

"He cannot understand the instructions regarding the setting of the standfirst," says Butler. "Wearily I tell him. Also there is a mistake in the leader. Some figures on Labour's tax plans are wrong. I groan. I had to make several changes in the leader last night. Was this my mistake? No chance of getting back to sleep. I had planned to get to the office around 1 pm but the thought of Andrew Neil jumping up and down makes me nervous. I head for the office and arrive at 11.30. A quick investigation and I am off the hook. I think the mistake was Andrew's but feel disinclined to ruin a promising career by telling him."

Ivan Fallon has also spotted mistakes in the overnight sections. Evelyn Rothschild had lost his knighthood, there are several misprints, and the wrong cat caught mad cow disease. The front page of the Business Section was being "replated" by 9.30. Neil, who has an encyclopaedic memory of what *The Sunday Times* has reported, had also made an angry call to Michael Williams. He has read in the morning papers that there are not going to be prosecutions after the Clapham rail disaster. Why therefore has *The Sunday Times* reported that there are? (A few months later Williams was vindicated when the driver of the train was gaoled.) The call to Williams is typical of Neil's restless style. On Saturdays, when he prepares for the day by an early morning visit to a gym, he is omnipresent, impatient, rarely satisfied, always prodding and pushing for better stories. Williams's predecessor, who moved on to edit a national daily, once confessed that he could feel the sweat in his armpits when he went into the editor's office on Saturdays.

Since big stories rarely break on Saturdays, Sunday papers as often as not lead the front page with a political story. That adds to the stress of the week for Michael Jones, David Hughes and Andrew Grice, the three political reporters. They worry all week, seeking leads and leaks that will give them a story that is new and exclusive by Saturday. Yet Sunday papers are as useful to politicians as they are to businessmen. A story leaked to Jones can set the political agenda for the next week. Sunday is another slow news day, so radio and television producers ransack the Sunday papers for subjects for the midday Sunday political programmes. Their interviews with leading Cabinet members or their Opposition rivals then make stories for the Monday papers. Aware of how the system works, Jones makes and gets a lot of calls on Saturday morning.

At 9.30 this morning he is dancing a jig of joy. He has just put down the phone on a call that he is certain has given him a story that will be the splash. He has been told that John Wakeham, the energy secretary, has been given special Cabinet responsibility for co-ordinating the government's information services. That means that Mrs Thatcher has bypassed two other obvious candidates, Sir Geoffrey Howe and Kenneth Baker. Jones begins to think that she is perhaps considering a 1991 general election. He starts to make more phone calls.

As production editors today, Simon Taylor, who left the office at 3.15 but was back by 9, and Ian Coxon are responsible for ensuring that the paper gets on to the presses by 6.30 tonight. Their job is to nag the subs to ensure that they keep the copy flowing so that the pages go down to the composing room in a steady flow. They are the pigs in the middle, cursed by the printers if the pages are late, cursed by the subs for harrying them when they fall behind. Their first job is to draw up the production schedule, setting out the times by which each of today's news pages should be designed, submitted to the subs, sent to the editor, "dumped" to the composing room and then completed for the presses. Today, for instance, page 4 must be designed by 11.15, copy sent to the subs by 12 noon, submitted to the editor by 1.30, passed to the composing room by 2 and "off-stone" by 4.15. The front page must be designed by 4.15 and off-stone (at least in theory) by 5.45. "Off-stone" is still a commonly used phrase, even though the stone, the iron desk where hot metal type was assembled by compositors in the days before electronic typesetting was introduced, is now an ordinary make-up table.

It is the job of Alex Butler to oversee the editing of the pages. As they are designed by Gordon Beckett, the design editor, each story is given a length as well as a style for the headline and the captions to pictures or graphics. Butler then assigns each story to a sub who edits it for sense, style, grammar and length and writes the headline. It goes then to the "revise" sub, who gives the story a final check, before it goes to the editor.

Saturday is also the day that Chris Nawrat, the Sports editor, goes to war. "It is the day when we have to run like an army in the field, no ifs, no buts, do it. The hierarchy from the editor to section heads to chief subs to reporters to subs has to be total. I wake up and rejoice. It is not raining. The thought of rain gives sports editors sleepless nights. Today we are covering every single cricket match and, obviously, have allowed space for all the scoreboards. If rain was to wash out all the day's play, I would have two blank pages. This week I don't, thank God.

After an early news conference chaired by Fallon, production of the news pages is in full swing by 11 am. The atmosphere is tense because of the pressure of deadlines but is relieved by endless wisecracks.

Peter Johnson, 61, sub-editor news and features, and writer on art market, *The Sunday Times*. Also freelances for art magazines; books on art, antiques, history. More than 40 years in journalism, 37 in Fleet Street. Track: *Evening Chronicle*, Manchester. *Daily Express*, London, from Beaverbrook days, parliamentary sub, picture editor, New York bureau, night editor. Long liaison with *The Sunday Times* began early 1970s. Wacky sidelines: curator, with wife Anne, of the Malcolm Forbes Museum of Military Miniatures, Tangier, Morocco; editor since 1975 of London-based the *Free Romanian* newspaper.

Peter Johnson

The badges of office of a newspaper sub-editor used to be the paste-pot, the scissors and the spike. A student of newsroom relations could reasonably argue that these oppressive objects probably did much to alienate "the subs" from their colleagues, the reporters, for whom they symbolised the various painful stages to professional obliteration. Now, after the overdue dawn of new technology, the sub-editors' ancient regalia have been consigned to the museum of journalism, and relations in the newsroom have perceptibly brightened. Both sides are united by the liberation of the VDU, which has not only sharpened writing skills but has improved the efficiency – and productivity – of the sub-editor.

The role of sub-editors, employed in large numbers on a national newspaper, is to prepare writers' copy for publication; they are the final link between the paper and its readers. Indeed direct input has handed the printer's mantle to the sub-editor, and when an edited story leaves him or her it should be "clean", free of literals, conveniently paragraphed and to the exact length required for the space allotted to it (electronic calculation has mercifully done away with the rule-of-thumb "casting off" methods by which stories were measured of old).

On the way to the final printing stage, a story may have received sub-editorial treatment ranging from a "ticking job" – leaving the copy largely as written, apart from simple corrections – to a complete rewrite. An adroit rewrite by a good sub-editor can transform a lacklustre story into a compelling read; equally important, however, it is a good sub-editor who knows when not to rewrite. Any sub worth the salt spends a good deal of the working day or night with his or her head in reference books or on the telephone to the office library, checking, checking, checking: spellings, names, dates, history, geography, quotations – scepticism rules and nothing is taken on trust in the quest for accuracy.

Headline-writing is fun, a sub-editor's privilege and pleasure. It represents a challenge to tell the gist of the story in a few pithy words. Some headlines require a humorous approach, but the skilful sub eschews the pun (unless it is a good one). Some headlines demand a direct approach, but this does not rule out colour and flair.

The calibre of its sub-editing staff can be judged by a newspaper's headlines; some of the most brilliant headline-writing is often to be found in the tabloids, exempting the antics of the shock-horror brigade. In the end the most effective head is the straightforward statement which tells the story and makes immediate impact. From a lifetime of headlines I commend one that was written for the front page of the *Daily Express* on the night of 22nd November, 1963. It said simply: KENNEDY ASSASSINATED. Although I was the author of the headline, I can claim little credit. It was a headline written by the news.

In the swamps of bad journalism an attempt is a bid, a surprise is a bombshell and a journey is a dash (preferably qualified by mercy, crisis, rescue or eleventh-hour); sheikhs are oil-rich, and scientists and businessmen are never less than top; hopes, airliners and poll-ratings plunge, prices rocket and circulation soars.

The reporters who perpetrate these clichés seldom talk the way they write ("The newsdesk called me in on my day-off, so I made a crisis dash to the office"). So cloying are these workaday expressions that they can lull a sub-editor into lowering his guard, unlike the more glaring clichés of shark-infested-Timor-Sea ilk. A good sub-editor constantly applies a simple test: would I say it like that? And, paradoxically, as he excises clichés he must firmly believe in one of the most common: rules are made to be broken. No one appreciated that more than Arthur Christiansen, the distinguished editor of the *Daily Express* in its heyday. "Clichés," he wrote in one of his famous daily bulletins to the staff, "should be avoided like the plague." The saying has a hallowed place in journalistic lore. A bad sub-editor, believing himself to be a good sub-editor, would have deleted the last three words of Chris's one-liner, thus impaling it on the spike of oblivion.

A chief sub's nightmares

by Liam McAuliffe, chief sub-editor (who succeeded Alex Butler when he left for *The Times*)

REAMS of complicated, over-length copy reaching the subs' desk seven minutes before deadline when you have sworn to the editor that the first edition will be off on time.

THE land offensive in the Gulf war being launched late on a Saturday night (as it was) when the only staff subs still standing had already worked 14 or 16 hours without a break. That is also, paradoxically, a Sunday paper chief sub's dream. The result was a *Sunday Times* triumph, and the subs were among the many who deserved a medal.

ILL-INFORMED "international" casual subs who arrive by recommendation for their first (and last) shift in a state of blissful ignorance: e.g. an Antipodean who thought the Isles of Scilly lay off Scotland, a South African without an inkling about the laws of contempt, and various American "copy-editors" conditioned not to change a word in reporters' copy are all real-life examples.

"DEAD" headlines (tedious, inactive, labelly) being written for a page due off-stone an hour before.

LAWYERS wanting to excise chunks of a story on the same page which is now one and a half hours late.

THE picture editor wanting to update the picture on the same page, which is now 2 hours late.

RUNNING out of cigarettes half an hour before the first edition.

TABLOIDESE creeping into a quality paper.

WRITERS/SUBS who have not read the house style book.

STORIES that "meet with" an angry chief sub "due to the fact that" they are "at this point in time" littered with Americanisms.

FINISHING a marathon shift five minutes after the pub has shut.

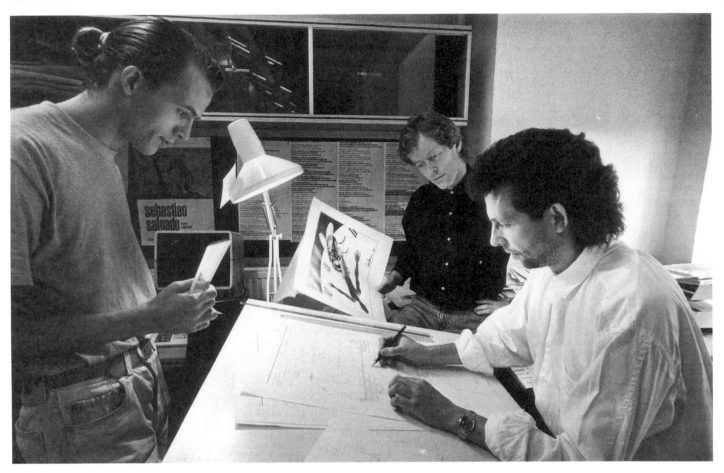

"Making it work": Beckett designs a page with Nolan and Dominic James (*left*).

"Make that story 70 centimetres," says the design editor.

"Why?" snaps Butler. "Do we want his life story?"

Williams, Witherow, Sullivan and Beckett are moving through the pages very quickly since all but five of the 17 pages have to be with the subs by 1 pm. So they select their stories, choose the pictures to go with them and design each page at a rate of one every 30 minutes. Williams constantly nags Collins for the stories she promises are ready – but reporters rarely understand deadlines and always want another ten minutes to ensure the story is perfect. Yet if every page is ten minutes late the paper would be an hour late on to the presses. That is why Coxon and Taylor nag Butler,

who nags Williams, who nags Collins, who nags the reporters.

As managing editor of News, Williams decides which story goes on each page and which is highlighted. He does the job by instinct but is always seeking to balance serious political reports with lighter human interest stories. It is a case of juggling people against policy and worthy-but-important against irrelevant but interesting.

For Beckett, working with Williams, the day is spent standing on his feet at a slanted desk, designing the pages with a pencil and ruler and "trying to beat the ads", as well as to make the pages presentable. With its big circulation and affluent readership, *The Sunday Times* is an advertiser's dream. So the news

Sizing pictures: Sullivan and Ray Wells, his deputy, check a page.

pages are full of big advertisements, often occupying two-thirds of a page at 38 cm by six columns on an eight column page. The advertising department loves them. They earn a lot of money and are considered prime positions. Yet they are so big that it is often difficult for Beckett to project the news around them.

Beckett is another pig in the middle. Sullivan wants to see his pictures printed big. Williams wants his story given length. With such big ads, Beckett has to suggest the compromises that satisfy both but also make the pages look good without ending up as lots of squares and rectangles. It is also important that the headlines don't clash. Since the pages will be changed at speed during the evening, he also has to en-sure that they can be taken to bits at midnight and reassembled without making too much extra work and delaying any changes made to stay abreast of late-breaking news.

Beckett describes his job as to understand what the section editors want and then to try to make it work, as well as to look appetising so that the reader is not even aware that a page has been "designed". News pages should look natural, he says. The aim is to give information as quickly as possible. Self-conscious design detracts from that although it can be more self-conscious for the Arts, Style and Travel sections, which are striving for different effects. So he starts with the news stories and pictures and gives them a physical form and tests that they will also fit whatever space is available on the page.

At 11.30 most of the news pages are prepared and Williams can start to prepare for the editor's 12.30 conference, where he will be severely grilled. Across the world, meanwhile, *Sunday Times* reporters are working to their afternoon deadlines. After a solid and often frustrating week's work, one has already been disappointed. When Jon Swain rang Witherow from Manila, he was told that his story wasn't running because of lack of space.

Aidan Sullivan is now assessing the state of his pictures. De Klerk is in the bag – but he is still hunting Tracy Edwards and her *Maiden* crew: Collier has not yet taken off from Blackbushe airport. He is awaiting news from a satellite link with the Whitbread race leaders. Sullivan is relying on Agence France Presse to cover the murder and a stringer in Gloucester is trying for family pictures of the murdered girl. He also has photographers at Simpson's in the Strand and McDonalds for the mad cow story and, with the arrival of another photographer from Paris, he has his pictures of the desecration of Jewish cemeteries in France. There are also good pictures from Moscow and of the Devon oil slick. All the news pages are covered – but he would still like to be able to offer the editor better pictures than he has so far got.

Over in the sports department Chris Nawrat has his own problems. This is not one of sport's great weeks. The soccer season is over and the World Cup is weeks away. He still does not know whether he will get pictures of the *Maiden*, so he may be forced to run cricket pictures on his first three pages,

which is not ideal. Scotland is playing Poland: if they lose he will use a picture from that match – but if they win it won't be a big enough news story. He has 18 reporters out in the field and their slots on the pages are allocated. Now he waits for the two hours from 4 until 6 when their reports arrive – and the six editions that will follow.

While John Karter, the racing correspondent, is on his way to Dublin for the Irish 2,000 Guineas, Sue Mott, tennis correspondent, is in Rome, where the day has dawned bright. Her first job is to finish a news story she has promised Nawrat on the closet payment of guarantees to players by the Association of Tennis Professionals, weaving in reports of the two men's semi-finals in the Italian Open as they happened. At 10.30 she has just sent 500 words back to Wapping via her Tandy – but now Nawrat has lost a picture he was planning to use and wants another 700 words to fill the gap. She sits in her hotel room and settles to write still more words.

Phil Green, the graphics editor, is overwhelmed. Not only is he doing four graphics to illustrate the Focus on the M1 air crash, he now has to do a graphic of the stranded Soviet astronauts. He worked until 2.45 this morning but he is still behind. "When journalists start late, I get the information late," he says. "Eventually I sat down with the *Daily Telegraph* to find the information I needed so that I could get started." He has four hours to draw the Soyuz graphic – but still has no information to work on.

Sitting a few desks away is Nick Newman, who draws the pocket cartoon. Today Newman, who also draws for *Private Eye*, *The Spectator* and the *Independent Magazine*, is working on mad cow disease, the

"When journalists start late": Phil Green tries to catch up. *Below,* the finished result four hours later.

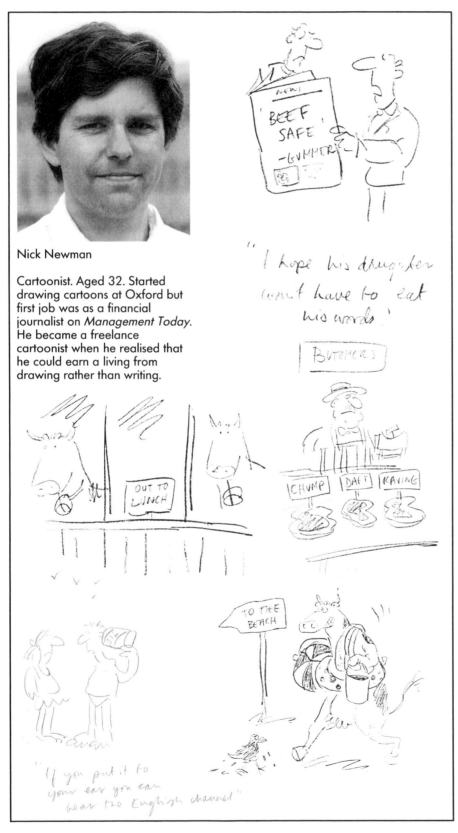

Nick Newman

Cartoonist. Aged 32. Started drawing cartoons at Oxford but first job was as a financial journalist on *Management Today*. He became a freelance cartoonist when he realised that he could earn a living from drawing rather than writing.

Devon oil slick and the cosmonauts. The ideas come quickly and he has already done ten cartoons. He makes the job of cartooning look easy, but his is an art that few possess – the ability to create gags out of the news that make the reader chortle or smile, and to do it day after day.

Tony Bambridge has been in the office since 9.30, has designed the front page index billing the contents of the paper, and is now sitting with Williams, acting as his mentor. After more than a decade in senior editorial positions on the paper, Bambridge, always snappily dressed and sporting a hat, is a *Sunday Times* character, a professional with a powerful and influential role in the making of the paper. His moods swing between elation at a well-written story to despair at the folly of young journalists. Now in his fifties, he has learnt stoicism about the quixotic decisions of editors. Among his colleagues, he is renowned for his spontaneous wisecracks about journalism.

When told he works too hard: "I have the interests of *The Sunday Times* at heart – not the sanctity of my own life."

On a Wednesday: "You know the trouble with this place? We have too long to produce a newspaper. If we did it every day, we wouldn't have to go through all this pantomime."

On a front-page headline: "What are we going to do when World War 3 breaks out?"

To a cartoonist: "I'm not here to draw them – just to criticise them."

To recalcitrant reporters: "Look, I have a simple view of journalism. If the editor says do it, do it."

Does a story work? "Give it the So-What test."

"The cock-up quotient in newspapers is enormous."

"Don't let anybody tell you the meek will inherit the earth."

"One of my main jobs today is to offer advice and support to Williams if he's worried about a story and also to make sure that copy is flowing to time," he says. "The paper is now so big that we cannot afford to fall behind schedule. We must be off by 6 pm and there must be no bunching of pages at the end. Each page has to be faxed to all the other printing centres. That takes time and bunching means a late start-up time.

"Equally if we're off late the presses may never catch up, which means deliveries may be missed – the first crime in all newspaper production. Everyone forgets that the actual words come only third in the list of newspaper priorities. First you must get the paper to the reader. No matter how brilliant it is, if he can't buy it you might just as well not have bothered. Second it must look good. If it doesn't look inviting, nobody will read the brilliant words. Third comes the words. Anyway it is always essential to be on time – because if anything goes wrong and we run late, the blame for everything will fall on us."

This morning Bambridge is working on the Insight story about the Third World tobacco scandal. He is not happy and is sitting in front of his screen brooding on how to improve it. "This is a bugger's muddle," he murmurs. "The story is all over the place. They have also taken the wrong angle." He goes back to the source material and the figures, rewrites the first third of the story and re-orders the rest before he is satisfied. "What matters is the last 5 per cent. What distinguishes good journalism is the last 5 per cent of effort to get a story absolutely right."

This was the result. As offered by Insight, the report said:

Thousands of tonnes of high tar tobacco are to be shipped to the Third World under a European Community scheme which is costing British taxpayers more than £100 million a year. New health regulations on the sale of strong cigarettes in Europe, agreed in Brussels last week, are expected to double the existing mountain of unwanted tobacco. Cigarette companies and dealers are to be allowed to profit from the surplus by selling it at knockdown prices in Africa. The move, which is expected to cost millions more in subsidies, has been condemned by the World Health Organisation, which said it would add to the growth of smoking-related diseases in poorer countries.

After Bambridge has finished, it reads:

Thousands of tonnes of high-tar tobacco are being shipped to the Third World under a European Community scheme that is costing British taxpayers more than £100 million a year in subsidies, and the community as a whole £740 million. The trade, which has been condemned by the World Health Organisation, is expected to increase sharply in the next few years following the ratification in Brussels last Thursday of a ruling to limit the tar content in cigarettes sold within the community. The ruling states that from December 31, 1992 no EC cigarette may contain more than 15 mtg of tar. Tobacco grown in Greece and Italy (the main EC producers) has a high tar content, and sales are falling fast as the West becomes more health conscious.

At noon the editor has arrived at the office – and the tension in the newsroom has risen perceptibly. Michael Williams is discussing the political prospects with Michael Jones and David Hughes so that he is armed for the 12.30 news conference with Neil. After a morning of calls Jones is now convinced he has a splash. He has learned – and wild horses would not drag his sources from him – that Thatcher is herself going to write the next election manifesto and that Britain will now put sterling into full membership of the European Exchange Rate Mechanism by November. That ought to take three percentage points off the interest rates (then 15 per cent) and push inflation below 5 per cent by summer 1991. That, plus the appointment of Wakeham, amounts to what he describes as the Tories' golden scenario. He presents it to Williams as "Maggie's secret masterplan".

Will the picture of the *Maiden* crew arrive in time for the first edition? It is beginning to look doubtful. Collier has arrived at Blackbushe airport and has been negotiating a charter flight with colleagues from thr *Observer*, *Sunday Express* and *Sunday Telegraph*. According to the latest satellite information, the *Maiden* is 300 miles off Cork. A Beech 200 executive jet has been chartered and the four photographers took off at 12.30 for Cardiff.

Editorial conference, 12.30.
Neil is not happy with the early news pages. Why is the story he wanted on industrial white elephants not in the paper? Why is the Bootle by-election being reported in the first edition, which doesn't go to Merseyside? "We can't design the paper solely for our Liverpool readers." Why is a picture of Neil Kinnock being used to illustrate the Labour tax plans story? "We all know what Kinnock looks like." Is the report on the oil slick being hyped? "We should be writing for our readers not for Friends of the Earth. Where is the evidence that any damage has been done? It may be that there has been a lucky escape but we are running a piece that looks for every bit of the worst evidence. That's not ethical journalism. The story is full of could-bes."

Then he turns again to page 4, the page devoted to Labour. Why has the most interesting item on the page, the table showing the effects of Labour's new tax policies, been buried at the bottom of the page with the big picture of Kinnock at

the top? "Put the table at the top please." He also points out that almost every page has a political lead story. "I don't want an endless diet of politics. I'm not having it. I'm sorry."

Now he turns to the stories offered for the front page. Williams ticks them off – the Tory golden scenario, Lockerbie, the tobacco scandal, de Klerk meets Thatcher, Baker meets Shevardnaze, Lithuania, the "cure" for breast cancer, Labour's tax plans, the murder in France, the stranded Soviet astronauts. Neil doesn't want to lead on the appointment of Wakeham and is more tempted by the tobacco scandal as the splash – but that decision can wait.

After the conference he is happier. "There is always huge pressure to put too much politics in the paper," he says, "but the Review section is chock-a-block with politics." He realises that Jones will be upset that he has decided against leading on Wakeham – "but that's a *Times* story. What will interest *Sunday Times* readers most is the scandal of taxpayers' money being used to sell high-tar cigarettes to the Third World, the Lockerbie bomber and the effect of Labour's tax plans." Some of the inside pages were boring. He had been forced to get life into them.

It is now 1 pm and the new decisions mean still more work for Williams, Beckett and Butler. Pages that were already finished have to be unscrambled and started again. That puts more pressure on Butler and his team. He has 14 subs working on shifts that begin at 9 am and end at 2 am, with another three "stone" subs working in the composing room where the pages are made up. At the start of the day he had 20 pages to finish for the first edition. Now he is way behind and every department is saying that the next story will be late. After Neil's new decisions, stories have moved between pages and have to be re-subbed to the new length. Suddenly that 20 pages has become 26. "Are we unhappy?" says Butler. He smiles ruefully and gets on with it.

On the foreign desk Witherow now has an hour to make his final dispositions. The drama in space is being covered by staff reporters in London, foreign news agencies and Blitz in Moscow, so that will not be his concern. There has been a train crash in Georgia with at least 11 dead. That too is left to the agencies. What he is most concerned about is the story from New York that serious racial violence is now likely. He decides to dump another story to get in the report from John Cassidy.

Around the backbench, where the managing editor of the news section decides which stories get used, the atmosphere is tense as the week enters its final four hours. Yet the only way to get the job done is to stay calm. Shouting and tantrums don't help at this stage. There is a final deadline for the first edition, a lot of work still to do – but it always gets done, especially if everybody conceals the inner hysteria.

Snap decisions are being made quickly all the time. Is the footballer Garth Crooks well enough known to allow the use of his name in a headline? Answer: No. So he becomes a "soccer star". Does *The Sunday Times* use "bosses" as a headline word – or is that too tabloid? Bambridge, now on the backbench, shouts for the Labour Party stories. They will be another ten minutes, says Williams. Bambridge shakes his head wearily. The editor asks to see the layout of the Whitbread race page. Then he insists on changes to make the pic-

tures stronger. Another extra page for Butler to sub.

Senior reporter Tim Rayment sits surrounded by yellowing cuttings as, assisted by Caroline Lees and two researchers, he tries to assemble the Soyuz story. One is studying previous space disasters, another is ringing space experts and another is speaking to the family of Britain's first astronaut. That is another worry for Butler. "He's writing 95 cm. A wonderful writer but notoriously slow," he mutters. James Blitz will be filing from Moscow, John Cassidy from New York. Using all their words, Rayment has to write a thousand words within the next three hours.

At 2.15 Williams is designing page 3. He leads on the story of the killing of 30,000 seal pups, which gives him two strong pictures to hold the page. He also wants to use a report about a five-year-old boy who is suing Marietta Higgs, the doctor at the centre of the Cleveland child abuse controversy; a report of a row over remarks made by Prince Philip about Ulster; and a turn from page 1 of the tobacco scandal. Beckett draws the page. Williams doesn't like it – the top looks too weak. Beckett draws it again. Williams is happy.

At 2.25 the backbench team think the editor has gone crazy. He is still not happy with the news pages and has demanded that another three should be changed. He wants page 9 re-schemed, the story on the oil slick moved from page 11 to page 2, and the story on classic cars moved from page 10 to page 11. The Scottish story he has been trying to get going all week – on Malcolm Rifkind and the aftermath of the Ravenscraig decision – is to go on page 10. At 2.35 only four pages have been finished and Butler is still waiting for the layouts for six

Sullivan and Williams plan the pages.

pages. That means that 16 have to go to press in the next three hours. The tension is mounting.

Meanwhile, as Simon Taylor warns Butler that he will have to "crash" the pages through, Williams has been reading the first report from Ian Glover-James, who has joined the paper as diplomatic correspondent from ITN, where he was Moscow correspondent. He is impressed and decides that it has to be placed on page 2. Another story will have to be ditched.

For Glover-James it has been his first week in a newspaper office since he left the *Daily Telegraph* for ITN five years ago. It is a very different experience, he says. "Two words sum it up: calm and concentration. Calm, because the newsroom environment at *The Sunday Times* is quiet. There are no booming television monitors. No one shouts. Nobody runs. And concentration, the opportunity to concentrate 100 per cent on being a journalist is a new experience after the multi-disciplines and demands of television.

"My unfamiliarity is partly due to the substantial changes that have taken place since the mid-1980s. Computers were then only just being talked of. It was a world of hammering typewriter keys, desks strewn with messy carbon papers and the faint aroma of hot metal setting down below. At the *Daily Telegraph* I spent most of my time abroad, filing from Africa and the Middle East by telex, typing my copy on a long-suffering typewriter I bought in Beirut.

"Most of my years as a television correspondent with ITN were also spent abroad, in Poland, the Soviet Union and Berlin. But even on the road a television reporter never manages to spend more than a percentage of his time working as a journalist. The rest is spent on logistics, planning, administration and accountancy. Running a television news bureau is a demanding, seven-days-a-week business. Reporting the news is merely the most enjoyable part.

"Television teaches you strict self-discipline. Each task you perform, each activity is worth only so much time. Anything more is wasteful, eroding time better spent elsewhere, eating into news budgets, wearing the stamina of colleagues who may not share a journalist's enthusiasm for a story.

"Getting back to thinking and writing like a newspaperman takes time. At first it seems you have all the time in the world, with merely the pleasure of reading and writing to fill it. The effort of concentration comes as a shock. Television develops a short, fast-moving attention span, with a premium on thinking out several problems at once and making it all appear effortless.

"Entering the new computer age of newspapers with these skills, and a memory of what went on in Fleet Street before that, I feel like a man returning home from a long exile. As I have spent the last three years living abroad, the effect is enhanced. Some things seem familiar, but often they are not. It is not an unwelcome experience. I would not have elected to make the change had I not profoundly missed the experience of writing for a serious newspaper."

Ian Glover-James sifts through pictures with photographer Jeremy Young.

Meanwhile for Sullivan the nagging question is whether there will be a picture of the *Maiden* crew in time for the first edition. It seems now that Williams and Nawrat are going to have to work without it. Collier cleared customs at Cardiff within 45 minutes and is now at

A moment of tension for Williams and Sullivan: will the front page work?

Cork, where the pilot is refuelling – but the first edition goes at six and he will not be back in England now until at least eight.

Whatever the nagging from Coxon and Taylor, Alex Butler knows for certain now that the subs have no chance of hitting the first edition deadline. At 2.20 he had still not received the finished layouts for six pages. Now he has eight pages with no copy. At least, however, the holes in the rest of the paper are being filled and he is climbing back.

At 3 pm there is another conference with the editor. Neil reads the headlines sent round every hour by the newsdesk and culled from radio, Reuter and PA. David Owen has said that the European Com-

munity should lift sanctions against South Africa. "We must get that in." Lithuania has announced that it will not make a declaration of independence. "Let's make sure that is reflected in the headline." Bill Keys, a former leader of the print union Sogat which caused so much grief to *The Sunday Times* is dead – a news in brief item. He asks for the latest news on the French murder, Lithuania, the Moscow arms talks and a speech by Michael Heseltine.

Then he starts to make the final decisions on the front page. He wants to lead on the Lockerbie story but is warned that it may not be as strong as was earlier suggested: there is no evidence of links at government level between Bri-

On the "stone": the front page is pasted up – but will it be off on time?

tain and Germany. The second-best story is the Tories' golden scenario and Neil wants the story on Labour tax plans published as a "box" within it. Then he wants the tobacco scandal, the breast cancer cure and the Moscow arms talks. The French murder is for page 2, "with a strong picture", as is the de Klerk–Thatcher meeting. There is still a choice to be made for page 1 between Lockerbie and the golden scenario.

He asks to read the two stories, and decides at 4 pm that the doubts about the Lockerbie report were justified. "There is no evidence that the German authorities did a secret deal. It's the sort of story the *Observer* would lead on, but we won't. Let's splash on politics." But what will the headline say? Neil broods. Then it comes. "Tories plot golden scenario for next election."

Now the decision on the front page picture has to be made by Neil. Sullivan presents de Klerk, already pasted on a page across eight columns to impress the editor. It's a good picture, says Neil, but is de Klerk, unknown in Britain, worth eight columns? The answer is No but he agrees that it is the best subject.

Neil is now content. He is breaking a strong news story with the splash, intriguing readers on income tax, outraging them over the tobacco scandal, and interesting women readers with the story about breast cancer. The balance looks good, he decides.

At 4 pm, Bob Collier still has not got his picture of the *Maiden* crew. After refuelling at Cork at 3 pm, he is over the Atlantic and within half an hour of the yacht, but there are clouds at 700 feet. After all this effort, it may be difficult to get the picture.

In Moscow, however, Blitz is working at full pelt. He has been waiting in the Moscow Press Centre for an hour – and worrying about whether anything is happening in Lithuania. James Baker has suddenly appeared and announced a big breakthrough in the arms talks. Blitz has rushed back to the office, called John Witherow, and been told to file immediately off the top of his head. Now he is having to deal with an irritated copytaker, who says he is being too slow. "Come on, mate, we've got tons of sports reports to do now." By 7 pm Moscow time the story is over to London and his week is nearly over. He watches the news two hours later, notes an item about a new Monarchist Party which could make a good subject next week, and goes home. His week is over.

Well away from Wapping, where the tension is now palpable, two writers are thoroughly enjoying themselves. With both his articles filed, Iain Johnstone in Cannes has been watching Gerard Depardieu in *Cyrano de Bergerac*. "So nice to relax and enjoy a film without reviewing it." Now he is at the Cannes English bookshop signing his novel. So far 40 copies have been sold.

On a gloriously sunny day in Cornwall Adam Nicolson, who writes for the Travel section, is walking round the Lizard Peninsula from Mullion Cove to Cadgwith for the Walk of the Month article he is due to deliver on Monday. The coast is swathed in banks of seaside flowers, the sea when the sun shines on it is a Caribbean blue. Never before, he wrote on his return, had he finished a day's walking with such a strong feeling that he would remember it for the rest of his life. It felt like a day made perfect.

"The simple creamy-white flowers of the Burnet Rose emerge singly, low among the heather. The thrift blankets acres of the clifftop pasture, the flowers of neighbouring tufts varying from almost white to rose-pink and raspberry, some near-purple. In places bluebells and white sea-campions pattern the ground like wallpaper and you can lie down among them on the woolly turf and find yourself surrounded by nothing but sky and flowers. This is the western side of the Lizard: flowery sweetness at your feet, blank flat landscape if you raise your eyes to the horizon, and the swilling of the sea, choking and gurgling below in the caves, the breakers cracking on the little beaches."

Three hundred miles away, where he cannot even see the sun or the sky, and no birds sing, Chris Nawrat, with a pocket television on his desk and the office television above him, is watching sport on two channels so that he stays abreast of the news. There is one setback. It is raining in Italy, which has wiped out his main tennis and golf reports. He is filling the suddenly empty spaces with news features written by Sue Mott, tennis correspondent, and John Hopkins, golf correspondent. Shivering in her shorts in Rome, Mott writes 700 words, a mix of politics and preview, to fill the space until the matches can start.

Soccer correspondent Brian Glanville is approaching the climax of his week at Wembley where he is reporting the FA Trophy cup final between Leek and Barrow. The telephone he had ordered was ready and he is due to write 850 words. "I was completely unacquainted with either team," he says. "But I managed to find out before the match at least the formation in which Leek would play. This is essential because at *The Sunday Times* we always set out both sides in the actual formation they adopt.

"But it is still a great problem to have to puzzle out the formation of either team, as I had to do today with Barrow, while the match is actually on. This prevents one putting the teams over before the game begins, which is the ideal situation. This was a 'runner' and I'm used to doing them. The method I adopt is unique. What I have is a chart consisting of a number of lines, each of 40 crosses. Every cross represents a word and is marked off as I dictate it into the telephone. The advantage is that I can keep watching the game and only have to make notes very briefly of what happens and do not perpetually have to get my head down writing the piece.

"Unfortunately you always seem to be cursed by goals being scored while you're on the telephone and cannot give them your full attention. Things happen so incredibly quickly in football that you have to make the most rigorous checks with colleagues, who usually help you out but occasionally give you a bum steer."

Today Glanville had virtually finished his report when the final whistle went and simply had to add the first three paragraphs.

Across London at Lord's, cricket correspondent Robin Marlar, a former Sussex captain and now a successful businessman, is reporting on the match between Middlesex and New Zealand.

As Marlar enjoys the cricket at Lord's, the night editor, Tony

Robin Marlar

For a specialist reporter on a Sunday newspaper Saturday is the working day, the day players make something happen in front of you, sometimes dramatic, sometimes banal, and you must find the words to describe and criticise.

You find them fast, these words. The space must be filled, and at cricket matches the first full-length account must be on the sub-editor's desk back at base by four o'clock or 4.30 at the very latest. Otherwise the ultimate crime is committed, a missed edition.

Except when the weather turns nasty, stumps are not drawn until 6.30 and since cricket has developed its own forms of go-slow, the powers have insisted that an allocation of overs per day must be completed. This means that overtime is almost always worked. Indeed Cup matches, whether 55 or 60 overs each side, have been known to continue into the gloaming and that can mean a scramble to get the result into the final edition, for which copy has to hit the desk by 8 pm. The chief cricket writer always has to write two complete stories at every major occasion, test matches, one-day internationals and cup finals, which can occupy as many as 12 of the 20 Saturdays of the average cricket season.

If the emphasis of play in a county match or a game involving the Tourists changes substantially, then rewrites are necessary. What with additional paragraphs for the in-between editions, usually two in number, I can expect to file between 2,000 and 3,000 words. For most of my 36 years in *The Sunday Times*, 20 as a cricket correspondent, it's been a case of rushing to a telephone wherever you can organise or find one to communicate and then rushing back to find out what's happened while you've been away.

Only recently has it been fashionable to have telephones installed on the desk. Some competitors have had telephonists: with my handwriting that would have been impossible! Most of the letters that hurt are those

complaining that the reader's particular edition did not have the final score.

All this may sound like a dog's life, full of pressure upon hardship, none of it appreciated. On the contrary it's been a wonderful experience, a weekly shot of adrenalin for an ever-ageing cricketer who has been able to travel the world and everywhere meets a host of friends. And to get paid for it! At one stage, such is the integrity of *The Sunday Times*, this included an 11-month period when there was an expenses-paid Australian visit during which not a word was published.

This Saturday was, at it turned out, a relatively quiet day, but an interesting one in that it highlighted a major point of principle, involving the relationship between the correspondent in the field and the sports editor. Time was when the cricket correspondent submitted a schedule at the start of the season to cover all the county teams – but with four Sundays competing at the top end of the newspaper market a more flexible approach has become necessary.

With soccer and rugby in a lull, on this Saturday a cricket report had to lead the front page of the Sports section and the Sports editor and I agreed at the start of the week that Middlesex against New Zealand at Lord's was the match to cover. This was the first day and Desmond Haynes, Middlesex's famous West Indian opening batsman, hit a huge century, almost a double, and belted the New Zealanders all over Lord's.

However there was an off-the-field occurrence of major importance for the England team. At that time they were chronically short of class players, not only because they were thin on the ground, but also because all the reserves had recently disqualified themselves from international cricket by playing in South Africa.

Gus Fraser of Middlesex was one of the successes of England's recently completed West Indian tour and he had been selected on the previous day as a key member of the England bowling attack for the one-day series against New Zealand. He had pulled a rib muscle in the West Indies and the selectors had gambled with him after just one county match earlier that week. On this morning he felt some reaction in an area of the body notoriously hard of healing and had pulled out of the Middlesex team. This news, and comment upon it, made an ideal subject for the first edition. In my judgement the news was so much more significant than the run of play that it could remain the lead throughout the day. So it did in most of the tabloids.

However, as the paper of record there was an argument for featuring Haynes's innings in *The Sunday Times* as the event of the day.

In the final edition my order of paragraphs was changed and a new introduction written on the sports desk. Some correspondents, particularly the peppery gentlemen in Fleet Street when I started, would have blown their top at this interference. However, one of my mentors when I started in journalism dinned into my head that "never complain, never explain" was the best policy for a journalist who wanted a long life.

Over the years, during which I have had the astonishing good fortune to have four, and only four, sports editors, all different but all outstanding and interesting to work with, my copy has been so often improved and, incidentally, saved from silly factual errors that I have had more reason to be grateful than to explode. I had no problem with this editorial judgement and its transposition. It was a close decision and when in doubt it's the desk, like the batsman, who always get the benefit of the doubt.

Allaway, who will work until 2.30 tomorrow morning, has arrived at the office. Allaway, who works during the week on *The Times*, is used to making quick changes to pages to keep up with the news as it breaks. Since he has no vested interest in what is used or discarded, Neil values his criticism of the news pages and his comments on the newsdesk's sacred cows. He also brings the practised skills of a daily paper, often absent from a once-a-week Sunday paper. Allaway handles all the editions after the first and acts for the editor when he has left the office. He starts by reading all the pages prepared for the first edition and then preparing the Irish edition, which goes to press only 30 minutes after the first.

Collier knows now that he is not going to find the *Maiden* but he has sighted *Steinlager 2*, the leader, below him. That will have to be today's picture. He is flying at 120 miles per hour, at 350 feet, with the boat only 300 metres away, and using a 200 mm lens. Now is when his skill really shows. The plane is jolting, there are three other photographers with him who also want the picture, and it has to be shot square through one window made of double perspex. He has got two minutes and the sweat is pouring off him. He gets through five rolls of film and thinks that he has got four or five shots that were bang on target. It's too bad if he hasn't – the plane has already turned back for Cork.

John Karter, the racing correspondent, is also sweating. He is covering the Irish 2,000 Guineas at The Curragh, 20 miles outside Dublin, and this is only his third Saturday in the job. On his first Saturday his Tandy had failed to work when he was covering the 2,000 Guineas at Newmarket, but today he is sure that he is fully prepared. Since the press room at The Curragh is hardly bigger than a dog-kennel, according to Karter, and he has been told not even to try to use a Tandy, he has hired a portable phone. Several test calls have worked perfectly.

"With the race finishing at about 4 pm, I was inevitably going to be under extreme pressure to get 850 words ready for dictation by 4.30. That was the easy part, however. No prizes for guessing what happened when I was actually ready to file my story. About a dozen times I got through to the copytakers on the portable phone. Each time after taking my name and catchline, the phone cut off. I tried using it inside and outside the building and in sev-

Collier: now is when his skill really shows.

eral different areas in case it made a difference to the transmission but the result was the same.

"By this time it was about 5 pm and I was going crazy. The two communal phones were still being used by Irish journalists with a queue waiting for them to finish. The secretary's office couldn't help. Eventually at about 5.05 I managed to grab a phone from another English journalist – the only one with his own line – and tried to dictate at a million miles an hour. I finished at about 5.20, some 50 minutes later than my deadline. Dismissal was a formality, I felt. Perhaps it would be better to resign and spare myself the indignity."

(That was not the end of Karter's troubles that day. When he arrived at the airport, the flight had closed and he had to persuade British Airways to let him on. "I raced through the departure lounge faster than the Guineas winner and collapsed exhausted in my seat. The final irony was that my last call on the portable phone – to check with the sportsdesk for any problems in my copy – went through like a dream. Next time I'll use a carrier pigeon.")

On the backbench in London it is 5 pm and the final deadline for the first edition is only 45 minutes away. The layout for the front page was due at 4.15. It is still being drawn. Michael Jones is still writing the splash, which should have been ready at 4.30. He finishes most of it at 5.10 and it is sent to Ivan Fallon to be read. "It is the most important story in the paper and I can look at it reasonably objectively," he says.

Voices are raised as the tension reaches a climax and the urgency of Saturday becomes genuinely urgent. Simon Taylor already knows that the last three pages will be late. Tony Bambridge is starting to write the front page headlines, the first that the reader sees and which may make the casual reader spend 60p to buy the paper.

On the Lockerbie story he has four lines to write, each with a maximum of 13 letters. If what he writes doesn't fit, the screen flashes a warning.

He tries:

> Germans talk
> to Lockerbie
> bomber about
> hostage deal

He isn't satisfied and tries another:

> Germans seek
> hostage deal
> on Lockerbie
> mastermind

That he thinks is better. But after it goes to the editor it emerges as:

> Hostages may
> be swapped
> for Lockerbie
> bomb suspect

The editor always has the last word.

At 5.21 Butler at last got the front page layout. His team have 24 minutes to sub and revise the stories and get them through to Neil. "The splash is written by Michael Jones, a guarantee that we will be late," he reflects ruefully. He is right: it is the last story into the editor's queue. At

The skill of the designer

No subject arouses more controversy among journalists or less interest among readers than newspaper design. Newspapers are such familiar objects that readers would be surprised to learn that complex design skills, juggling with advertisements, text, headlines and pictures, have been at work behind every page.

A former editor of *The Sunday Times*, Harold Evans, described the design of newspapers as one of the "magical" experiences of journalism. "We begin with a blank sheet of newsprint and a mosaic of ideas we want to communicate. It is the function of newspaper design to present that mosaic in an organised and comprehensible way."

The mosaic of *The Sunday Times* started to change in June 1990. The sections were given numbers instead of letters (and the pages were given numbers and section numbers), a comprehensive index was introduced on page 2, there were new headline faces and a re-ordering of the editorial content.

Andrew Neil, the editor, said: "*The Sunday Times* has been through massive changes over the past few years. Some were forced on us almost overnight by the move to Wapping. Some, such as how to produce a multi-section paper, had never been done in Britain before. We had to learn on the job. The time has now come to stand back and to get more elegance into our design."

The job of assessing what needed to be done was given to Stephen Hitchins, graphics director of the Business Design Group, who worked with his colleague Barry Dunnage and Gordon Beckett, design editor of *The Sunday Times*.

One of the more interesting aspects of the redesign, as the photographs show, was Hitchins's work on the paper's masthead. Hitchins started with the masthead because he believes that the first signal a newspaper gives to its potential readers of what it stands for is the quality of its signature. So he spent hours testing new mastheads before deciding that what he had was right.

All that was required, he decided, was to redesign the masthead so that it was drawn with sufficient clarity to withstand printing on the new Wapping colour presses. Unless it had been redrawn the lion over the masthead would have become a blur. As for all Hitchins's ideas on mastheads, Neil decided to stick with the existing typography, but to redraw the crest with the new lion.

Some of the ideas put forward by Hitchins. Few were adopted.

5.30 Neil, alone in his office, is reading the stories on his screen. Rupert Murdoch likes hands-on editors and no news story appears in *The Sunday Times* that hasn't been read and approved by Neil. With several stories arriving late, the last half-hour is going to be a rush, making it difficult for him to give the most important reports in the paper the scrutiny they deserve.

He checks the news headlines on the wires, presses a button on his phone and checks with Witherow that the report on the murder in France is up to date. He reads Glover-James's story on de Klerk, is quickly satisfied, and sends it onward to the composing room simply by pressing another button as his word processor. He starts to read the tobacco report and rings Williams to ask if it is getting an Insight byline. It isn't. So he tells Williams to make sure it does. He is pleased with the report and calls Nick Rufford, the Insight editor, to congratulate him – but asks him to revise it for later editions to ensure he gets across the message that the scandal is perpetrated with "our money".

It is 5.40. Up comes the breast cancer report. He sends it out but dislikes the headline, which uses the word "battle". That belongs to a tabloid. The income tax report is now on his screen. He makes a small amendment to add the point that there would be a top ceiling of 59 per cent if the ceiling on national insurance contributions was abolished.

It is 5.45, all the pages should be off-stone, but Fallon and Bambridge are still writing headlines. On the stone, 500 yards away in the basement, the final six pages are still being worked on. Phil Green's brilliant graphic of the Soyuz has been finished just in time but still hasn't been processed.

6.05. Page 3 is finished.

6.08. The Soyuz graphic arrives. The back page can go.

6.10. Neil is rewriting the splash. There is still a big hole on page 1.

6.11. John Karter's copy from Dublin is ready.

6.15. Still no splash.

"It's no use shouting and screaming once it's through to the editor," says Butler. "He knows the deadline. If he wants to work on a story and take us past the appointed hour, that's up to him."

Reg Limb, the production director, who is hovering in the composing room awaiting the final pages for the presses, explains why deadlines matter. He oversees the printing of the *News of the World* as well as *The Sunday Times*. The start-up times of the presses are staggered so that there is an orderly procession through the platemaking and fax systems (the pages go to Scotland and Manchester where they are separately printed). If one paper is late the system breaks down, since the *News of the World* and *Sunday Times* pages hit the system simultaneously. That costs 25 minutes on the presses or the loss of 80,000 copies, all of which has to be made up during the night.

6.27. The splash arrives at last. But it is two paragraphs over the required length. There is an instant solution – the stone sub simply cuts the last two paragraphs.

6.30. The paper is off-stone and on its way to the presses.

6.31. The compositors start making up four pages for the Irish edition. Nawrat is changing pages to update the cricket results.

6.32. Butler checks the front page. The editor has written a literal into the introduction.

For many of the staff there is now a relief in the tension. Neil, Fallon,

The sports pages are changed to keep up with late results.

Bambridge and Jones relax for half an hour in the editor's office, swapping gossip, watching *Blind Date* and awaiting the printed paper. It is a good night for Jones. He has written the splash. Without the nightly deadline of his daily rivals, he was able to spend Thursday night in the Commons talking to ministers and MPs – he will talk to at least 30 MPs a week at Westminster on lobby terms – and first learned that there had been an intriguing announcement that morning at Cabinet. Then a source in Cabinet had told him on a strictly confidential basis about the new job for Wakeham.

After calls to Number Ten and Wakeham himself, Jones's suspicions were confirmed. Now that he knew the main element of the story, it suited Downing Street to explain to Jones what was going on, in a way that would defuse any potential damage if he built up his report as a row over why the job had not gone to Howe or Baker. He was given a full and frank account of why they were not chosen. As he made his calls, he was tipped off elliptically that the next election manifesto would be written by Thatcher herself. Using the judgement he had acquired from all his years in the Commons, he decided that his tip was "hard", that it was true.

Sitting alongside him at Wapping was David Smith, the economics editor. Smith had been working all week on a story about the EMS and had decided that joining the ERM was definitely part of the government's strategy. Jones welded that information into his report and made it into a golden scenario for June 1991.

It turned out to be a story with legs. It was followed by rival Sunday papers and ran in the dailies through the week, mainly because the political correspondents read their rivals' reports and trust to the nods and winks contained in them for clues to what is going on. Yet even as he joins in the laughter in the editor's office at the antics on *Blind Date*, Jones knows that his is a short moment of glory. Then his moment of "pure joy" is over and he starts worrying what his rival Sunday political editors will have on their front pages. Tonight he is lucky. There are no rival scoops.

For the newsdesk and the subs, meanwhile, there is still another eight hours to go and the tension remains. Butler is sending down stories for the Irish edition, reading the proofs of all the first edition pages, correcting any literals, and improving headlines. He now has

ten pages to do for the 7.45 and 8.45 editions.

The relaxation in Neil's office is brief. Every Saturday night *The Sunday Times*, the *Observer* and the *Sunday Telegraph* swap their front page headlines. They soon know if they have been scooped by their rivals – and if any are running stories that are so good that they can be checked and got into their own later editions.

At 6.45 Vic Chapple, the night news editor who works on weekdays for the *Sun*, arrives in Neil's office with the main headlines from the *Observer*. It has splashed on a report that the boss of the National Farmers' Union has attacked John Gummer, the agricultural minister, over his policy on mad cow disease. At *The Sunday Times* there is a general air of disbelief that this is a story worth leading on. The view is that the *Observer* has "codded up" the report to get a front page lead. The opposition also has a front page report on a row over the Oberammergau passion play (which *Sunday Times* reporters are at present writing), a picture of de Klerk with Thatcher, a report on the Moscow arms talks, and an offbeat story about Stephenson's rocket.

There are some Saturday evenings when everybody grudgingly admits that the *Observer* has got itself some good stories. This is not one of them. Meanwhile the *Sunday Telegraph* has got a good story by commissioning an opinion poll on mad cow disease. That gets placed in the paper's unique What The Other Papers Say column, which allows *The Sunday Times* to report briefly on the main stories in all the rival Sunday papers.

Simultaneously Donald Trelford, editor of the *Observer*, and Trevor Grove, editor of the *Sunday Telegraph*, are assessing *The Sun-*

day Times. Trelford went to a briefing on the de Klerk talks. Neil was not there and Trelford was worried that the reason for his absence was that Neil had his own scoop. Now he is relieved to find that he was wrong. At the *Observer* they roar with laughter at *The Sunday Times*'s splash, and the associated story about Labour's tax plans, both, they believe, inspired by Neil's anti-Labour politics. They do, however, acknowledge the Wakeham scoop. The rest of the front page they dismiss, either as not worth following up or as stories for *The Sunday Times* but not the *Observer*.

Let's change the front page says
Neil.

Grove was also impressed by the Wakeham report and asks his political editor to check it. Yet, like Trelford, he is not impressed by the "golden scenario" emphasis of *The Sunday Times*'s splash, and thought its picture of de Klerk was boring. He was, however, jealous of the reports on the *Maiden* crew, the row over Malcolm Rifkind and mad cow disease, all better than his own.

With *Blind Date* over, the next date is the 7 pm conference.

Neil is now going through the first edition page by page for the next main edition at 8.45. Surely the de Klerk talks should be on the front page, says Ivan Fallon. So what would you take off, asks Neil. It's a big story of the day, Fallon insists. De Klerk has announced

that he "won't waste a second" to scrap apartheid. But it's already on the front page, says Neil. OK, let's change the headline over the picture so that it better reflects the significance of the meeting, says Fallon. "Done," says Neil, adding that the story should also include the remarks from de Klerk.

Several other quick decisions are made. The Oberammergau report is to be beefed up, a report on a London murder got in as a panel, the picture of soccer star Garth Crooks changed ("The report says he's a nice guy," says Neil, "but the picture makes him look like an intimidating mugger"), the main headline on page 9 is changed, and everybody hates page 11. That, Neil decides, is where the Oberammergau report should go, with pictures. Is there a good picture? Yes, says Sullivan. That settles it. Witherow wants to get a newly arrived picture of Ceauşescu's grave in the paper. Agreed. The story on the arms talks is to be updated.

At 7.10 the paper arrives. So does the *News of the World* and there are occasional guffaws at some of its outrageous stories. Neil now turns his attention to the Focuses. He has enjoyed reading about the journey of the *Maiden* crew and congratulates Tyrer on a good read. But the spread on the M1 air crash is considered a mess. It is agreed to adjust the graphics. Nor does anybody understand the Soyuz graphic on the back page. Amendments are agreed.

At 7.25 the newsdesk is reacting to a news "snap" from the Press Association. Two light aircraft have collided in mid-air and crashed close to the M25 near Reigate, Surrey. The news and picture desks respond quickly. A reporter is making phone calls from the office and a local Surrey freelance has been sent to the scene of the crash. A staff photographer is also on his way. Meanwhile the PA report is rushed into the paper.

By 8 pm Collier's pictures of *Steinlager 2* are at last arriving at Heathrow, where a despatch rider is waiting to rush them to Wapping. Phil Green is still working on the Soyuz graphic. Alex Butler is back on an even keel after the second edition, but now there are 11 pages to sub for the third, due off in 45 minutes. Nawrat has managed to get all the close of play scores into the paper for the Yorkshire edition, and now, while he starts to plan for next Saturday, he is waiting for the *Whitbread* pictures.

In Rome, where it has stopped raining, Sue Mott is filing regular updates from two three-set marathon tennis matches and her day is at present far from over. With her story on the Devon oil slick spiked, Margarette Driscoll is half-way home on the M4. Michael Jones is rewriting the splash and David Hughes is trying to check the *Observer* story on the NFU. In Manila Jon Swain, whose week's work seemed wasted when his Philippines story was spiked, has now been asked – at 2 am Manila time – to write the story on the *Goddess of Democracy* radio ship that he had contemplated on Tuesday but rejected. This story, so quickly written, is used.

The first editions of the *Mail on Sunday*, *Sunday Mirror* and *People* have arrived. Nothing to worry about. But then the *Sunday Express* arrives. It is splashing on a strong story that mothers who stay at home will not have to pay poll tax. If true, it has to be followed up. Hughes calls Downing Street. Neil is now reading the revised splash. It is longer and includes a report of a speech by Michael Heseltine, as well as an extra story from Hughes that there is a question mark over Britain's fourth Trident nuclear submarine.

At the 8.15 conference attention turns now to the main edition of the night, due off at 10.30. This is the edition which goes to homes from The Wash to Southampton, the heartland of *The Sunday Times*'s readership. Neil is now satisfied with the front page so he asks for only a few changes. He decides to abandon the London murder ("too fish and chippy"), and says that the NFU story (from the *Observer*) should go in if it stands up (it does). Nothing is moving in foreign news. Allaway wants to cut back the tobacco scandal story. Neil says No.

Note the changes from the first to final edition.

It is now almost the end of the day – and the week – for Neil, but he still feels dissatisfied. He has an agenda-setting splash on the golden scenario but the Lockerbie story is not as strong as he had hoped and he would have liked more human interest stories. With Ravenscraig, mad cow disease, beggars and drugs as the main news stories, the diet is a bit relentless. But the foreign pages have two very good stories on Marlon Brando's son and the children of the dust, born to American fathers in Indo-China, only to be abandoned, and who are now despised by the Vietnamese.

He has also hammered the resistance to some of the stories that he particularly wanted to see in the paper – Labour's income tax plans, the IRA, and Ravenscraig. He is happy with the work of Insight and neither the *Observer* nor the *Sunday Telegraph* has a scoop. He is now going out for dinner, but will have a mobile phone on the table so that the office can call him and he can call the newsdesk.

At 9.30 Williams also calls it a day and hands over to Allaway. It has been a long week and a gruelling day.

"The fresh air as I leave the office smells like champagne," he says. "I tot up – 31 of the past 36 hours have been spent in the office. So why do I do it, with never a normal weekend, no Friday night movies or Saturday night dinner parties and exhausted on Sunday? As I turn the key in the ignition and point the car towards home, my adrenalin gives me the answer – I'm addicted to it. And, you never know, I might get to be editor one day."

Most of the staff have now left for the weekend, but those who remain are still hard at work on the Scottish edition (where the Ravenscraig story is put on the front page) and the 10.30 edition, which involves changes to seven pages. Tim Rayment, however, is still updating the Soyuz story, and David Hughes, making his final call, discovers that European Community officials have agreed that the European Reconstruction Bank should be based in London. It makes a short news digest. He leaves at 10.20 after a 14-hour day. So does Liam McAuliffe, Butler's deputy, who also has worked 14 hours.

After 10.30 the pace slows down, though Neil has just come on the phone to ask how the print run is going (236,000 copies so far) and whether there is any news (the plane crash is the only new story). The sports desk is almost at the end of its day, especially now that it has been able to get in a big picture of the Whitbread race. Collier, the photographer, is now on his way back to Blackbushe airport to get his car (and won't get home until 11.30 after a 5 am start), but at least he got his pictures, even though the cost was £850.

Sue Mott has filed her final report from Rome. Her evening ends damply at 11. "I cannot remember a precise description of the bottle of Chianti that followed," she says, "but it was very welcome and empty by 11.30."

As he prepares to leave at 11, Nawrat is a satisfied sports editor, especially satisfied with the *Steinlager 2* picture which he has rushed into the paper and which will get into 750,000 copies. He has a report of every first class cricket match, which has never been done before, and, alone among the Sunday papers, he has got in the result of the Preakness, America's equivalent of the 2,000 Guineas, in a paragraph on his front page. He has also planned next week's sports pages, including a front page on

Sussex against New Zealand, the Monaco grand prix and PGA golf. Brian Glanville has been allocated a fourth division play-off. "Basically it was a very straightforward day. The system didn't crash. No copy was lost or sent to the wrong newspaper. The system never became inordinately slow. We always knew how to handle the rain in Italy." Tomorrow the weekly cycle will begin again when he calls his writers to tell them his plans for next week.

At 11.20 Moscow denies that the Soviet cosmonauts are marooned. Tim Rayment starts rewriting his story yet again.

Journalists write and edit newspapers, but they also have to be printed and distributed. All night long lorries and vans are leaving Wapping, Manchester and Glasgow with copies of *The Sunday Times* and the *News of the World* which will be on sale at more than 40,000 newsagents shops tomorrow.

Over in the main printing plant a solitary spotlamp shines in the darkness of the office of Reg Limb, the production director. An Australian who moved from Sydney to help see through the Wapping revolution when it was still being secretly prepared, the genial Limb is responsible for *The Sunday Times* (as well as all the rest of the Wapping papers) from the moment it leaves the journalists until it leaves the plant on lorries. He oversees the production of more than 30 million newspapers a week at the biggest printing plant in Europe. One result of the Wapping revolution is that there are now only 125 staff in the press room compared with 1,000 in Fleet Street.

The Sunday Times is printed over three days. On Friday morning 1.3 million copies of the Style and Books sections are printed; on Saturday 900,000 copies of the Business, Arts, Review and Appointments sections are printed between 8 am and 3 pm (the rest are printed at Manchester and Glasgow); and another 900,000 News sections are printed on Saturday night and Sunday morning. At 11.30 tonight the screen in his office tells Limb that 320,000 copies have been printed, with 600,000 still to go. It is a good run. His men will be finished by 4 am.

The nerve centre of the production operation is the Tote Room, manned by three staff faced by six screens which record what is happening on each press, how many papers have been printed and which lorries are loading. At midnight they can tell that 369,000 copies have been printed, the Oxford lorry has just been loaded and the Ashford lorry is now loading. That is due to leave at 1.31 with 382 bundles of newspapers – and 298 have now been loaded. This is the command room where instant decisions have to be made when presses break down or printing is running late.

The circulation department also never sleeps. It is manned 24 hours a day. Tonight the circulation manager is Jack Woollard. He is checking that the printing schedules are being maintained at the three printing centres and ensuring that the correct editions get to the right areas – that Yorkshire, for instance, gets the edition with the full Yorkshire cricket scorecard. The sheet on his desk, detailing how 1.3 million copies of an eight-section *Sunday Times* plus two magazines gets to 40,000 newsagents from Land's End to John o'Groats (and across the world), reads like the battle orders for the D-Day landings. It covers six closely-typed pages detailing the movements of more than

Nerve centre: the Tote Room.

60 big lorries. It starts at 18.32 and finishes at 4.39 with the last run, which goes to Watford.

20.13	Taunton	11,975 copies
20.25	Plymouth	14,475
21.11	Swindon	50,885
21.24	Exeter	14,890
21.41	Salisbury	19,350
22.06	Swansea	9,860
22.25	Newport	21,790
22.49	Norwich	10,620

That is simply the start of the distribution of *The Sunday Times*. The Plymouth lorry, for instance, drops 6,790 copies at two wholesalers in Plymouth at 2 am, then 1,900 to W. H. Smith in Bodmin; plus 620 for Newquay, 1,895 at Truro, 1,300 at Redruth and finally 1,300 at Hayle, near Penzance.

Special circulation "bills", small posters announcing what news is in the paper, go out with each bundle in the hope that newsagents will display them outside their shops – especially if there is a good scoop that will sell more papers. The two news bills tonight say: "Thatcher sights on spring election" and "New hope in cancer battle."

Back in the newsroom the world has gone to sleep and the few editorial staff who remain are relaxing, even though Allaway is restlessly reading Reuter for any last scraps of news he can steer into the paper. But even Reuter is silent now:

Moscow and Washington also enjoy a weekend off.

Butler has had a busy night. Since 10.30 he has done another two editions, including the last at 1 am, and has made changes to 49 pages since 6.30. At 1.59 he has one last job, still on his mind since the angry memo from the editor last Wednesday. He bollocks the sub who changed "fish supper" to "fish meal", causing him so much aggravation.

At 2.30 Allaway goes home to Muswell Hill – but the presses roll on until 4.19 when the last copy is printed, and the last van leaves Wapping, as dawn breaks, for Watford. Until the reporters from *The Times* arrive in a few hours' time to plan Monday's paper, the thunder of the presses gives way to silence and you can even hear a few birds singing as the sun rises behind Tower Bridge. Andrew Neil and his staff are asleep – but Neil has a mobile phone by his bed just in case.

The editor

Several months after the week on which *Deadline Sunday* is based, Andrew Neil sat down one Saturday afternoon and wrote a long leading article attacking the behaviour of the Royal Family. Angered by the antics of the minor royals when British soldiers were fighting in the Gulf, he wrote a powerful philippic.

"The Queen needs urgently to summon the royals to Windsor for a chapel meeting," Neil declared. "The country is at war, even though you would never believe it from the shenanigans of some members of Her Majesty's clan. As usual it is not the most important members of the royal family whose behaviour has been less than we have a right to expect, though the performance of even the inner circle since hostilities broke out has hardly been faultless.

"It is the exploits and public demeanour of the minor royals and nearly royals which cause most offence. Britain's armed forces are waging war against the fourth largest military machine in the world. They stand on the brink of the biggest land battle since the Second World War, a battle in which some of the nation's finest young men and women are expected to risk their lives. Yet, on the home front, too many of the young royals and their entourages carry on regardless with their peacetime lifestyles, parading a mixture of upper-class decadence and insensitivity which disgusts the public and demeans the monarchy. The Queen should put a stop to it."

The leader was typical of Neil, an editor who never flinches from attacking Establishment targets, whether of the left or right, when he thinks they are behaving badly. Even as Neil wrote that leader, he knew it would create an uproar – which it did – and that he would become the editor at the centre of the media maelstrom, a target of public abuse. Yet the uproar provoked by editorials that express strongly held opinions is for Neil precisely what editing *The Sunday Times* is about. Using the authority and prestige of *The Sunday Times* to start a controversy rolling and then to see its impact, he says, is one of the pleasures of editorship.

It was a pleasure he also enjoyed when he published a story on the front page saying that the Queen was at odds with Mrs Thatcher, or when *The Sunday Times* revealed the connection between Arthur

Saturday night: Neil orders the final edition changes.

Scargill and Libya during the miners' strike, or Mordecai Vanunu's story of Israel's secret nuclear bomb; or in 1991 when he projected across eight columns at the top of the front page a report showing that the big high street banks were crucifying small businesses with penal rates of interest.

"Upsetting a few powerful people on Sundays is a measure that we are doing our job," Neil comments. That means naming the chairmen of companies that are polluting rivers or using tax funds overseas to evade income tax or the men behind restrictive practices in the television industry; it doesn't matter whether the targets are on the right or the left.

There are several skills to being an editor, according to Neil. One is to have a nose or an instinct for what readers want to read on a Sunday, to follow your instincts and hope that they coincide. Another is an insatiable curiosity, yet another an ability to get angry or outraged by events. "That shouldn't be manufactured, as it is in some papers. It should be genuine outrage or anger. That is what gives a paper its personality."

With his belief in the regeneration of Britain, Neil was horrified by the brutal tactics and restrictive practices of the print unions which still exercised a stranglehold over Fleet Street – and especially *The Sunday Times* – when he arrived as editor at the offices in Gray's Inn Road in 1983. "I was arguing for a modern Britain – but we were still living in an antique Britain," he says.

That made him a strong supporter of Eddy Shah when he was embroiled in his dispute with the National Graphical Association who were picketing the plant where his *Messenger* group of free newspapers were printed at Warrington. The Battle for Shah became his first big campaign – the intimidation and bullying of Shah by the NGA represented everything Neil most hated in British life. Within weeks of assuming the editorship, he devoted the centre four pages of *The Sunday Times* to the Shah story and wrote a leader, The Battle for Britain, which stamped on the paper the policy that became Neil's hallmark.

"If decent entrepreneurs cannot survive and prosper in Mrs Thatcher's Britain there is little hope for the country, and less for the government," he wrote. "All over the western world the jobs of tomorrow are being created by such people today. Unemployment in Britain is still stuck over three million partly because enterprising spirits who try to grasp the potential of the new information technology are blocked by the job-destroying power of certain unions. Those such as Eddy Shah who dare challenge this state of affairs risk being threatened by such brute force that minor disputes are turned into a national crisis."

Shah's eventual victory also speeded Rupert Murdoch's plans to get out of Fleet Street to Wapping and Neil was an enthusiastic proponent of the plans to switch to new technology and dump the unions. After the move occurred, he spent the following year with two personal bodyguards as militant pickets surrounded Wapping, and there were frequent and often bloody clashes with mounted police. Yet it was the success of the move to Wapping which enabled *The Sunday Times* to expand to eight sections on the American model that Neil so admired.

He remains bitter that *The Sunday Times* under his editorship has never been given the credit he thinks it deserves for retaining the strengths of the Thomson era and remoulding them for the new climate of the 1980s. "Harold Evans fought for the Crossman diaries and the victims of thalidomide," he says. "I have fought for *Spycatcher* and fair treatment for haemophiliacs. Our investigations and campaigns have been stronger than ever and we have attacked left and right. We haven't been in anybody's pockets. It is a pity that the old guard cannot bring themselves to credit that achievement. Why we have not been forgiven is that we turned a lot of the techniques they used against their establishment."

His liberal critics believe that Neil is the creature of the reviled Rupert Murdoch. Yet he insists that this is not the case – and his senior staff would support him in that view. What Murdoch really did in appointing Neil was to install an editor who shared his free-market beliefs and who was often ahead of him.

"I have never discussed any editorial with Rupert Murdoch, except the leader supporting Michael Heseltine when he challenged Margaret Thatcher," says Neil. "On that occasion he did not try to argue me out of doing it but said he disagreed. I have survived as editor because a lot of what I believe is what he believes. Any proprietor wants an editor who reflects his interests. The values and attitudes and stories that *The Sunday Times* has pursued under my editorship have been mine not his. The idea that I am anybody's puppet is ludicrous – and can only be put about by people who don't know me."

His staff have learned to live with him, even though, as an unmarried workaholic, he sets an exhausting pace, always has a phone by him and is never far from a fax machine, even on holiday. When he visited the Gulf to see British troops in action during the war, he could be contacted at the press of a button. His staff worry about his moodiness, his lack of social skills and small talk, and his inability to delegate. "Human relations are not his strong point," says one. "He is a hard man to work for and not a pleasant man. He was a real bastard at the beginning." He leads by fear rather than inspiration and often distrusts advice from his own executives, say others. He stamps his own views on news stories. He has blind spots – for instance about theatre and the visual arts. The chips on his shoulder are still too visible. He can be bully in a group but not face-too-face. As an unmarried man he does not understand the suburban life of mowing the lawn and family Sunday lunch.

Yet those selfsame staff also respect his "supreme intelligence", the sharpness of his intellect, his homework when he wants to inform himself about a subject, his restless, demonic energy, his popularist instinct, his respect for the English language and the independent spirit which makes him refuse to suck up to Rupert Murdoch or to defend the excesses of the *Sun*. Above all they respect his decisiveness.

"That is the greatest attribute of an editor. Even if the decisions are wrong, it doesn't matter because he gets things moving," says one assistant editor.

"I enjoy working for him," says another. "The frustration of working for an autocrat arises when he isn't there. An absent dictator makes life difficult. Terror works."

"He is the best all-round editor I have known," adds another who has worked for three.

Memo to staff, February 1991

THE SUNDAY TIMES
MEMORANDUM

From: The Editor   To: Please see list

Date: 27th February 1991

Though it was a long night for all of us, your sterling efforts seem to have been rewarded. Our 6am edition drew plaudits from many broadcasters, including a wonderful plug on Frost on Sunday. The results have been encouraging: early indications are we rose 35,000 on Sunday to almost 1.23 m, which is a fantastic result in a four-paper quality market, achieved without any TV promotion. By contrast, The Telegraph and The Sindie fell, The Observer was no change. Our reputation is clearly such that they turn to The Sunday Times when big news breaks.

Thank you for the long hours. Congratulations.

Andrew F Neil
Editor

"He yomps along rather than treads a thin line, combative and controversial, often happy to ruffle some feathers ... He makes no concession to polite society or the establishment he scorns. Neil's senior executives have been known to pray he might wed and settle down to a less punishing routine. For he is married to his job, a bachelor who bulldozes his way through a punishing schedule and expects the same commitment from his journalists . . . He commands, argues, exasperates, bullies, cajoles and never leaves his team in any doubt as to what he wants, whether they like it or not."
Robin Morgan, former managing editor (features) of The Sunday Times *and editor of the* Sunday Express, *on Andrew Neil: Campaign, April 1991.*

Second Sunday

Each week the circulation department of
News International delivers 38 million
newspapers to newsagents and wholesalers
throughout the United Kingdom and to
81 countries abroad. *The Sunday Times*
is the most difficult to get distributed.

As the presses shut down, the newsagents start their work of assembling the papers, and the weekly cycle has now come full circle. It is now the job of the circulation department at News International to ensure that this paper is distributed throughout the United Kingdom and to 81 countries around the world.

That is not its only job. The department is also responsible for distributing *The Times, Sun, Today, News of the World* and Murdoch magazines, all of which are owned by News International. Each week it delivers 38 million newspapers to newsagents and wholesalers. There is a staff of 160 including eight area managers, 61 area representatives and another 25 who look after the 6,300 newsagents in London.

Nick Sheldon is circulation manager of *The Sunday Times*. It is the most difficult paper to get dis-tributed, since it is printed over four days at four printing plants. That is the most important reason why the delivery of *The Sunday Times* is planned to the last detail, starting nine days in advance of publication, since the magazine starts being distributed on Mondays and it is the circulation department which sets the print order, the number of copies that will be printed.

Each paper sets a tight budget for its percentage of "unsolds", the number of papers that don't get sold. Readers who want *The Sunday Times* expect to find it. If they don't they will buy a rival, so there must always be copies to spare. Yet printing the paper costs so much that a lot of money is wasted if too many copies are unsold. That is why the judgement of the likely sale of the paper by the circulation manager is so important.

The print order is based on a detailed weekly statement of how many copies of *The Sunday Times* were sold last week in every town in Britain, whether the sales were up or down, and in which areas they were up and in which they were down. On bank holiday weekends or during the summer orders drop in the big cities but go up on the coast. Sheldon has to judge how many to add to the seaside orders so that no readers complain that they could not get their *Sunday Times*.

By Saturday most of the work is done, and the bulk of the paper has been delivered. The circulation manager checks with wholesalers that there have been no difficulties with the Friday and Saturday deliveries and that they have a stock of contents bills. On Saturday night he ensures that production runs smoothly and makes any last-minute adjustments. If there is a big news story based in Yorkshire or Sussex, he will send extra copies to those two counties.

Unlike weekdays, the selling period for Sunday papers is only about six hours: most newsagents shut by 1 pm. The first job of the area rep this morning is to check with his local wholesalers to get hints of what the opposition is up to – are the *Observer* or the *Mail on Sunday* adding extra copies because they were advertising a special promotion on television last night? By 8 am he is touring newsagents' shops to check they have ordered enough copies. If not, he will give them extra copies from the back of his car. He will also make quick assessments of which papers are doing well or badly. By noon he will be talking to the wholesalers again to order extra copies into shops that are in danger of selling out, or switching copies from a shop where sales are slow to one where they are in short supply.

At lunchtime he will have made

his own assessment of how *The Sunday Times* has sold and will ring in his estimate to Wapping so that the circulation department can answer calls from Andrew Neil, or Rupert Murdoch when he is in town. He types his report today and it is on the circulation manager's desk tomorrow.

As Sheldon says, the circulation reps are spies – the eyes and ears of the company – the quickest to know when the paper has done well, or badly.

As the newsboys strolled along Britain's streets this morning, the last link in the chain that made paper from a tree in a Welsh forest into *The Sunday Times* they are delivering to more than a million doorsteps, Iain Johnstone is on his way back from Cannes. The woman sitting next to him in the plane is reading *The Sunday Times* and he catches sight of his photo. That lifts his spirits. Then, when she discards the paper, he reads the review of *Cannes: The Novel*. That sends them down again. It is a personal attack on him by Chris Peachment, the Arts editor, masquerading under a pseudonym. The woman beside him has, however, kept the magazine, where the first article she turned to was on its inside back page – A Life in the Day of Josephine Barstow, the opera singer.

A Life in the Day . . .

After a glance at the front page, it is a fair bet that the item in *The Sunday Times* that most readers turn to first is the feature published every week on the last editorial page of *The Sunday Times Magazine*. A Life in the Day of the hundreds of men and women it has featured since October 16th, 1977 is perennially fascinating and allows an easy start to Sunday, a peep through a neighbour's keyhole, before settling down to all the serious politics in the paper.

All magazines look for a short appetiser article to tempt the readers and make them stop and start reading as well as a digestif, another short article, to end the magazine meal. A Life in the Day is the digestif; Relative Values, a weekly conversation about their relationship between a mother and a daughter or a father and a son, is the appetiser. They are described by Philip Clarke, editor of the magazine, as "beacons".

The idea of Life in the Day started over a lunch between Hunter Davies, then the editor of the magazine, and Susan Raven, who has edited the page since it began. Searching for beacons, they originally thought up two ideas. The first was Sacred Cows, an opportunity for a lively writer to attack a pet hate, such as the Country Cottage, Paris or the rules of tennis. That lasted only a year. You soon run out of pet hates. There are only so many.

Then Davies turned to A Life in the Day, a thought inspired by Patrick Nicholson, chief sub-editor on the magazine, who had mentioned in conversation that he drew up a weekly plan of what clothes he would wear each day. It was that sort of intimate fascinating glimpse into another person's life that convinced Davies that this was an idea which might work.

Susan Raven and Davies thought that it might last eight weeks and among their first eight subjects were Guy the Gorilla, A. J. P. Taylor, Catherine Cookson and Sue Lawley. They were wrong. It has never stopped and there would be an outcry from readers if any editor thought of

killing it. Among those it has featured are Nancy Reagan, Colonel Gadaffi, Princess Grace, Andy Warhol, Yoko Ono, Clint Eastwood, Luciano Pavarotti, Placido Domingo, Lord Carrington, Sir Geoffrey Howe, Benazir Bhutto and Rudolf Nureyev. Whether unknown or famous, Raven insists that all the authors or interviewers stick to the same framework, that the article starts at the beginning of the day and ends when they go to bed.

Apart from the articles she commissions herself, Raven gets at least 20 unsolicited offerings a week and tries to use an "unknown" once every six weeks. It is often the unknowns who make the most riveting reading. "You get a marvellous view of British lives from Life in the Day," she says. "We get a lot of unsophisticated people talking directly to the reader, many of them happy in spite of the hardness of their lives. It doesn't matter how boring the person seems so long as their life is interesting. Life in the Day works if you think, 'Fancy that, they're just like me' or 'Their life is much more boring than mine'. I don't mind if famous people are dull because the article is not about jobs but lives."

One unknown who really caught the attention of readers was Mary Philpott.

Mary Philpott

Aged 55, a derelict.
I am a single woman and live in an old rented terraced house in a down-at-heel street in Wallington, Surrey.

I am totally alone except for my cat Tosca, who, like me, is one of today's rejects. She was thrown out by her previous owners, and made her way to me. She is old, and swears and spits occasionally, more from habit than anger, and this I understand. She too has a reason to feel bitter, and she and I recognise kindred spirits, and get on very well.

My day begins at 7.30 am when I

feed my cat and have my breakfast, which invariably consists of two cups of tea. Then I empty the teapot, wash the cup, and make my bed. Later, I go to the shops, where I buy a tin of cat food, and, if I can afford it, a tin of vegetable soup for my own dinner. Fortunately I am a vegetarian, so not having the money to buy meat does not worry me unduly, although it would be nice to be able to buy luxuries occasionally, like cakes, fruit, particularly bananas, or a strong piece of Cheddar.

I've been virtually penniless since my father died, some two years ago. My mother, whom I loved dearly, died in 1968. I still mourn her, and remember her with absolute love.

For a few months, the Social Security Office in Sutton allowed me a small sum to cover my rent, rates, heating, etc., but this was stopped abruptly by the Dickensian officials, who in their wisdom decided I had not made enough effort to get a job. Unfortunately it had not occurred to these latter-day Bumbles that a woman of 55, with no recent experience, had very slight chance indeed to get work, particularly in view of the un-

Mary Philpott, aged 55, who describes herself as a de[relict]

A LIFE IN THE DAY OF MARY PHILPOTT

" I am a single woman and live in an old rented terraced house in a down-at-heel street in Wallington, Surrey.

I am totally alone, except for my cat Tosca, who, like me, is one of today's rejects. She was thrown out by her previous owners, and made ʰer way to me. She is old, and ˑˑasionally, more

Born in Brockley, London. S[t] work. Left employment in 195[3]

these latter-day Bumbles [t] woman of 55, with no recent

ars in a local radio and valve factory, and later went into personnel invalid mother, and, latterly, widower father. Both parents now dead

. Then, around 4p.m., I have r cup of tea, and a bread roll | movement in the second half. Again, I will play Dvorak's New World

employment prevailing at the moment. Even the stamps for interviews were a major expenditure, and I don't think I received one reply!

Sutton Council, on the other hand, were very good, and allowed me a full rebate of rent and rates, and this lifeline is one I fully appreciate. But back to my average day . . .

After I've fed Tosca, I heat my soup, and make myself another cup of tea. One of the not inconsiderable blessings of tea is that it does serve to deaden the appetite.

In the afternoon I go to my local library. In the winter it is warm there, and in the summer it's a place to go, a transient escape. I've had no holiday since 1961 and I like to look at the travel books, and dream.

They are very understanding, not to say tolerant, in the library, and if ever they get tired of the sight of me poring over their books, or sorting through their recordings, they are too tactful to show any displeasure. Quite possibly, since I am an anonymous figure, they do not notice me.

When I return home, I talk to Tosca, and feed the birds in my back garden. Then, around 4 pm, I have

another cup of tea, and a bread roll and cheese spread.

I'm not a great conversationalist, which again is fortunate for me, for from the time I get up until I retire thankfully to bed, I doubt if I say more than half a dozen words to anyone. I've no friends, and there is just no point in talking, anyway. Perhaps a few words when I'm in the supermarket and good morning to the milkman, and that's it.

I find much more to say to the birds and Tosca, and although understandably they do not reply, I feel sure they understand. I get a great deal of pleasure from the birds who visit my garden, and Tosca, happily, has no killer instinct, and is quite content to watch them swooping down for my offerings of bread. They seem to realise that they have found a sanctuary of a sort, and pay no attention to the cranky little spotted cat who eyes them reflectively.

Some years ago I was able to buy myself a record player, and this I've hung on to grimly, although almost all my other personal possessions have been sold. My evenings are usually spent in the company of Mozart's Third Violin Concerto, which I love, particularly the slow movement in the second half. Again, I will play Dvorak's New World Symphony, which never fails to make me weep, possibly because of its sheer nostalgia. One of the additional joys of the library is that I can obtain four records monthly, and I can indulge myself with the classics.

I have clung too, with equal tenacity, to my weekly copy of *The Sunday Times*, which I cannot imagine being without.

My other indulgence is my treasured typewriter, an ancient Royal model which I found languishing in a junk-shop some years ago. I bought it, lovingly cleaned, oiled and generally refurbished it, thus I can sit back and type little efforts like this, partly to assuage the dreadful monotony and poverty of my existence, and partly to try to convince myself I'm not really on the scrap heap. Most probably, though, I set this down so there will be some record that I exist at all. Sometimes I doubt it myself.

Finally my day ends, and I say goodnight to Tosca and go to bed. If I try not to think that I have another day to face tomorrow I might even be able to sleep.

Of all the 400 or so Life in the Days Mary Philpott's aroused the greatest response from readers: hundreds of letters to us and to her, presents for herself and Tosca, invitations, offers of friendship, holidays, jobs. She was overwhelmed, thrilled, and felt she could at last "overcome that sense of being lost, of being non-existent". The local newspaper and a couple of publishers got in touch with her; a professor of English wrote that he hoped we realised she was a born writer; an American sailor on weekend leave turned up on our doorstep saying he'd "like to take Mary out on the town" that evening. Alas, it couldn't be arranged: she had no telephone.

She still has no telephone, but she writes (still from her old address) to say as she now qualifies for an old age pension she is not in such desperate straits financially. But "one sad piece of news is that my old Tosca died 18 months ago, at the great age of 22 years". Otherwise, she says, her life is more or less unchanged, except that "Mozart's Third Violin Concerto has given way to, I blush to say it, a recording of La Cage aux Folles."

Second Monday

At his home in North London Matthew Engel has been brooding on the invitation from Chris Nawrat, the sports editor, to join *The Sunday Times*. He has decided against, for reasons that Andrew Neil would recognise and which explain why, when challenged, he cannot refrain from attacking the *Sun*, even though it is published by the same stable.

"I am sure that my independence on *The Sunday Times* would be as great as on the *Guardian*," Engel writes. "But this week I was totally scandalised by what *Today*, the *Sun* and the Screws did to Bobby Robson [England's manager in the World Cup]. With the best will in the world (which I am sure you would have), I cannot see how I could have written about that for you without feeling in some way compromised. And this has reinforced my gut instinct that I do not want to be employed by any of the megalomedia organisations if I can help it."

Nick Sheldon is compiling his circulation report for yesterday's *Sunday Times*. It sold 1,130,000 copies, slightly down on the week before. So were the rivals, with the *Sunday Telegraph* selling 570,000, the *Observer* 541,000, the *Sunday Correspondent* 180,000 and the *Independent on Sunday* 323,000. Not a bad week for *The Sunday Times*, considering the competition from two new papers, but not a brilliant one either. The *Sunday Mirror* has rerun the Callanetics articles first published in *The Sunday Times*. Once again Callanetics has worked. Sales of the *Sunday Mirror* were up by 63,000.

As Sheldon makes his calculations on the sixth floor of the main building at Wapping, David Walsh, a floor below, is comparing the advertising performance of *The Sunday Times* against its rivals. With 240 columns (well down on the budget target of 289 and last year's performance of 275), against 214 the week before, its market share declined slightly from 28.95 per cent to 28.56 per cent of the quality market, consisting (then) of five papers. The two closest rivals were the *Observer*, with 165 columns, and the *Sunday Telegraph*, with 149, followed by the *Independent on Sunday* with 173 and the *Sunday Correspondent* with 112. Given the onset of the 1990–91 recession, however, Walsh is not dissatisfied.

Nor is Neil. Even though it has not been a strong week for news,

Thatcher's "golden scenario" has become the main political story of the week and is running in all the other papers. The *Sun* has followed up the Garth Crooks story; the *Daily Mirror* has reported Insight's Lockerbie scoop; and both the *Daily Mail* and the *Daily Express* published the table on Labour and income tax. "Once again, though, *The Sunday Times* has set the news agenda."

More than a hundred letters are also on their way to the editor as readers start reacting to what they read in the paper yesterday. Most are about Labour's tax plans, with sales of high-tar tobacco to the Third World and Lockerbie as the two other most popular subjects. Eighteen were published the following Sunday. This is what some of them said:

THE SUNDAY TIMES 27 MAY 1990

Letters

We're not afraid of Labour's tax plans

BAD BUSINESS: Under the new business rating system, once the phasing arrangements come to an end, we will be paying a real net (after tax) increase in rates of about £4,000. This is considerably more than you claim a single man earning £50,000 a year will lose under Labour's tax proposals. Our joint income this financial year is unlikely to exceed £25,000.

I DISAGREE strongly with your editorial on taxation (News Review, last week). As a computer systems manager earning well over £20,000, I would lose, although not by much, under Labour's plans. If inflation stays anywhere near its current level, the matter would be largely irrelevant.

I am already losing out, thanks to the chancellor's decision not to raise the threshold for the higher tax bracket. I look for my wages to keep pace with inflation and to reflect the level of my company's profits. But it is not wage increases that are the incentive to my working more effectively, as your editorial suggested. For this I look to a good working environment, properly regulated job conditions and a good social infrastructure.

If Labour plans to raise some extra taxation to sort out the mess which these are currently in, I won't be objecting.

Keith Martin
London N17

While I agree with the arguments set out in your editorial, there is no doubt that our votes for the Tories in 1987 have cost us a lot, and that a vote for Labour next time will be much cheaper.

The Tories might find it more profitable electorally to remove the enormous costs the new rating system in the south has imposed on many of their staunchest supporters rather than to make unfounded statements about how much a Labour government would cost the taxpayer.

John Venn
Chichester, W Sussex

NO BENEFIT: Many people are in the same position as Mr Richards, the fireman who was "singed over car tax" (Personal Finance, May 13).

I am a civil engineer with British Rail and am on call continuously. I am required by my employer to take a car home at night and at weekends in order that I can respond quickly to a call-out. I am not allowed to use the car privately; like Mr Richards, I have my own car, too.

Nevertheless, I and many others in BR are taxed as if we had full private use of the car when not at work. I am taxed on a benefit I do not have.

Some time ago, you ran a campaign against building societies which charged a higher interest rate on larger loans. You shamed them into abolishing the differential. Many of us would welcome a campaign to shame the inland revenue into changing the rules in cases such as these.

Graeme Monteith
Giffnock, Glasgow

Selling coffin nails to the 'natives'

I READ your Insight investigation headlined "Africa, ashtray of the world" with great interest (Focus, May 13). My initial gut feeling was utter disbelief, followed by anger at the way BAT, the powerful tobacco multinational conglomerate, is taking advantage of susceptible Africans.

The plight of individuals is sad; viewed nationally, it amounts to a major health alert, rivalling that of malaria and tetanus. Africans continue to be fools to themselves by allowing these marketing strategies to create havoc within their borders.

It is about time the African continent united to counter this aggressive marketing. Governments must curtail these unethical practices, which can only be detrimental to the people.

S Osei
Harlow, Essex

DOUBLE LIFE? Your article quoted BAT's spokesman as saying "Our view is that smoking has not been established to be the cause of disease". You also mentioned in the same article that BAT has purchased two life insurance companies, Eagle Star and Allied Dunbar.

It is well known that life insurance premiums are substantially higher for smokers than non-smokers. Premium rates computed by actuaries are based on statistical facts, and not on opinion. Is this a case of the left hand not knowing what the right is doing?

David Gamse
London W1

● *If you have views on any subject in the paper, write to the Letters Editor. Please post your letter early in the week, or fax it to 071-782 5120.*

The M1 crash and Lockerbie: lessons we have to learn

YOUR article about the M1 air crash made compulsive reading (Focus, last week). But to me it raised one important question: why did so many people die when the aircraft did not catch fire?

In 1958 I was a passenger in an aircraft which had to do a "wheels-up" landing. It was a piston-engined aircraft, and despite the fact that it had jettisoned most of its fuel it still had some petrol in its tanks. The aircraft was on charter to the air ministry and so all its seats were rearward facing. When it skidded to a halt, the seat mountings held and the passengers, who had their heads down between their knees, were forced back into the seats.

In the M1 disaster, I assume that the seats were not held in their fixings and were thrown forward or, if they did hold, then the passengers themselves were hurled forward — the aircraft lap belts are worse than useless in this respect. How many more people would have survived if the seat mountings had held and if the seats had been rear facing?

Ronald Taylor
Mossley Hill, Liverpool

SECURITY: Dr John Swire's inconsolable grief over his daughter's death in the Lockerbie disaster is wholly under-standable (Valerie Grove, last week). But I believe he is misguided in trying to put the primary blame on Pan Am.

I am sure Pan Am's security system was inadequate — but security on all American and British airlines was, and is, much the same. It is tempting to pick on a large, highly visible target, but attacking terrorism, not its outcome, must be our main aim.

Clearly, a fail-safe back-up of airline security is highly desirable, but consider the practicalities. At present, most passengers at check-in are asked a few very fundamental questions about their baggage, which is then passed through a primitive imaging machine. If the operator sees something he cannot identify, he may pass the bag over for a superficial inspection by hand.

If checked baggage is stowed but the owner is not on board, it must be taken off the aircraft. To allow time for these procedures, passengers are asked to turn up two hours before departure.

Are these procedures adequate to put paid to an even moderately determined terrorist? I doubt it. Although the loopholes cannot be entirely closed, the following precautions would probably suffice:

All aircraft from arrival at the gate to push-back should be attended by guards with authority to search baggage-handlers at any time and examine any item of luggage if they suspect that security seals have been tampered with — or, indeed, turn out the entire hold for a spot check.

All baggage, both checked and carry-on, should be thoroughly hand-searched by trained operatives with sniffer dogs. Passengers, too, should be rigorously searched — not just a quick pat on the clothes. Only one single small carry-on item per passenger should be allowed, which must remain with the owner at all times. Baggage left unattended should be automatically confiscated and its owner subjected to a punitive fine.

There should be a mandatory check-in time of three hours before departure, and no passenger turning up later should be allowed to travel on that flight.

These precautions are by no means foolproof, but if they were in place, the blame for another successful terrorist attack could, perhaps, be fairly placed on the airline and airport authority concerned. The question is: are we prepared to pay the price?

Jonathan Ingrams
Heronsgate, Hertfordshire

Don't forget the superbomb spotter

MRS Thatcher congratulated the customs officials who drew attention to the tubes said to be part of Iraq's projected supergun. She added that we had good reason to be grateful to them, although, according to most military opinions I read, it seemed that the gun wouldn't even work.

Her tribute contrasts strangely with the reward Vanunu was given for the comparably greater service he rendered in alerting the world to Israel's ability to make 2 nuclear weapons and the even more deadly neutron and hydrogen bombs. We scarcely protested after he was held from this country by a Mossad agent, and Italy shrugged shoulders over his subsequent kidnapping in Rome.

Vanunu was sentenced 18 years in prison, and in his fourth year of this confinement. When considering the fate of kidnap victims let's spare a thought for ...

Dolgellau, C...

BIRTHDA...

TODAY: Dr Henry ... former US secretary ... Dr Eric Anderson, he... Eton, 54; Christoph... and Vincent Price, ... film stars; Pat C... Wimbledon cha...

British fur trade will not touch baby seal coats

IN your article on the Soviet seal cull (page A3, last week). Mark Glover, who is the director of Lynx (1986) Ltd, an organisation dedicated to the abolition of the fur trade, expressed concern at the suggestion that whitecoat furs, a byproduct of the Soviet seal cull carried out to protect fishing stocks, might be being imported into Britain.

The British Fur Trade Association, which represents responsible members of the fur trade, was the first organisation in Europe to volunteer to discontinue the trade in whitecoat furs, and it did so well before the passage of the European Community directive banning the importation ...hitecoat furs into its mem-...ates.

...at your article did not ...s that once the whitecoat ...ups have moulted, the ...of the fur changes and ...ease to be white, thus ...ing the alleged attrac-...the whitecoats.

...der that readers of your ...per should be in no ...the British Fur Trade ...ion, on behalf of its ...s, states unequivo-...t there has been no ...ion of whitecoat furs ...mbers since well be-...passage of the EC ...banning such im-...into member states; ...urprisingly, no such ...n of whitecoat furs ...om the Soviet seal ...g to take place.

David Liney
Acting Executive Officer
British Fur Trade Association
London EC4

Out to lunch without even leaving the office

HOW sad that The Sunday Times fell into the old trap of glamorizing the workaholic by reference only to the great and the good (page A5, last week). Power and control can be a heady mix, and the 16-hour work day gets a lot more tolerable when it includes "lunching with chums" and taking so-called contacts to the opera or ballet, so often sponsored as corporate fun.

The reality of the workaholic lifestyle is less pleasant. Our research among thousands of middle managers over the past few years shows ...asing desper-... ...eight minutes fo...

from 43 hours in 1972 to 49 hours in 1989. New working methods have upped productivity for many types of workers, but managers still muddle along as ever and cut into their leisure and family time to pay the price.

For too many children the white-collar father is a remote figure, leaving home early and coming back late simply to eat and fall asleep in front of the television before the daily grind begins again. The early start and late finish actually show a total inability to deal with interruptions (on...

on the desk taking three hours a week, for example.

The results are diminishing returns and higher costs from crisis managers; the average corporate telephone bill could fall by 12% if the users were more organised.

It can't go on. Signs of stress and burnout are already common among the managers in the key 25-35 age group, and the problem is clearly growing. Unless they can learn how to work smarter, not harder — and quickly — managerial mis-ery at ...